The
CRITICAL
WRITING
WORKSHOP

The
CRITICAL
WRITING
WORKSHOP

Designing Writing Assignments to Foster Critical Thinking

Edited by

Toni-Lee Capossela

Boynton/Cook
Heinemann
Portsmouth, NH

BOYNTON/COOK PUBLISHERS, Inc.
A Subsidiary of
Reed Publishing (USA) Inc.
361 Hanover Street Portsmouth, NH 03801
Offices and agents throughout the world

"Three Friends Cross The Water" originally appeared in *A Treasury of African Folklore*,
Ed. Harold Courlander. New York: Crown, 1975. Reprinted by permission of the
author.

Library of Congress Cataloging-in-Publication Data

The Critical writing workshop : designing writing assignments to foster critical
thinking / Toni-Lee Capossela, ed.
    p. cm.
    Includes bibliographical references.
    ISBN 0-86709-319-6
    1. English language—Rhetoric—Study and teaching. 2. Critical thinking—
Study and teaching. 3. Writing centers. I. Capossela, Toni-Lee.
PE1404.C75 1993
808'.042071'1—dc20   93-9449
                                                                    CIP

Cover design by T. Watson Bogard
Printed in the United States of America on Acid Free Paper
93 94 95 96 97 9 8 7 6 5 4 3 2 1

Contents

Introduction

The idea for this book grew out of a workshop entitled "Designing and Sequencing Writing Assignments to Foster Critical Thinking," given by the editor and four contributors at the 1988 Conference on College Composition and Communication and at the 1989 National Conference of Teachers of English. We realized we had struck a responsive chord when the openings in our first program filled up immediately. The morning of the workshop, many teachers waited outside the door in hopes of a last-minute vacancy. They were enrolled in other workshops, they said, but this was the one they really needed, and they would be happy to forfeit their second enrollment fee if there was room for them at one of our tables. Clearly, teachers are interested in critical thinking.

We also discovered, when the day was over and we had examined the evaluations, that participants found our varied approaches helpful, and they especially liked the comprehensive, holistic definition of critical thinking that was our point of departure. As one participant wrote in her closing remarks, "Critical thinking now goes beyond the cognitivist approach that I feared it might exclusively be interpreted as here and elsewhere."

We knew that group activity was of primary importance the day of the workshop, so we kept our theoretical comments to a minimum. But at the same time, we knew that the theoretical underpinnings of our presentations were crucial; trying to stuff them into a brief orientation session and a massive set of handouts had not worked. Our desire to combine a thorough presentation of theory with classroom and workshop applications provided the impetus for this book, and it is directly reflected in chapters 2–6. Although the authors of chapters 7–12 did not participate in the workshops, they extend the range of this collection to other important areas in which concepts of composition and critical thinking converge.

The Goals of the Book

This book invites readers to share a number of approaches to exploring the connection between thinking and writing—more specifically, the role that college writing can play in the development of holistic critical thinking, which we alternatively refer to as "reflection."

Most of the contributors have backgrounds in rhetoric or composition theory; however, we think the book will also be useful to educators whose primary interest is critical thinking. As chapter 1 documents, writing teachers and teachers of critical thinking are discovering a wide and fertile area of common interests. Critical thinking specialists often refer to the benefits of writing as a method of inculcating the skills that interest them. The degree to which critical thinking teachers are interested in writing was graphically demonstrated when one of us attended the 1988 Sonoma State University Conference on Critical Thinking, and spent four days listening to presentations on writing as a way of fostering critical thinking skills. A relevant paper was presented during every time slot of the conference, and it was not possible for one person to attend all the sessions that explicitly connected these two topics.

Chapter Summaries

By way of establishing a common context for the contributors' varied approaches, chapter 1 formulates a definition of critical writing and relates it to traditional and revisionist definitions of critical thinking.

Libby Jones (chapter 2) and William Zeiger (chapter 3) share an approach based on dialectic and multiple perspectives; they recommend forms that encourage exploration and the entertainment of contraries rather than closure. Jones uses Jack Meiland's *College Thinking* as the basis for an interactive process of questioning and reasserting a thesis; she shows how this approach works in workshop and in classroom settings. Zeiger defends both dualism and pluralism, seeing them as complementary aspects of critical thinking. In his workshop, story telling provides the frame for approaching a given issue from three different directions.

Toni-Lee Capossela, in chapter 4, connects writing and critical thinking to William Perry's research on ethical and cognitive development, with emphasis on the assets and liabilities of various pedagogical applications of Perry's scheme. She outlines an assignment sequence in which students guide themselves through Perry's scheme and then reflect metacognitively upon the journey.

In chapter 5, Betty Pytlik examines the ways in which assignment sequencing promotes critical thinking by helping students construct new knowledge structures on existing foundations. Pytlik describes a sequence based on the theme of family and designed to conform to William Coles's sequencing theories and James Moffett's levels of abstraction.

Lois Rubin (chapter 6) recommends tagmemics as a way of promoting critical thinking in both personal writing and literary analysis.

Rubin relates how workshop participants and writing students use tagmemics to identify an element that puzzles, surprises, or disturbs them in a text, first stating the problem and then exploring it.

Martha Birken and Anne Coon (chapter 7) investigate the positive consequences of shifting emphasis from answers to questions, and they discuss recursive questioning, looking beyond the answers, and the connection between intuition and critical thinking. Then they analyze a course in problem solving that they team taught from the perspectives of math and English. Richard Jenseth (chapter 8) explores important theoretical and pedagogical connections between critical thinking and epistemic rhetoric—and, briefly, deconstructionism—and shares two assignment sequences that "attempt to enact these common concerns" and pose "questions about the nature of interpretation, understanding, and composing." Kate Sandberg (chapter 9) summarizes research on the links between critical thinking and collaborative learning, lists six elements necessary for successful small-group collaboration, and explains one workshop and one classroom application. Joel Nydahl (chapter 10) evaluates recent developments in computer-aided instruction in terms of the degree to which they encourage—or inhibit—reflection and critical thinking in student writers. Sandra Lawrence (chapter 11) uses two case studies to delineate the circumstances and contexts in which journals become effective write-to-learn instruments and promote metacognitive awareness. Carol Booth Olson (chapter 12) explains a research project that challenges students to "de-center," to consider alternative approaches, and to think about their own thinking: three aspects of growth in critical thinking.

How to Use the Book

We hope you will find yourself returning to this book after your initial reading and using it in a variety of ways. For instance, it is possible to treat the book as simply an anthology of essays about the theory and practice of teaching; on this level, the consensus and collaboration originally demanded by the workshop make the essays as a sequence more coherent and mutually reinforcing than most collections.

In addition to their theoretical discussions, the workshop leaders who contributed chapters (2–6) have attempted to preserve the active, participatory nature of a professional workshop. We think that at some time during your use of the book you will find this approach stimulating and helpful. To some degree, it is possible to experience the workshops as they occurred—sometimes through a conflated "script" that is a distillation of several versions of the workshop (chapter 6), sometimes through summary and example (chapters 2–4). We have included enough details about workshop mechanics so that you can also create your own teacher training or faculty development workshops, using the procedures and source materials contained in these chapters. Workshop suggestions are also included in chapter 9.

Should you decide to undertake your own workshop, we have two suggestions based on our own experience. First, don't use the authors' accounts, or previous workshop outcomes, to shape your expectations. Preconceived assumptions about what *should* happen are lethal to the immediacy that makes workshops stimulating for participants and leaders. Second, take the trouble to tape your sessions. A successful workshop in full spate is a perfect example of James's "blooming, buzzing confusion"; as a participant-leader, you will not have the leisure or the spare brain cells to make sense of things while they are happening. After the fact, the tapes will suggest all kinds of interesting patterns and themes and will give you ideas for subsequent workshops.

Acknowledgments

We would like to thank workshop participants and our students, whose enthusiasm and intelligence gave us a wealth of information to draw from, and whose appreciation encouraged us to undertake this book.

1

What Is Critical Writing?

Toni-Lee Capossela

A History of Critical Thinking

Socrates is sometimes labeled the first critical thinker, because of the importance he gave to ideas and their role in the conduct of everyday human life. The modern history of critical thinking, however, began with John Dewey's coining of the term in the thirties. This was followed by a series of events, each of which sparked extensive and renewed interest in critical thinking: that is, the publication and adoption of the Watson-Glaser Critical Thinking Test in the forties, the back-to-basics movement in the fifties, and a rash of reports on the state of American education in the eighties (Paul 5).[1]

Current interest in critical thinking can be traced back to 1980, when formal instruction in critical thinking was mandated throughout the California State University system (Lazere 1). Another catalyst was a rapid-fire succession of reports decrying the decline in critical thinking skills among American students of all ages, e.g., *A Nation at Risk* (National Commission on Excellence in Education, 1983), *Involvement in Learning* (National Institute of Education, 1984), *Higher Education and the American Resurgence* (Newman, 1985), *The Writing Report Card: Writing Achievement in American Schools* (ETS, 1986), and *An Imperiled Generation Saving Urban Schools* (Carnegie Foundation, 1988).[2]

It seems reasonable to suppose that a concept so frequently invoked would long ago have acquired a clear-cut definition, but in fact the opposite is true: with each new appearance, critical thinking becomes less rather than more clearly defined. A book or article on critical thinking invariably begins with an elaboration of the author's definition — usually an addition to the always-ballooning list — and an explanation of how it is superior to its predecessors. In 1963 a graduate class assigned by Edward D'Angelo to survey educational journals came up with thirty-five definitions of critical thinking (5), and Brookfield outlines eight categories of critical thinking definitions (8–12). This proliferation is due partly to the fact that, as Blair and Johnson point out, the attempt to define is persuasive as well as analytic: all definitions are in essence "recommendations about how the term should henceforth be used...." (105).

In her study of the evolution of critical thinking, Karen Kitchener returns to John Dewey, who coined the term in conjunction with synonyms such as *problem solving, inquiry,* and *reflection* (76). In the ensuing years these terms have been used to distinguish between different kinds of intellectual activity. More frequently than not, such well-intended semantic maneuvers, often by Dewey's own disciples, have impoverished his rich and evocative concept and reduced it to a set of subskills.

Dewey's Definition of Critical Thinking

Dewey, who preferred the term *reflective thinking,* defined it as "active, persistent, and careful consideration of any belief or supposed form of knowledge in the light of the grounds that support it and the further conclusions to which it tends" (9). For Dewey, reflective thinking was a way of thinking, a disposition, rather than a succession of steps to be followed. This disposition included a willingness to live with uncertainty: "One can think reflectively only when one is willing to endure suspense and to undergo the trouble of uncertainty," he wrote (16). The metaphors he used to describe critical thinking included turning over, diving into, and probing, all of which suggest creativity and risk rather than a specific methodology or set of component parts.

According to Dewey, the reflective thinker had to draw not only on intellectual but also on affective powers, such as open-mindedness, wholeheartedness, and responsibility—"Note that all three are traits of character, not intellect," Dewey pointed out (33), and then warned, "...with respect to education, no separation can be made between impersonal, abstract principles of logic and moral qualities of character" (34).

Dewey made a clear distinction between *actual thinking,* of which reflective thinking was the highest form, and *formal logic.* The basic distinction was that between process and product. The great value of logic, according to Dewey, was that it set forth the result of thinking; its limitation was that it did not reflect how thinking took place (74).

Dewey did not describe critical thinking as a group of subskills to be taught in isolation or steps to be followed like a paint-by-numbers kit. He saw relationships, like context, as crucial to critical thinking, and so his approach was holistic rather than atomistic and reductive. "All reflective thinking is a process of detecting relations" (77). And later, "Only when relationships are held in view does learning become more than a miscellaneous scrap bag" (185). Not only did Dewey discourage the division of his concept into reductive parts, but he also avoided the use of polar oppositions like concrete/abstract and denotation/connotation, preferring to wed them with a memorable image: "Things are clothed with the suggestions they arouse" (220). Dewey understood the divisiveness of what Ann Berthoff calls "killer dichotomies" ("Killer" 13) and synthesized them at every opportunity.

On the other hand, Dewey abhorred pure formalism. He did not acknowledge the existence of generic "thinking" as a "single, unalterable faculty," but rather pluralized thinking as "the various ways in which things acquire significance for the individual" (46). He saw atomistic and formalistic approaches to epistemology as opposite sides of the same false coin: "The mind needs to be defended against the deadening influence of many isolated particles, and also against the barrenness of a merely formal principle" (273).

In short, Dewey described reflective or critical thinking as a complex, transactional, context-based web of activity involving the whole person.

The Move Towards Quantification

The impoverishment of Dewey's theory coincided with the development of the Watson-Glaser Critical Thinking Appraisal and a resultant absorption in assessment. As Michael Carter points out, there is an unavoidable trade-off between theoretical complexity and the power of empirical research (563). Predictably, when educators set out to measure critical thinking, they had to dissect Dewey's concept into parts in order to render it quantifiable. The legacy of this reductivism and its connection to measurement-as-assessment survive today: Kitchener finds that the instruments used to assess critical thinking ignore the basic epistemological assumptions on which critical thinking rests (78).

The most common method of cutting Dewey's concept down to size is to slice it into subskills, which supposedly can be empirically verified, then put back together to equal the composite called critical thinking. Justification for this methodology is traced to what Dewey called "the indispensable phases of reflective thinking": ideas, intellectualization to form a problem, formulation of a hypothesis, reasoning, and testing the hypothesis (107). However, Dewey called these units phases rather than stages, and he emphasized that their sequence was not fixed, precisely because he did not want his theory to be interpreted as a whole equal to the sum of its parts. This realization is echoed by

Snook: "To imagine that thinking can be broken down into its component parts which are then programmed is to misunderstand the nature of thinking" (154–55). But many educators ignored Dewey's disclaimers in their eagerness to pin down critical thinking so that its mastery could be measured.

Subskills definitions of critical thinking are characterized by exhaustive lists of steps or components. D'Angelo, who set his students to counting definitions, lists fifty skills and ten procedures in his own definition (7). Ennis gives his definition twelve aspects and three dimensions (83–85). Other theorists recycle developmental models such as Bloom's taxonomy and make critical thinking a matter of climbing to the top of a particular developmental ladder: in Bloom's case, mastering factual knowledge, comprehension, application, and analysis, in that order (201–5).

Problem Solving: The Scapegoat

Those who are uncomfortable with a subskills approach but ambivalent about completely surrendering it distinguish between problem solving and critical thinking, making problem solving the subskills scapegoat and freeing critical thinking to acquire less reductive connotations. Thus, two terms that Dewey proposed as synonyms come to appear as opposites. Kinney, for instance, makes the distinction that problem solving is a narrowing process, whereas critical thinking is an expanding process (5). Brookfield lists among the qualities of a genuine critical thinker the rejection of standardized problem-solving formats (115). In a less extreme attempt to distinguish between the two terms, Beyer claims that problem solving and critical thinking are at different stages in a hierarchy of strategies, with critical thinking occupying a higher position (27). Chet Meyers states that critical thinking, unlike problem solving, does not always begin with a problem and move toward a solution (5). D'Angelo explains that problem solving involves fewer skills—some of them nonevaluative—than critical thinking does (19). Ann Berthoff dismisses problem solving as "an activity carried out very well by trouts" because it does not include the crucial element of metacognition, or "thinking about thinking" ("Is Teaching" 743).

Plus Ça Change: The Trend Toward Holistic Definition

By and large, the back-to-basics movement of the fifties reinforced a subskills approach to critical thinking, because "the basics" were usually defined as discrete elements such as the rules of grammar, mechanics, spelling, lists of dates, and details of geography. Today, although the subskills approach to critical thinking is alive and well and generating a dizzying number of publications, many articulate voices are beginning to echo Dewey's original description of critical thinking as an attitude and a disposition with affective as well as cognitive dimensions — a process rather than a product, and one that is sensitive to and interactive with context. To a great extent this shift in sensibility is due to a growing interest in interdisciplinarity, as well as to the sense of crisis projected by the reports of the '80s. When critical thinking becomes everybody's business, then it begins to look like a meta-subject rather than a set of subskills.

Some theorists try to keep a foot in each camp. For instance, Beyer says that critical thinking is both a set of attitudes and dispositions (holistic) and a collection of specific operations (subskills); he warns that critical thinking is not a strategy, and that the operations can be used together or alone, in any sequence (33). But because most of his book deals with detailed descriptions of these operations, replete with sequential charts, the overriding impression is that the operations constitute critical thinking. Similarly, Halpern begins with a definition that appears holistic: critical thinking is "thinking that is purposeful and goal-directed," "a purposeful attempt to use thought in moving towards a future goal" (3). But her chapter headings, which are merely a list of subskills, reveal her true allegiance, and a final "Applications" chapter is little more than a feeble attempt at synthesis. Robert Ennis, who begins with a definition so generous as to be almost meaningless ("the correct assessing of statements") (81) quickly gets down to the real business of describing the twelve aspects and three dimensions by which assessment is achieved (84–85).

A wholehearted return to Dewey's rich version of critical thinking is best represented by McPeck, Meyers, and Petrosky. It is reflective of the growing interdisciplinarity of critical thinking concerns that McPeck is a philosopher, Meyers an educational theorist, and Petrosky a composition theorist.

McPeck explains that critical thinking is both a propensity and a skill, both affective and cognitive (17), both a task and an achievement phase, and that the term does not necessarily imply the successful completion of a task (13). "'Critical' is a function of the way a result is pursued, not the result itself," he states (44). Rather than consisting of a specific series of steps, the "way" is characterized by "seeing the facts in both their most persuasive and their most vulnerable lights" (157), a description reminiscent of Peter Elbow's distinction between "the Doubting Game" and "the Believing Game." McPeck concludes that epistemology rather than logic should be the foundation of a course that addresses critical thinking at a meaningful level (158). In other words, just as one does not write writing, one does not think thoughts, but rather thinks about something in particular. The curricular implication of this attitude is that critical thinking should be taught in the context of a particular discipline.

Although Chet Meyers asserts that teaching critical thinking is everybody's business (5), he does not see critical thinking as a generalizable set of skills; rather, he sees it as the context that should frame every course. Like McPeck, he asserts that the core of critical thinking is the basic epistemic of each discipline (6). Problem solving and logic, either of which is sometimes the framework for a critical thinking course, are most useful as points of departure for investigations rooted in a particular discipline, he asserts (5). Meyers's definition of critical thinking is "the ability to formulate generalizations, entertain new possibilities, and suspend judgement" (28) — components of a process rather than the achievement of a specified goal or product.

It is significant that the teaching methods that Meyers recommends to promote critical thinking are those most common in the writing classroom. For instance, he suggests an inductive approach (tantamount to a decentered classroom), because presenting deductive abstractions first (tantamount to a teacher-centered or lecture-based course) robs students of the pleasure of discovery, a pleasure that is a positive prod to critical thinking (30). He states that student interaction — such as that which exists in writing workshops, peer response groups, and other forms of collaborative writing — creates disequilibrium, an uncomfortable state that impels students to seek a resolution by examining new possibilities (31).

Anthony Petrosky, although he calls his article "Critical Thinking, Qu'est-ce Que C'est?" quickly introduces the synonym "reflective thinking" to underscore the fact that he is not talking about subskills, but rather about "a speculative or questioning stance towards knowledge and experiences" (3), a stance that is useful when one faces an "ill-structured" problem for which there is no clear solution. This definition implies that the critical thinking stance is just as integral to disciplines such as literature, which require students to grapple with "ill-structured problems," as it is to mathematics or the sciences, where problems may appear to be more obviously "well structured."

From Critical Thinking to Critical Writing

Like Petrosky, we were anxious to find a term that signals that this book does not deal with a subskills approach to critical thinking. Because we are interested in using writing to promote the kind of critical thinking that lends itself to holistic description and definition, the term we came up with was *critical writing*. Critical writing, then, is writing that creates, encourages, or prolongs McPeck's "way," Petrosky's reflective stance, and Meyers's metacognitive approach. Such writing involves both affective and intellectual dimensions, is sensitive to context, and extends the writer's ability to delay closure, entertain contradiction, and deal with uncertainty.

Although the term may be new, the connection between writing and advanced forms of cognition has been described and explored from many perspectives. From the early days of their respective disciplines, psychologists, philosophers, linguists, and educational theorists have been fascinated by the connection between thought and language, between thought and literacy, and between writing and learning.

Language and Cognition

Language theorists agree that there is a pivotal relationship between thought and language, although their ideas about the nature of the relationship differ.

Many researchers assert that the complex modes of organization required by higher order thinking are dependent on language. I. A. Richards calls language "the supreme organ of the mind's self-ordering growth" (9); Cassirer describes it as "the mighty and indispensable vehicle of thought — a kind of flywheel that carries thought along with its own increasing momentum" (qtd. in LeFevre 104). Sapir flatly states that thought "is hardly possible in any sustained sense without the symbolic organization brought by language" (15).

Susanne Langer, who calls language "the only general precision instrument the human brain has ever evolved" (201), formulates a theory that incorporates nonverbal as well as verbal conceptualization: "New ideas usually have to break in upon the mind through some great and bewildering metaphor." But, she adds, "the ideas become real intellectual property only when discursive language rises to their expression" (201). Becoming "real intellectual property" is similar to Sapir's idea of "sustained thought" — and both require language.

Vygotsky's seminal work *Thought and Language* arises out of his dissatisfaction with earlier analyses of the subject. He posits that thought and language do not have the same roots (33). By way of proof he reports the results of animal experiments, as well as the existence of both pre-verbal thought and pre-intellectual language in children. But when a child is about two years old, Vygotsky claims, he or she discovers "the symbolic function of words." As a result, thought and language "meet and join to initiate a new form of behavior" and from then on, "the knot is tied for the problem of thought and language" (43).

Michael Polanyi's attitude towards thought and language is particularly interesting, because one of the characteristics of his concept of "personal knowledge" is that it is inarticulate, or tacit (70). However,

Polanyi describes in powerful terms the dialectical relationship between thought and language:

> ... every use of language to describe experience in a changing world applies language to a somewhat unprecedented instance of its subject matter, and thus somewhat modifies both the meaning of the language and the structure of the conceptual framework ... (104–5)

Hence, in spite of their varying approaches and explanations for the phenomenon, these theorists all describe language as necessary for advanced cognition (see also Dowst, Hullfish and Smith, and Schaff).

Literacy and Cognition

For the purposes of our discussion, a literate culture is one in which mastery of a written language is necessary for full participation, and a literate person is one who is competent in that language.[3] The centrality of written language to higher forms of cognition is a more controversial issue than the centrality of language in general, which includes oral and inner speech. Until recently, most theorists agreed that written language allowed individuals as well as cultures to achieve more sophisticated feats of intellection than oral language.

Goody and Watt, in describing the results of literacy, use the same vocabulary as critical thinking theorists. For instance, Goody and Watt claim that written language results in the kind of distancing required for objectivity, because it establishes "a less direct, more abstract relationship between the word and its referent" (331). The historical development of a fully articulated written language, they argue, led to the growth of logic, a sense of the human past as objective reality, and the ability to distinguish between myth and history (332). The evaluative, questioning stance that is part of critical thinking is also fostered by written language: "Insofar as writing provides an alternative source for the transmission of cultural orientations it favors awareness of inconsistency" (337). Finally, writing puts into an individual's hands the tools needed to create a personal interpretation of reality, as opposed to the common version embodied in oral tradition:

> ... insofar as an individual participates in the literate, as distinct from the oral, culture, such coherence as a person achieves is very largely the result of his personal selection, adjustment and elimination of items from a highly differentiated cultural repertoire; he is, of course, influenced by all the various social pressures, but they are so numerous that the pattern finally comes out as an individual one. (347)

Although Goody in a more recent publication acknowledges that he may have overestimated the benefits of literacy and understated the importance of context, his earlier work with Watt remains influential.

Eric Havelock, in *The Origins of Western Literacy*, points to the cultural achievements of archaic Greece as proof that nonliterate civilizations can be highly sophisticated. But his analysis of Greek and Roman civilizations, "the first founded on the activity of the common reader" (2), leads him to conclude that conceiving, absorbing, and building on new ideas does require a language based on an alphabet, a development that he calls "a psychological and epistemological revolution" (49).

> The advance of knowledge ... depends upon the human ability to think about something unexpected—a "new idea." ... Such novel thought only achieves existence when it becomes a novel statement, and a novel statement cannot realize its potential until it can be preserved for further use. (50)

The ability to work with, evaluate, and build upon new ideas is described here as the cultural equivalent of critical thinking.

Like Havelock, David Olson examines the development of written language as embodied in the Greek alphabet, but in addition he traces the cognitive shifts effected by later language developments. Both individuals and civilizations, he says, follow a developmental sequence that leads from utterance to text: writing serves as "an instrument for making explicit the knowledge that was already implicit in their habits of speech and, in the process, tidying up and ordering that knowledge" (267).

Recent studies have challenged the claim that higher cognitive processes require literacy; for summaries, see Fox (91−98) and Hollis (122−25). Arthur Applebee, after surveying the literature on both the cultural and the individual consequences of literacy, concludes that the connection between writing and reasoning has been accepted as a given more often than it has been supported with evidence. He argues that historical studies of the cultural effects of literacy are highly inferential, and that contemporary studies confuse the effects of literacy with the effects of schooling (582).[4] Applebee concludes:

> ... the notion of writing as a unitary phenomenon, differing in a clearly specifiable way from spoken language or from cultural traditions, and thus having clearly specifiable effects on either individual or cultural development, is much too simplistic. (581)

To avoid this oversimplification, Applebee calls for examination of "the functional roles that writing and literacy play in particular cultural or individual settings" (581) (see also Heath).

Applebee also takes issue with studies that claim to show the connection between writing and thinking on an individual level, using as his primary example the protocol analyses of Linda Flower and John R. Hayes. He states that such research neither proves nor measures the understanding that purportedly occurs through writing (583).

According to Applebee, future researchers who wish to verify this connection must formulate "a more rigorous conceptualization of the functions that writing can serve, each of which might be expected to have a different relationship to the development of reasoning skills" (591).

Applebee's suggestions for future research strike a note of optimism in the midst of his skeptical rigor: the implication is that a more complex, contextual body of research may yield stronger evidence for the connection between writing and thinking than earlier studies have produced. This is the connection that teachers of writing and critical thinking are employing in their classrooms and documenting in their research.

Writing and Cognition in Academic Settings

During the initial enthusiasm for quantitative assessment, there was little possibility of dialogue between proponents of measurement and proponents of writing; their attitude towards each other was basically antagonistic. Proponents of measurement argued that writing was messy, and that its evaluation was unquantifiable and subjective. Proponents of writing countered that critical thinking was better demonstrated through writing than through easily quantifiable assessment instruments, no matter how ingeniously designed. Mike Rose points out that the "fundamentally behaviorist model" upon which quantification depends reduces writing to "a behavior that is stripped of its rich cognitive and rhetorical complexity" ("Language" 341−45). Now that holistic definitions of critical thinking are becoming more widely accepted, however, writing teachers and teachers of critical thinking are finding that they have much to learn from each other—what was once confrontation is evolving into conversation.

This book is one voice in the conversation. Underlying each chapter is the premise that writing improves thinking and that writing should be an integral part of any effort to help students think critically and reflectively.

Other voices can be heard in *Thinking, Writing, and Reasoning*, whose editors celebrate the centrality of thinking-writing connections by presenting the subject from the varying perspectives of three disciplines: informal logic, cognitive psychology, and composition theory. As Maimon, Nodine, and O'Connor point out, these disciplines have been borrowing from each other for many years, and some contributors who appear in the "Writing" section could just as accurately be grouped in the "Thinking" section (xvii).

Critical thinking theorists are coming to recognize that writing both demonstrates and fosters critical thinking. Nickerson, Perkins, and Smith, in a book devoted to teaching thinking, recommend a close examination of writing pedagogy because "writing is so paradigmatic a case of thinking" (247). They point out that "to teach people to write better is to teach them to think better" and that methods that help students write better should be incorporated into courses aimed at improving their thinking skills (247). As noted above, Meyers's recommendations for critical thinking pedagogy are already common in composition classrooms (see also Hullfish 225−28; Quinn; Ruggiero).

On the other side of the dialogue, the link between writing and thinking is fundamental to several influential and rival composition theories.[5] For instance, research based on cognitive psychology, represented by the work of Flower and Hayes, uses an information-processing model and portrays writing as a problem-solving process − "a complex cognitive skill" that is particularly interesting because it is "both a strategic action and a thinking problem" (449). If writing is an example of problem solving, then it follows that applying the general principles of problem solving to this particular manifestation will yield useful information about how people write.

Patricia Bizzell finds this cognitive "inner-directed" approach to writing incomplete, relying as it does on the assumption that there are "invariant, universal structures of human cognition" (227) and that problem solving is "an unfiltered encounter with the underlying structure of reality" (231). Bizzell proposes that the inner-directed model be enlarged by the outer-directed approaches of sociolinguistics and discourse analysis, which make room for context, convention, and other social forces shaping the decisions writers make as they compose (229). The discourse analysis model, which asks "Why" questions, provides important information that the cognitive model, with its "How" questions, has no room for; in addition, Bizzell claims, there is no acknowledgement in the cognitive model of "the dialectical relationship between thought and language" (223), the foundation on which another influential writing theory rests.

Proponents of epistemic rhetoric claim that language creates knowledge, rather than merely clothing it in words. As Kenneth Dowst explains,

> It is by means of writing that one stands to learn the most, for writing is the form of language-using that is slowest, most deliberate, most accessible, most conveniently manipulable, and most permanent. (71)

Janet Emig asserts that writing is not just a learning tool, but a form of learning, "not merely valuable, not merely special, but unique" (123). Specifically, she points out that writing possesses four characteristics common to successful learning strategies:

1. Writing is "uniquely multirepresentational and integrative."

2. Writing is a powerful form of "self-provided feedback.",
3. Writing provides many kinds of connections.
4. Writing is "active, engaged, personal," and "self-rhythmed." (129)

In addition to grappling with the fundamental issue of writing and thinking, composition teachers are borrowing from the specific vocabulary and methodology of problem solving and critical thinking. Larson, for instance, identifies two components of problem solving as particularly useful to writing teachers: evaluating the consequences of choice, and being aware of options (629). He recommends that, to promote the aims of liberal education, composition teachers use problem solving as an invention heuristic, as an analog for formulating and testing hypotheses, as a method of organizing essays, and as a tool in analyzing literature and evaluating their own work (see also Coe and Gutierrez; Kiniry and Strenski; and Odell).

Finally, to complete the conversational loop, composition theorists are attributing the success of their pedagogy—the pedagogy that is being adopted by teachers of critical thinking—to its foundation in critical thinking concepts. For instance, Ken Bruffee claims that collaborative writing succeeds because it requires students in groups to exercise judgment—"the part of knowledge that's social: decision making, discrimination, evolution, analysis, synthesis, establishing or recognizing conceptual frames of reference and defining 'fact' within them" (181). The implication here is that critical thinking is a socially acquired capacity.

Herrington and Cadman claim that peer reviewing helps students produce more effective work precisely because it encourages "active, reciprocal decision-making," rather than the unquestioning acceptance with which students frequently adopt teachers' suggestions. The authors show how the comments of student writers who have received peer reviews reflect "processes of weighing alternatives and then deciding how to act" (184), a pithy description of critical thinking even if it is not labeled as such.

In short, critical thinking and composition theory are converging in so many ways and on so many fronts that it is difficult—and probably pointless—to figure out who is borrowing from whom. Rather than thinking of them as separate fields, it is more fruitful to conflate them into a single self-referential metacognitive endeavor—hence the term *critical writing*.

Endnotes

1. Resnick points out that the history of critical thinking in the twentieth century is distinguished from earlier movements by an effort to situate critical thinking in the context of mass education. Only within the past sixty years,

Resnick observes, have the two separate strands of mass and elite education been intertwined. One result of this merger is that higher order skills are now included among the objectives of mass education, which previously dealt only with minimal proficiency levels (4−5).

2. Dinkelman, however, shows that two of these studies place little "substantive emphasis on the development of critical thinking" (5).

3. *Competence*, we realize, is a problematic word. Many provocative literacy studies examine various kinds of competence, particularly as they relate to polarities, such as resistance vs. accommodation, revision vs. ratification of accepted versions of reality, subversion vs. absorption of value systems (Bizzell; Brodkey; Freire; Hoggart; Hollis; Kintgen, Kroll, and Rose; Rose, *Lives*; Shor; Trimbur; Ward). Because the primary thrust of our discussion is the oral-written distinction, we regretfully confine our discussion to the more limited definition of literacy.

4. In a study unusual for its attempt to distinguish between the cognitive effects of literacy and the cognitive effects of schooling, Scribner and Coles claim that literate subjects demonstrated no significant differences in any of the study's cognitive measures, and that there was no significant drop in metalinguistic skills among illiterate subjects (see also Gere).

5. Carter studies the common genealogy of these rival camps, and he attributes this irony to the existence of two opposed "theories of problems." He proposes a "pluralistic theory of problems" that will accommodate both the information-processing and the epistemic models of problem solving. His description of the pluralistic model is strongly reminiscent of Dewey's original definition of critical thinking.

Works Cited

Applebee, Arthur N. "Writing and Reasoning." *Review of Educational Research* 54 (1984): 577−96.

Berthoff, Ann. "Is Teaching Still Possible?" *College English* 46 (1984): 743−55.

———. "Killer Dichotomies: Reading In/Reading Out." *Farther Along: Transforming Dichotomies in Rhetoric and Composition*. Eds. Kate Ronald and Hephzibah Roskelly. Portsmouth, NH: Boynton/Cook, 1990. 12−24.

Beyer, Barry K. *Practical Strategies for the Teaching of Thinking*. Boston: Allyn & Bacon, 1987.

Bizzell, Patricia. "Cognition, Convention, and Certainty: What We Need to Know About Writing." *Pre/Text* 3 (1982): 213−43.

Blair, Anthony, and Ralph Johnson. "Informal Logic: A Thematic Approach." *Thinking, Reasoning, and Writing*. Ed. Elaine Maimon, Barbara Nodine, and Finbarr O'Connor. New York: Longman, 1989.

Bloom, Benjamin S., ed. *Taxonomy of Educational Objectives* Vol. 1 New York: Longman, 1956.

Brodkey, Linda. *Academic Writing as Social Practice*. Philadelphia: Temple University Press, 1987.

Brookfield, Stephen D. *Developing Critical Thinkers: Challenging Adults to Explore Alternative Ways of Thinking and Acting*. San Francisco: Jossey-Bass, 1987.

Bruffee, Kenneth. "The Structure of Knowledge and the Future of Liberal Education." *Liberal Education* 68 (1981): 177–86.

Carter, Michael. "Problem Solving Reconsidered: A Pluralistic Theory of Problems." *College English* 50 (1988): 551–65.

Coe, Richard M., and Kris Gutierrez. "Using Problem Solving Procedures and Process Analysis to Help Students with Writing Problems." *College Composition and Communication* 32 (1981): 262–71.

D'Angelo, Edward. *The Teaching of Critical Thinking*. Amsterdam: B.R. Gruner, 1971.

Dewey, John. *How We Think*. Boston: D.C. Heath, 1933.

Dinkelman, Todd. "Critical Thinking and Educational Reform in the 1980's." *Illinois Schools Journal* 69 (1990): 5–14.

Dowst, Kenneth. "The Epistemic Approach: Writing, Knowing and Learning." *Eight Approaches to Teaching Composition*. Eds. Timothy R. Donovan and Ben McClelland. Urbana, IL: NCTE, 1980. 65–85.

Elbow, Peter. "Appendix Essay." *Writing Without Teachers*. New York: Oxford University Press, 1973. 147–91.

Emig, Janet. "Writing as a Mode of Learning." 1977. *The Web of Meaning*. Eds. Dixie Goswami and Maureen Butler. Montclair, NJ: Boynton/Cook, 1983, 123–31.

Ennis, Robert. "A Concept of Critical Thinking." *Harvard Educational Review* 32 (1962): 81–111.

Flower, Linda, and John R. Hayes. "Problem-Solving Strategies and the Writing Process." *College English* 39 (1977): 449–61.

Fox, Thomas. *The Social Uses of Writing: Politics and Pedagogy*. Norwood, NJ: Ablex, 1990.

Freire, Paulo. *Education for Critical Consciousness*. Trans. Myra Bergman Ramos. New York: Continuum, 1983.

Gere, Ann Ruggles. "A Cultural Perspective on Talking and Writing." *Exploring Speaking-Writing Relationships*. Eds. Barry Kroll and Roberta Vann. Evanston, IL: NCTE, 1981, 111–23.

Goody, Jack, ed. *Literacy in Traditional Societies*. Cambridge: Cambridge University Press, 1968.

Goody, Jack, and Ian Watt. "The Consequences of Literacy." 1972. *Language and Social Context*. Ed. Pier Paolo Giglioli. Baltimore, MD: Penguin Books, 1972. 311–57. *Comp. Studies in Society and History*, 304–26, 332–45. Vol. 5 1962–63.

Halpern, Diane F. *Thought and Knowledge: An Introduction to Critical Thinking*. Hillsdale, NJ: Erlbaum, 1984.

Havelock, Eric. *Origins of Western Literacy*. Ontario: Ontario Institute for Studies in Education, 1976.

Heath, Shirley Brice. *Ways with Words: Language, Life and Work in Communities and Classrooms*. Cambridge: Cambridge University Press, 1983.

Herrington, Anne, and Deborah Cadman. "Peer Review and Revising in an Anthropology Course: Lessons in Learning." *College Composition and Communication* 42 (1991): 184–99.

Hoggart, Richard. "The Importance of Literacy." *Journal of Basic Writing* 3 (1980): 74–87.

Hollis, Karyn. "Building a Context for Critical Literacy: Student Writers as Critical Theorists." *The Writing Instructor* 7 (1988): 122–30.

Hullfish, Gordon, and Phillip G. Smith. *Reflective Thinking: The Method of Education*. NY: Dodd, Mead & Co., 1961.

Kiniry, Malcolm, and Ellen Strenski. "Sequencing Expository Writing: A Recursive Approach." *College Composition and Communication* 36 (1985): 191–202.

Kinney, James L. "Why Bother? The Importance of Critical Thinking." *Fostering Critical Thinking*. Ed. Robert E. Young. San Francisco: Jossey-Bass, 1980.

Kintgen, Eugene, Barry Kroll, and Mike Rose, eds. *Perspectives on Literacy*. Carbondale, IL: Southern Illinois University Press, 1988.

Kitchener, Karen. "Educational Goals and Reflective Thinking." *Educational Forum* 48 (1983): 75–95.

Langer, Susanne K. *Philosophy in a New Key*. Cambridge, MA: Harvard University Press, 1942.

Larson, Richard. "Problem-Solving, Composing, and Liberal Education." *College English* 33 (1972): 628–35.

Lauer, Janice M. "Writing as Inquiry and Some Questions for Teachers." *College Composition and Communication* 33 (1982): 89–93.

Lazere, Donald. *Critical Thinking in College English Studies*. ERIC, 1987. ED 284 275.

LeFevre, Karen Burke. *Invention as a Social Act*. Carbondale, IL: Southern Illinois University Press, 1987.

Maimon, Elaine, Barbara Nodine, and Finbarr O'Connor, eds. *Thinking, Reasoning, and Writing*. New York: Longmans, 1989.

McPeck, John. *Critical Thinking and Education*. New York: St. Martin's Press, 1981.

Meyers, Chet. *Teaching Students to Think Critically*. San Francisco: Jossey-Bass, 1986.

Nickerson, Raymond S., David Perkins, and Edward Smith. *The Teaching of Thinking*. Hillsdale, NJ: Erlbaum, 1985.

Odell, Lee. "Piaget, Problem-Solving, and Freshman Composition." *College Composition and Communication* 24 (1973): 36–42.

Olson, David R. "From Utterance to Text: The Bias of Language in Speech and Writing." *Harvard Educational Review* 47 (1977): 257–81.

Paul, Richard. "Critical Thinking: Fundamental to Education for a Free Society." *Educational Leadership* 42.1 (1984): 4–14.

Petrosky, Anthony. "Critical Thinking: Qu'est-ce Que C'est?" *The English Record* 37.3 (1986): 2–5.

Polanyi, Michael. *Personal Knowledge: Towards a Post-Critical Philosophy*. Chicago: Chicago University Press, 1958.

Quinn, Mary. *Critical Thinking and Writing: An Approach to the Teaching of Composition*. Diss. U of Michigan 1983.

Resnick, Lauren B. *Education and Learning to Think*. Washington, DC: National Academy Press, 1987.

Richards, I.A. *Speculative Instruments*. New York: Harcourt Brace, 1955.

Rose, Mike. "The Language of Exclusion: Writing Instruction at the University." *College English* 47 (1985): 341–59.

———. *Lives on the Boundary*. New York: Penguin, 1989.

Ruggiero, Vincent. *Teaching Thinking Across the Curriculum*. New York: Harper and Row, 1988.

Sapir, Edward. "Language." *Culture, Language and Personality: Selected Essays*. Ed. David G. Mandelbaum. Berkeley: University of California Press, 1956. 1–44.

Schaff, Adam. *Language and Cognition*. New York: McGraw Hill, 1973.

Scribner, Sylvia, and Michael Coles. "Literacy Without Schooling." *Harvard Educational Review* 48 (1978): 448–61.

Shor, Ira. *Critical Teaching and Everyday Life*. Boston: South End Press, 1980.

Snook, I.A. "Teaching Pupils to Think." *Studies in Philosophy and Education* 8 (1974): 146–62.

Trimbur, John. "Literacy and the Discourse of Crisis." *The Politics of Writing Instruction: Postsecondary*. Eds. Richard Bullock and John Trimbur. Portsmouth, NH: Boynton/Cook, 1991. 277–96.

Vygotsky, Lev. *Thought and Language*. Trans. Eugenia Hanfmann and Gertrude Vakar. Cambridge: MIT Press, 1962.

Ward, Jay. *Cognitive Development as Literacy*. ERIC, 1987. ED 280 074.

2

Exploring Beliefs Through Dialectical Thinking

Libby Falk Jones

The 1991 ASHE-ERIC Higher Education Report *Active Learning* is among the latest in a series of national studies of education to call for increased intellectual exchange and active learning in our classrooms (Bonwell and Eison 2–4). In a world of rapid change, all knowledge bases have inherent limitations; learning to create, investigate, and manipulate any knowledge base is more important than simply acquiring knowledge. We need to be teaching our students not to receive knowledge passively but to think critically through issues and beliefs, to engage in "systematic reasoning about what they read and write" (Applebee, Langer, and Mullis 9).

According to Edward M. Glaser, educator and developer of the Watson-Glaser Critical Thinking Appraisal, critical thinking includes three principal elements:

1. An attitude of being disposed to consider in a thoughtful perceptive manner the problems and subjects that come within the range of one's experiences;

2. knowledge of the methods of logical inquiry and reasoning;

3. skill in applying those methods. (25)

Glaser goes on to say that "the knowledge and skill components of critical thinking involve the examination of a stated belief ... to see if the evidence or reasoning presented supports it" (25). To conduct this examination, critical-thinking educators are moving away from the teaching of narrow, technical reasoning skills such as the ability to construct a syllogism or label a particular logical fallacy—skills that may not be readily transferable to complex real-life situations — and toward the teaching of flexible strategies used holistically to sort through complex issues. The underlying goal is less to teach particular techniques and more to develop an orientation, a predisposition, to reflection and inquiry.

The Value of Dialectical Thinking

One useful strategy for developing critical thinking abilities is dialectical thinking: a process of examining a subject by positing chains of contrary views. According to Richard Paul, director of the Center for Critical Thinking and Moral Critique at Sonoma State University, dialectical reasoning "meets the needs of persons ... to work out an amalgamation of ideas from various dimensions of experience, to achieve ... intellectual, emotional and moral integrity" (Glaser 25). Five characteristics of dialectical thinking differentiate it from formal logic and render it useful in teaching critical thinking. Dialectical thinking

- Is a generic rather than a discipline-specific means of structuring an on-going process.
- Is generative and exploratory as well as evaluative.
- Provides a means of coping with the complexity and comprehensiveness of issues and arguments.
- Integrates the seemingly contrary elements of doubting and believing, thus encouraging connection and ownership.
- Encourages the development of thinking as a collaborative activity.

In the following sections, I'll discuss these aspects of dialectical reasoning and establish their value in the teaching of critical thinking.

1. Thinking: Generic Versus Discipline-specific

The academy is currently debating the relation of thinking skills to the subject matter to which the skills are applied. Do thinking skills constitute a discipline in themselves, relevant to every subject matter? Or does the discipline, as constructor and orderer of knowledge and determiner of value, dictate the sort of thinking skills necessary for inquiry in that field?

The value of dialectical reasoning is that it can exist happily on the horns of this dilemma. Because dialectical thinking can be discussed and practiced on any subject matter, it can be used generically across the curriculum. Since it is a framework rather than a content, and since that framework can be loosely defined, it is also capable of being made field-specific: the field can determine what constitutes acceptable objections and responses, while the thinker is still operating within the dialectical structure. It's true that some fields are more receptive than others to arguments presented dialectically. But dialectical thinking can be used as a heuristic even in fields where dialogic presentation is not appropriate. Further, dialectical thinking can be practiced by students at various levels of the educational process, from high school through postgraduate.

2. Thinking: Inquiry, Not Advocacy

In our culture, the process of reasoning about an issue is generally called argumentation. For most people, argument has two primary associations: emotion and persuasion. The first association, argument as heated discussion, precludes the possibility of rational thought. The second association, argument as persuasion, is more useful in that it opens the possibility that thought can occur, can be structured and analyzed. Communication scholars confirm that argumentation is a means of persuasion. According to one textbook, argumentation is "a form of instrumental communication relying on reasoning and proof to influence belief or behavior through the use of spoken or written messages" (Rybacki and Rybacki 2). The implication of equating thinking with advocacy is significant.

In James Kinneavy's terms, persuasive discourse focuses on the decoder, or recipient, of communication (39). As defined in a representative composition text, the Trimmers/Sommers shorter edition of McCrimmon's *Writing with a Purpose*, persuasion is "verbal communication that attempts to bring about a voluntary change in judgment so that readers or listeners will accept a belief they did not hold before" (329). Persuasion is thus audience-directed and product-oriented; whatever doubts the writer or speaker may have experienced in formulating a stance, her persuasive voice is knowledgeable, confident. The rhetorical structure too is audience-dominated, based on a thesis known from the outset; the writer or speaker is urged to order points from weakest to strongest so as to end with the most convincing, and to introduce objections only in order to refute them.

Though advocacy is an important and natural outcome of systematic reasoning, equally important is the thinking that seeks to discover rather than to persuade. In contrast to persuasion, thinking as inquiry is self-directed and process-oriented. Rather than convincing an audience, the writer is testing for her own benefit the strength of a position; development is governed not by exemplification and support of an already determined thesis, but by a continuing search for truth. In Kinneavy's terms, this discourse is referential, stressing the ability of language to designate or reproduce reality, and more specifically, exploratory, since the reality "is not known or is being sought" (39). If finding out is more important than proving, as William Zeiger has argued, then we should offer students a form more open than traditional thesis-support exposition. A dialectical structure, in which assertions are tested through oppositions, facilitates exploration of a belief. Further, where the structure for proving/persuading inclines always to closure as soon as necessary agreement has been reached, the dialectical structure encourages maximum development of ideas and in fact serves as a heuristic to help the thinker generate more material. As John Gage notes, the implication of dialectic is that "knowledge can be created in the activity of discourse" (157).

3. Thinking: Beyond Dualism to Relativism

As an open-ended exploration that discourages early closure on an issue, dialectical thinking is a natural antidote to a dualistic mind-set. Dualism, the first stage in the cognitive model posited by William Perry, consists of a belief in absolutes, a conviction that truth is simple and fully knowable, and a reliance on outside agency rather than self to determine truth. In order to be able to think critically, the student must move beyond such a mind-set. Dialectical reasoning helps students to see that there are many viewpoints and that truth can reside in more than one view. At the same time that dialectical thinking moves a student toward Perry's last stage of contextual relativism, it also provides a concrete structure for conducting the exploration of complexity, thus satisfying the thinker's transitional need for solidity in the midst of change.

4. Thinking: Connecting Doubt and Belief

Doubt as a mode of inquiry has a long and distinguished history. Including a cluster of behaviors described by Belenky et al. as *separate knowing* (adversarial, impersonal, logical), doubt has been established as the academy's primary means of determining truth. This predominance is suggested by the implications of the word *critical* in critical thinking. Since dialectical thinking demands that assertions be tested through objections, this process of reasoning encourages development of critical skills.

Yet doubt is only one means of knowing — and for some learners, not the primary one. *Connected knowing*, as defined by Belenky et al., depends not on doubt but on belief. Connected knowing requires an initial suspension of judgment while the knower tries on another's view, immerses herself in that view. Where doubt demands detachment, belief demands empathy; where doubting asks us to suppress the self, believing asks us to consider the self in light of the point at hand. The strength of believing as a mode of inquiry, Peter Elbow argues in *Embracing Contraries*, is that belief prevents a superficial dismissal of views that we don't share (258–63). Before we can reject a position, we must truly believe it: we must genuinely see what the world looks like from inside that position.

My argument here is that dialectical thinking encourages precisely the contrary movements of doubting and believing. The structure demands that an assertion be countered by an objection (a doubt). Once the doubt is stated, however, its effectiveness in exploring the truth of the issue depends on the degree to which it can be believed. That is, truly to test the issue at hand, the thinker must fully inhabit each stage of the developing dialectic. Though the structure of inquiry is dictated by doubt, the thinker must believe in the position advanced at each stage of that structure and make the strongest possible case for the truth of that stage. In this way the strength of the different positions can be seen clearly and evaluated.

A final important element of connected knowing is the knower's ability to relate the discussion to her own self. Dialectical thinking, rather than removing the writer from her beliefs, provides a methodology for examining those beliefs in order to understand them more fully. By encouraging students to apply dialectical thinking to their own beliefs, we help them to see that thinking is not simply an academic activity but a life skill leading to personal growth.

5. Thinking: Collaboration

Implicit in the connected knowing model is the assumption that knowing is, in Parker Palmer's terms, a communal act. If we are to get beyond the objectivism (with its emphasis on detachment, analysis, and manipulation) that dominates the academy, we need to engage in collaborative learning in the classroom. Collaborative learning, as theorists such as Kenneth Bruffee, Anne Gere, Clark Bouton, and Russell Garth argue, assumes that knowing is a constructive, not a receptive, act; that dialogue is essential to learning; and that the development of abilities is integral to the acquisition of knowledge (Bouton and Garth 75). In dialectical thinking, as Gage notes, knowledge is "something that people *do* together" (157). Dialectical inquiry can readily form the basis for group exploration of a position, as members of the group work together to generate reasons, objections, and replies. As I explain below, I have devised an assignment that requires students to collaborate in thinking dialectically.

An Assignment in Dialectical Thinking

Having established, then, the value of dialectical thinking in the teaching of critical thinking, we can turn to a means to implement this form. The method I have chosen is based on the framework outlined by Jack W. Meiland in his book *College Thinking*. Meiland advocates the writing of a major argumentative essay as a means of learning how to think. Various authorities, including Ernest L. Boyer, emphasize the importance of writing as "the means by which critical thinking—the essence of good education—can be pursued" (33).

Simply put, Meiland demands that the writer examine a belief by testing the strength of the reasons for holding such a belief. He describes a formal dialectical structure for the essay:

1. Statement and brief explanation of the question or problem, justifying its importance.
2. Statement of the position you are testing.
3. First argument (reason) for the position.
4. Objection to this argument.
5. Reply to this objection.
6. Continued objections and replies until all material related to this argument is exhausted.
7. Second argument for the position.
8. Objection to second argument.
9. Reply to this objection.
10. Continued objections and replies until all material related to this argument is exhausted.
11. Third argument for the position, followed by objections and replies until all material is exhausted.
12. Continued arguments, until all arguments have been presented and tested.
13. Conclusion: assessment of original position, in light of testing of arguments.

   Several features of this assignment are crucial.

1. Each stage should be clearly labelled and each should be a separate paragraph. The writer must not simply state a reason or objection or reply; each stage must be identified, developed, and supported. Since the goal is to test the strength of the reason, the strength must be allowed to emerge. Developing each stage prevents superficiality.

2. Further, each argument should be pursued until material related to that reason is exhausted. Since the goal is not to convince a reader of the strength of a reason but to test that strength, the writer must continue to bring up objections even if there are no replies to them.

3. Since the writer is testing a position rather than persuading an audience, the position does not need to be one in which the writer herself believes. In fact, inquiry may be more genuine, may result in fuller consideration of other viewpoints, when the writer is testing a position with which she does not agree.

4. The essay resulting from this assignment must be long enough to allow the writer to pursue her thinking fully and deeply. For an essay without research, I ask for 1,000 words; with research, 1,500—2,000 words. For both, I ask students to test at least two reasons for the position and to develop each through at least one objection and reply.

Classroom and Workshop Administration

My approach to this assignment in dialectical thinking is to ask students to experience it. After a brief review of the steps Meiland outlines, we take a sample topic, frame a question, pick a position to test, brainstorm reasons for that position, and divide into small groups to test these reasons. An hour spent in experiencing the process forms the best foundation for the longer assignment that will follow. In a class not researching their topic, the whole assignment can be completed in two weeks, with sharing of papers and revisions taking a third week. In addition to explaining the approach and allowing students to practice it briefly on the first day of the assignment, I also give or read to them sample papers or sections of papers responding to this assignment.

In workshops for high school and college faculty, I've asked participants to try out the approach through a sample topic, then discuss its philosophy and results. At the conclusion of the workshop, teachers have devised ways to adapt the assignment and its administration to their own environments. Faculty workshops have generally lasted one and a half hours, with fifteen—twenty participants in each.

Choosing a Topic

For the longer assignment, to further collaborative investigation, I demand that the class agree on a single topic. For classes in which the essay will result in a research paper, I ask that groups of four to six students choose a single topic.

Topics chosen by my classes during the last several years include mandatory drug testing, public school attendance by children with AIDS, legal drinking age, college admission requirements, choice of sex of unborn children, inclusion of creation theory in school curricula, and book censorship. The best issues have been contemporary and unresolved ones; at the time my first class explored mandatory drug testing, for example, there had not been any court ruling on its legality. For the faculty workshops, I've chosen an issue similarly unresolved, one that should genuinely interest the participating teachers: the yoking of the teaching of writing and literature.

Stating the Question

Turning the issue into a question is not an automatic step. "Should there be mandatory drug testing?" fails to specify a number of important elements: Testing for what drugs? When? Of whom? By whom? Posing the question is a valuable group exercise illustrating the need for limits and clarity in defining a problem. My class, deciding not to include drug testing of athletes, settled on this question: "Should companies and the government be allowed to require periodic testing for illegal drugs of any or all employees?"

For the faculty workshops, to save time, I've posed the question: "In secondary and postsecondary institutions, should programs of writing be separated from departments of literature?"

Stating the Position to Be Tested

Because I want to stress that critical-thinking skills can be used to examine any belief, and because I want my students to work to understand the opponent's position, I do not allow them to choose their positions on the question. Instead, I arbitrarily assign half the group to test the position that affirms the question, the other half the position that denies it. Freeing students from commitment to the position being examined can help further their reasoning skills; once developed, their skills can be applied to beliefs they do hold.

Brainstorming Reasons

Students and workshop participants must then come up with some reasons to test. Here are reasons participants have generated within five minutes to support the position "Yes, writing and literature should be separated."

1. English teachers who love literature may neglect the teaching of writing.

2. When writing is the sole focus of a course, a wider variety of styles and subjects can be addressed.

3. Many literature teachers have not been trained to teach writing.

4. Separate writing classes would please the public, businesses, corporations, professionals, all of whom feel schools are currently neglecting writing skills.

5. Separating the programs could more easily involve faculty across the curriculum in the teaching of writing.

6. Separation would increase the status of writing teachers and the money available for writing instruction.

7. Separate writing courses would make available the time needed to pursue fully the writing process.

Here are reasons given by participants — again, in five minutes — to support the position that writing and literature should not be separated.

1. Reading and writing are complementary exercises; they are best taught together.

2. Literature teachers make the best teachers of writing.

3. Literature provides useful models for writers.

4. Keeping writing and literature together increases the financial resources of the English Department.

5. It avoids the disciplinary fragmentation and isolation that already plagues most curricula.

6. It avoids unnecessary and expensive proliferation of administrative structures.

Note that even though some of the reasons on each side speak to the same issues, they are not mirror images of one another; the shape of an essay testing the positive position will not be the simple reverse of one testing the negative position. This is why it is useful to have half the group test reasons supporting the positive position, and half test the negative position.

Testing a Reason's Strength

In the next step, students or workshop participants work together to test the strength of one reason for the position. It's important that each reason be tested separately, though some overlap with other reasons may occur as the testing develops. Only separate testing can indicate the relative strength of each reason; the relative strength of all the reasons tested will become the basis for the writer's assessment of the validity of the position. Testing means first supporting the reason, then objecting to it, then replying to the objection, and so on.

Here is a testing chain developed by one group of workshop participants in approximately ten minutes. They were testing the fourth reason for not separating the two programs: Keeping writing and literature together increases the financial resources of the English Department.

> *Support*: You have more dollars for professional development, travel, etc.
>
> *Objection*: Even if the department is receiving more money, this does not necessarily mean more money for writing teachers. Travel funds may be allocated on a per person basis — not spread among all faculty. And in the typical department, literature teachers get more of such money than do writing teachers.
>
> *Reply*: Even if distribution of funds is unequal, it's still true that the more funds there are, the more there will be to distribute and the better chance there is that all faculty will benefit.
>
> *Objection*: Even if some of this money filters down to writing teachers, it's still not as much as they would get if they were in fact a separate department with a budget of their own — even if that budget were smaller than the original English Department budget.
>
> *Reply*: Even in a separate department, some hierarchies could emerge — some research could be valued more than others so some individuals still might not be fairly treated.

The group felt that it had not yet exhausted the material on this reason. In an argumentative essay, of course, not only would the chain be pursued until no more objections or replies could be given, but also each step in this skeletal chain would be supported as strongly as possible. I include this short skeletal chain here to illustrate the way in which the structure facilitates critical thinking through the argument — and in a short time. Note too that the essentially linear structure can branch: testing a reason might involve raising (and replying to) three or four different objections. By labelling each stage of the developing argument, the writer ensures that complex logical processes become clear.

Here is a section from a student essay on drug testing, examining as a reason against testing the claim that testing is an invasion of privacy.

> One argument for this position [that testing should not be allowed] is that the testing is an invasion of privacy. The employee, as well as his employer, has a private life that is his and his only. If the employee wishes to use drugs, it is his choice. The employer has as much right to check for drugs as he does to check what time the employee gets in on Saturday night (or Sunday morning). It is the employee's concern if he wants to take drugs ...
>
> But then there is the objection that the company is only doing the drug testing because they are concerned with the welfare of the employee. The employee's safety, health, and longevity may be the

primary reasons for the subjected drug testing. If the employee is found to be a user, the company may just want to help him get over his problem. If so, it is only for the employee's benefit and the drug testing should be allowed.

But, if an employer is allowed to stop an employee from taking drugs because it is bad for the employee's health, should he also be allowed to tell the employee he can't eat certain foods or smoke cigarettes? The meaning is the same. The employer has as much right to tell the employee to stop his usage of drugs as he does telling him to stop eating french fries. Both are detrimental to his health and decrease the longevity of his life. Yet the employer, no matter how good his intentions, has no right to make the employee stop because it is the employee's life, not the employer's.

An additional objection to this reply might be that the employee's good health benefits not only the employee, but the company, which loses money and time when employees are ill and away from work. The company's need for productivity from employees could mandate drug testing. Then this objection might be answered and the chain continued until all material on this reason has been exhausted.

Testing Gone Awry

Testing the reason can fail when participants abandon the reason and begin to debate the position. In one workshop, participants testing the position that the programs should be separated began with the first reason, that literature teachers often neglect writing because they love literature. Rather than testing that reason, they listed reasons for teaching literature: the variety of materials available, literature's ability to give students the opportunity to discover the world and themselves and to develop critical thinking skills. Then they listed problems with the teaching of literature: community values may not permit full exploration of literature, while reading others' writing may stifle rather than enhance creativity. This material is relevant to the issue, but groups of claims about the value of literature do not test the strength of the first reason for separating the programs. One objection to that first reason might be that literature teachers' neglect of writing results not from their love of literature but from their lack of training in teaching writing. This objection would need to be supported and then, if possible, answered. Another objection might be that even if writing per se is being neglected, teaching literature is actually a good indirect means of teaching writing. This objection could also be supported and answered and a testing chain developed.

Sometimes problems occur when the writer omits pieces from her chain of reasoning. Here is a paragraph from a student essay testing the position that social fraternities should be allowed on the university campus.

One argument for my position is that social fraternities provide a wide variety of social and recreational opportunities. However, an objection may be taken by stating that the many social activities can lead to a decrease in grade point averages. Too much emphasis on social events tends to overcome the importance of studying. A reply to this objection is that fraternities help members avoid the feeling of loneliness by holding certain functions in order to meet other people. Members of fraternities do not need invitations to their socials. Therefore, the active members introduce their pledges to friends. Guys that are not members may need invitations to attend the events. When attending the events, the non-members may feel inferior to the others because they are unfamiliar with the members.

The initial reason-objection-reply structure is clear. The passage begins to become confusing at the stage of the reply, when the reader wonders just how avoiding loneliness relates to studying. The rest of the paragraph may seem irrelevant to the argument. However, elaborating the abbreviated statements reveals their underlying logic. At the reply stage, the writer's point is that fraternity-sponsored social events, while taking time away from studying, contribute to solving another problem that can also cause a decrease in grade-point averages and even withdrawal from school: loneliness. The writer's objection to this reply is that students don't have to be members of fraternities to attend their social functions, that these functions are available to non-members as well. In reply, she claims that fraternity members are more likely to take advantage of the social events since they don't need special invitations and since they know other members who will introduce them around. Nonmembers who attend may feel inferior to others and are thus less likely to attend and more likely to experience loneliness. Thus fraternity social events are more likely to prevent loneliness among their members and to encourage them to continue their studies.

This student writer needs to make clear each stage of her reasoning; in particular, she needs to allow a full paragraph to support each stage and to make clear its relationship to other stages. Another issue is scope: this writer tried to test five different reasons in support of fraternities in 1,000 words. Revising to test the three best reasons resulted in a stronger essay.

Putting Together the Whole Essay

The essay consists of at least two arguments, each tested at least through the reply stage. Because the writer is testing the strength of the position rather than convincing an audience of the truth of her position, she should begin by testing her strongest reason and progress to the weakest. Though many students — particularly first-term freshmen—think initially that a 1,000-word paper assignment is too long, most discover that they need more words to develop their two arguments. Many of my students test more than two reasons and pursue them through more stages.

In the conclusion, the writer must assess the strength of the reasons tested and accordingly affirm, deny, or modify the position with which she began. Giving the writer permission to reject the assigned position, if its supporting reasons have been shown to be weak, marks this assignment as one of genuine inquiry. In practice, most students seek to negotiate between the two extremes of affirming and denying. Here are concluding paragraphs from two student essays:

> As a final statement, I believe that fraternities are neither all good nor all bad. I withdraw my previous statement that says that fraternities should not be allowed at the University. In its place I shall say that social fraternities should be allowed at the University, but only under stipulated rules and policies such as those I have suggested in this paper. With the proper guidance a fraternity can be a productive useful asset to the University.

> I believe the position I have taken that first quarter freshmen should not be responsible for the new admission requirements is justified by arguments throughout my paper. But I also believe, from the objections in this paper, that it would be good for college students to have taken the new required classes. A solution, or maybe better said, a compromise, would be for the requirements to be a college graduation requirement instead of an admission requirement. Being a graduation requirement, it would give all students an opportunity to meet the requirements, if not before enrollment, then during college at their own pace until graduation.

Though I have had as many as thirty students writing on the same topic, I have never received duplicate papers. Because they are working together to explore ideas, I tell them that I expect to see some of the same reasons, objections, and supporting evidence in their final essays. With each reason spawning several possible objections, each objection several replies, and the potential for supporting evidence virtually unlimited, the likelihood of carbon copy essays is small.

Some students object that labelling each stage of the argument ("An objection to this reason is . . .") limits their ability to make the graceful transitions they've been taught mark good writing. Yet the final essay exhibits a different kind of power: clear thinking.

Teacher's Response

I coach students' thinking for depth and breadth, pushing them to additional stages in the chain that tests each reason and proposing additional reasons that could be tested. In my marginal comments, I also request evidence for their claims and point to logical flaws. I've found that Meiland's structure makes my job easier: the track of thinking is laid out so clearly that it's easy to see when the student writer gets derailed. And because I'm focused on one or, at the most, five topics, I can think those through more fully than if every student were writing on a separate topic. Students must revise their essays to answer my comments; some rewrite sections of the essays. This revision extends the dialectical approach to reasoning, with the teacher's voice continuing the dialogue the student has begun in the paper. Revising also reinforces the concept of thinking as a process, rather than a finished product. To celebrate achievement and illustrate diversity of thinking, I select a good essay on each position to read aloud to the class.

Dialectical Argumentation and Research

I find one of the strengths of Meiland's approach is that it provides a means of learning reasoning skills without doing the extensive research necessary for truly informed belief. Further, Meiland's structure works to clarify the questions — the accuracy of drug tests, for example — that can be answered only through research. When I use Meiland's method in classes without extensive research opportunities, I urge students to indicate in their essays the points at which research is needed to establish conclusively the strength of that reason.

Perceiving the value of an approach that defines clearly the questions to be researched, I've adapted this argumentative essay assignment for a composition and research class. Working in groups of four to six, students choose a topic and write the initial argumentative essay based on their own knowledge and, if they desire, some preliminary outside reading. I respond with comments on the structure and substance of their thinking; I ask them, as part of their self-assessment, to list questions research might answer. Over the next five weeks, students develop and execute a team research plan to answer those questions and produce revised and expanded argumentative essays (6–10 pages; many are longer). The researched essay still follows Meiland's structure; material from the sources is incorporated into the testing of the reasons. A particular value of this assignment is that it requires students to research all views of the issue, not only those with which they agree, and to use a full range of research material; objections to reasons, as well as reasons and replies, require research support.

Here is a section from a student research paper, testing the position that random drug testing should be allowed. Note the ways in which information from research deepens each stage of the argument:

A second argument for drug tests is one that should be viewed from a legal standpoint. The drugs that the government is primarily concerned with are marijuana, cocaine, amphetamines, opiates, and PCP (Holden 744). Without a prescription, to have possession of these drugs is illegal. This makes users of these drugs criminals, and isn't it the responsibility of an American corporation to bring criminals to justice? Addicts with expensive habits are also more likely to "steal cash from a company safe, products from a warehouse, or even equipment from a factory" (Bible 612). Isn't theft still a crime in this country? Drug tests would reduce the illegal drug market, cut down on imports of marijuana and other unlawful substances, as well as "take a bite" out of organized crime.

However, from the same legal standpoint, isn't "invasion of privacy" a criminal act as well? The fourth amendment specifically provides "the right of people to be secure in their person, houses, papers, and effects, against unreasonable searches and seizures" (Adams 96). Drug testing obviously denies employees of this constitutional right. O'Keefe mentions that a "urinalysis can reveal who is pregnant, who has asthma, and who is being treated for heart disease, manic-depression, epilepsy, diabetes, and a host of other physical and mental conditions" (38). It really isn't any of the employers' business to ascertain an employee's personal and confidential circumstances. Recently, in a Suffolk country court case, it was ruled by the Appellate Division of Justice, 2nd department, that "mandatory urine-testing of probationary schoolteachers for drug use before they are permanently appointed by a Suffolk county school district is a violation of the fourth amendment and an invasion of personal privacy" (Fox 1, 3). This is just one of many illustrations of the intrusive means of obtaining a drug-free workplace. The idea that we are going to do something about organized crime by invading the rights of millions of innocent workers who have never used drugs and aren't even suspected of using drugs is ridiculous.

Nevertheless, drug testing is nothing more than a tool, much like the polygraph test, by which employers can insure that certain conditions of work are met. ...

Students' Responses

Among the more than a hundred students with whom I've used this assignment, response has been overwhelmingly positive. Comments on self-assessment sheets submitted with the essays indicate that students like this structured dialectical approach for its ability to stimulate their thinking, to help organize their thoughts, and to enable them to achieve a balanced view.

First, students recognize the intellectual demands of this assignment. One student wrote, "It made analytical thinking an essential." Another wrote of "having to totally rack my brain for thoughts that had never really been there before!"

Mentioned frequently is the value of Meiland's structure in organizing thoughts. Many students liked knowing "what was expected in each paragraph" and found it helpful to have "a specific point about what you are writing." Though some writers found the form limiting ("At times I felt like I couldn't write something because it didn't fit"), more echoed this student: "The major weakness in my writing is my tendency to ramble on ... In writing this particular argumentative paper, I was able to overcome this tendency and still explain things thoroughly."

Many students also spoke of the unusual ease they experienced in writing: "It surprised me how smoothly the ideas flowed onto paper, once I got started." Another noted, "Once I got on a roll, it was hard stopping."

Almost every writer spoke of the value of achieving a balanced view of the subject. One wrote that this method "allows you to see if you might change your mind." Another acknowledged that this approach "made me explore areas of my subject that I normally would leave out."

For some students, given the emphasis on persuasion in past writing classes, developing both sides was difficult. One wrote, "All of my other writings ... have been of a one-sided viewpoint ... When you are forced to look at a topic from both sides and prove both the good and bad points it takes mental adjustment." Yet most valued the chance to be open, recognizing that "propaganda can be nothing more than an argumentative paper with one side cut out." Meiland's "more open and honest approach" is preferable to persuasion "since no one has to slide objections under the rug."

Given their appreciation of the value of multiple perspectives, it is not surprising that students reported alterations in their own beliefs about their topics. Most found that initially easy answers dissolved into complexity: "I started out a definite yes and became a definite maybe." Another wrote, "I'm still not in favor of the drug tests, but I can see *both* sides of the issue. It is obvious why there is so much debate."

Some students reported genuine change in their beliefs, especially when testing positions not their own. One student noted, "I learned that I often have biased unfounded views." Changed beliefs often resulted from researching the topic. A student writing on preselection of a child's sex was opposed to preselection at the end of her original essay: "I don't believe it is morally right to mess with something God has been doing a good job of for a long time." At the end of her research paper, she wrote: "My belief has changed. I believe the right to choose the sex of your child should be available, but personally, I will opt not to use the choice."

Clearly these students are moving toward the cognitive and ethical maturity Perry defines as contextual relativism: the ability to perceive alternatives and to make reasoned personal choices. My goal in the assignment, of course, is not to advocate change for the sake of change but to provide a stimulus and a structure for students to examine the bases of their beliefs.

Summary

In my experience, then, dialectical argumentation is a successful means of helping students examine beliefs — their own and others'. Meiland's approach as I've implemented it helps students to recognize and probe the tacit knowledge we all hold, leads them to understand the nature of their own and others' determining frames of reference, and provides them with the means of constructing and examining truths that matter. By coupling rationality and belief, dialectical thinking avoids the pitfall of sophistry. Instead of encouraging empty intellectualizing that serves only to confirm irrational beliefs, dialectical thinking helps to nurture what Richard Paul labels the rational passions: "a passionate drive for *clarity*, accuracy, and fairmindedness, a fervor for getting to the bottom of things, to the deepest root issues, for listening sympathetically to opposition points of view . . ." (142). Since learning to think dialectically means learning to embrace rather than deny contradictions (Basseches 55), teaching dialectical thinking is a primary means of equipping our students to cope with a world of change.

Works Cited

Applebee, A. N., J. A. Langer, and I. V. S. Mullis. *The Nation's Report Card: Learning to Be Literate in America*. Princeton: National Assessment of Educational Progress, March 1987.

Basseches, Michael. "Dialectical Thinking and Young Adult Cognitive Development." *Adult Cognitive Development*. Ed. Robert A. Mines and Karen S. Kitchener. New York: Praeger, 1986. 33–56.

Belenky, M. F., et al. *Women's Ways of Knowing*. New York: Basic Books, 1986.

Bonwell, Charles C., and James A. Eison. *Active Learning: Creating Excitement in the Classroom*. ASHE-ERIC Higher Education Report No. 1. Washington, D.C.: George Washington University, School of Education and Human Development, 1991.

Bouton, Clark, and Russell Y. Garth. "Students in Learning Groups: Active Learning Through Conversation." *Learning in Groups*. Ed. Clark Bouton and Russell Y. Garth. San Francisco: Jossey-Bass, 1983. 73–81.

Boyer, Ernest. "Critical Thoughts on Education." *National Forum* 65 (1985): 33–34.

Bruffee, Ken. "Liberal Education and the Social Justification of Belief." *Liberal Education* 68 (1982): 95–114.

———. "The Art of Collaborative Learning: Making the Most of Knowledgeable Peers." *Change* 19.2 (1987): 42–47.

Elbow, Peter. "Methodological Doubting and Believing: Contraries in Inquiry." *Embracing Contraries*. New York: Oxford, 1986. 253–300.

Gage, John T. "An Adequate Epistemology for Composition: Classical and Modern Perspectives." *Essays on Classical Rhetoric and Modern Discourse*. Ed. Robert Connors, Lisa Ede, and Andrea Lunsford. Carbondale: Southern Illinois University Press, 1984. 152–69.

Gere, Anne Ruggles. *Writing Groups: History, Theory, and Implications*. Carbondale: Southern Illinois University Press, 1987.

Glaser, Edward M. "Critical Thinking: Educating for Responsible Citizenship in a Democracy." *National Forum* 65 (1985): 24–27.

Kinneavy, James. *A Theory of Discourse*. 1971. New York: Norton, 1980.

Meiland, Jack W. *College Thinking*. New York: New American Library, 1981.

Palmer, Parker J. "Community, Conflict, and Ways of Knowing: Ways To Deepen Our Educational Agenda." *Change* 19.2 (1987): 20–25.

Paul, Richard W. "Dialogical Thinking: Critical Thought Essential to the Acquisition of Rational Knowledge and Passions." *Teaching Thinking Skills: Theory and Practice*. Eds. Joan B. Baron and Robert J. Sternberg. New York: Freeman, 1987. 127–48.

Perry, William. "Cognitive and Ethical Growth: The Making of Meaning." *The Modern American College*. Ed. Arthur W. Chickering. San Francisco: Jossey-Bass, 1981. 76–116.

Rybacki, Karyn C., and Donald J. Rybacki. *Advocacy and Opposition*. Englewood Cliffs, N.J.: Prentice Hall, 1986.

Trimmers, Joseph, and Nancy Sommers. *Writing with a Purpose*. 8th ed. Boston: Houghton Mifflin, 1984.

Zeiger, William. "The Exploratory Essay: Enfranchising the Spirit of Inquiry in College Composition." *College English* 47 (1985): 454–66.

3

Freedom of Imagination: A Workshop in Writing from Multiple Perspectives

William Zeiger

In an episode of *Star Trek*, Captain Kirk confronts an irascible robot that is bent on a course of destruction toward Earth. The ship's weapons have no effect. The situation is critical. So Capt. Kirk does some "critical thinking." In conversation with the robot, he leads it down a Socratic path to a self-contradiction and snarls, "I put it to you that you are in error." The robot, programmed both to persist in its own course and to correct errors, goes into a funk, then into a tizzy, and finally into oblivion.

The two opponents in this battle of wits caricature two poles of a dichotomy in education between *dualism* and *pluralism*. In the dualistic view, the conceptual world is clearly divided into two parts, "right" and "wrong." Education in such a world rigidly metes out information and evokes correct answers. In a pluralistic view, on the other hand, the conceptual world is composed of many potentials, and education in this world proposes alternatives and evokes shrewdly reasoned, adaptive responses. In the scene from *Star Trek*, Kirk gets the upper hand because he is a pluralist: he has the advantage of being able to cast his mind over many possibilities and to piece together a response uniquely adapted to his situation. The dualist robot, however, cannot cope with a problem to which there are two or more right answers.

Anthony Petrosky, a well-known commentator on teaching in high school and college, gives fuller descriptions of these two modes of thought and identifies the pluralist mode as critical thinking. The distinguishing feature of critical thinking to Petrosky is its fluid adaptability, its ability to weigh alternatives and choose among them. As applications of critical thinking, he cites essay tests, discussions, spontaneous writing, and reading a text interactively. *Rote learning*, on the contrary, observes strict precision and adheres to an external, absolute authority. It encourages a limping pseudo-thought that mechanically fills slots with what-the-teacher-wants. Petrosky calls it "regurgitation" and says it "handcuffs" a writer and saps "anything useful" from the act of reading (3). As vehicles of rote learning, Petrosky includes multiple-choice tests, workbook exercises, writing from an outline, reading for a fixed main idea, and even some informal logic. These rote techniques restrict thinking and narrow it to a single path. Pluralistic techniques, however, liberate thinking to discover and explore different paths. "Genuine tasks" for education are not those that lead the student through a formula to a correct answer, but those "that have more than one plausible solution" (2). The variety of possibilities puts students in a position to "state, explain, and justify their interpretations" (3).

Petrosky's views represent the widespread opinion in education that we have had enough of narrow, dualistic thinking and that we need more free-ranging, pluralistic thinking. I share this opinion. But in favoring an emphasis on multiple perspectives, I do not reject the dualism that Petrosky and others have so little use for. I think that Petrosky's definition of critical thinking is too limited. Critical thinking can mean weighing alternatives and creating solutions, but it can also mean finding one solution and contrasting it with all others. If getting a "correct answer," as Petrosky says, means thoughtlessly applying a formula, then it is a profitless educational exercise. But the impulse to define a single position and to defend it against all comers seems to me a hearty exercise in critical thinking, as indeed it has to university examiners from the Middle Ages into our own century. Galileo, for example, in muttering that the Earth moved, was insisting on a single, correct answer and adhering to a firm, external standard. The precision and rigor of such "right-wrong" thinking are essential to decision making and to the refinement of ideas. Dualism enacts hypotheses that pluralism creates. Without such testing in action, pluralistic alternatives would be merely academic. Thus pluralism, the tendency to project a multitude of answers, and dualism, the tendency to reject all but one, are partners in critical thinking.

In presenting this workshop on writing from multiple perspectives, I will advocate pluralism and defend dualism as complementary aspects of critical thinking. I believe, with many others, that in our schools and in Western culture in general we have had too much of a good thing — too heavy an emphasis on binary logic and its derivatives and imitations. To correct this imbalance, however, we need not eliminate dualism, but simply emphasize anew the openness and freedom of reflective thought. The workshop that I will describe emphasizes openness by leading writers to approach a given issue from three different directions. Three, because three is the simplest expression of multiplicity—greater than two and not commensurable with duality.

Duality Versus Multiplicity

The difference between two and three as conceptual strategies is more than numerical. A system composed of two parts may conjoin its alternatives as opponents or as partners. If opponents, they "fight" until one "wins." If partners, they complement each other like yin and yang. In either case, they occupy a narrow field—narrow not only in the sense that there are few options, but in the sense that the system tends toward unity. The winning "opponent" is a unitary result; and the paired opposites compose a symbiosis in which, practically speaking, the individual identity of each partner diminishes. A system of three elements, however, is not so easily reduced, and the trio tend to retain their separate identities.

As an illustration, consider stage drama. When there are two simple characters on stage, each must have a distinct quality: one may be wise and the other foolish, one eager and the other reluctant, or one angry and the other fearful. Whatever the difference between the two characters, their interaction tends to polarize along a single line— the angrier the one grows, the more fearful the other becomes—and this is the heart of the drama. When three characters appear together, each character still must have a distinct quality. Three distinct elements make a broader range of possibilities than two. A trio like the Three Musketeers or Dorothy's companions in Oz create a field of play among them, a system of shifting interactions. If one becomes jolly, a second may become embarrassed, and the third, exasperated. The scene is less predictable than with two characters. Whereas duality leans inward, toward unity, a three-part division leans outward, toward complexity.

The delicate but significant difference between duality and multiplicity, then, is the difference between a linear train of thought and a field of various options. When the mind has only two options, its action is narrow and focused. When it has three, its action is expansive and variable. This is the key difference between duality and multiplicity as conceptual strategies.

Multiplicity: The Ground of Being

In our present cultural context, multiplicity means not just greater variety and opportunity, but a "more real" reality. The duality of logic, of "either-or" thinking, dwells in structure or system, but multiplicity implies departing from system and approaching unordered being. For

example, Gary Zukav describes the New Physics as a sort of escape
from the old logical structure into "enlightenment," which "entails
casting off the bonds of concept ... in order to perceive directly the
inexpressible nature of undifferentiated reality" (270). In the liberal
arts, similarly, Hélène Cixous urges us to abandon conventional forms
of writing and to express our own raw substance as a new "chaosmos."
When every event or entity is unique and valuable, the universe is a
welter of color and motion that has no order other than its own
impulses. By increasing the number of options or entities in any area
from one or two to three or many, we seem to draw nearer to that
"undifferentiated reality," that pure being. In our current political
context, for example, pluralism appears in demands for the autonomy
of ethnic minorities and in calls for freedom of speech. These causes
reflect the sense that more participants, more voices, will bring about a
more just approximation of myriad reality.

At the same time, the limiting concept of duality currently excites
mostly adverse associations. Petrosky regards it as reductive and confining. In their studies of cognitive development, both William Perry
and Mary Belenky and her colleagues ascribe to duality the qualities of
authoritarianism and hostility; and their advocacy of pluralism has
been used as a basis for rejecting conventional academic writing in
favor of new, more liberating styles.

The Perry Scheme

In Perry's analysis, dualism is the lowest level of knowing. At this
stage, a person divides the noetic world between the *familiar* (right)
and the *strange* (wrong) (59–71). In other words, dualism is not the
coexistence of two equals, but a division between "good" and "evil."
Truth is understood to be absolute, and so only one opinion may be
right at a time. This attitude gives rise to dogmatic assertion rather
than to speculation and inquiry. A more advanced cognitive stage is
multiplicity, in which a person appreciates that differing opinions may
have equally respectable claims to truth. This acceptance of multiple
possibilities is the basis for still more advanced cognitive positions.
Whereas dualism is associated with comparative ignorance and personal
limitations, these more advanced positions are associated with subtle,
mature modes of thought and personal freedom.

Belenky et al. assert a hierarchy of values similar to Perry's, from
the simplest and most rigid to the most complex and flexible. They
clearly prefer the position of multiplicity, or "subjective knowledge"
(51–70), to the position of dualism, or "received knowledge" (41–50).
In their interpretation, emerging from dualism into multiplicity is not
just an increase in complexity, but the achievement of a morally higher
position.

Dualism's reputation, more than just that of a restrictive pattern of thought, is downright evil. When only two positions are available, one "right" and one "wrong," the mind is forced to make a choice; free play is prohibited. Both Perry and Belenky et al. see the division of the noetic universe into opposed positions as leading to authoritarianism and hostility. For Perry, whose study focuses on men, these attitudes beget narrowness and intolerance. For Belenky et al., whose study focuses on women, these attitudes engender self-denial and self-reproach. Conceptually, duality, the act of polarization whereby only one pole is good, is the act of painting oneself into a corner.

Multiplicity in Composition Pedagogy

Positing that the qualities of good thinking are also the qualities of good writing, compositionists have sought ways to liberate the teaching of writing. Drawing on Perry, on Belenky et al., and on other proponents of multiplicity, much recent commentary asserts that conventional academic writing is dualistic and constricts the writer into narrow thought paths that permit little scope for mature and expansive expression. Several, including Chris Anderson, Pamela J. Annas, William A. Covino, Olivia Frey, Shirley Brice Heath, Clara Juncker, Catherine E. Lamb, Thomas Newkirk, W. Ross Winterowd, and myself, point out that the essay in its natural form is a flexible medium capable of expressing the many voices of subtle thought, but that college writing requirements tend to force the essayist to use a single, dominating voice. The resulting academic composition, these commentators say, indiscriminately suppresses ideas of potential value.

These objections in different ways identify duality as the quality that restricts academic writing. The restricting element in each case is equivalent to either authoritarianism or hostility. Authoritarianism is the exaggerated tendency to consider one's own view correct; hostility is the quickness to challenge and discredit an opposing view.

As a concept, then, duality bears a heavy weight among educators as an obstacle to free inquiry. It is possible, nevertheless, to see that this reaction against duality is a temporary phenomenon, and that the evils associated with duality are incidental and not essential to its nature.

Duality and Authoritarianism

For example, let us look closely at authoritarianism, one of the negative qualities we attribute to duality. Lamb's "Beyond Argument in Feminist Composition" shows that a destructive situation results when opposed parties consider their own positions correct and refuse to compromise.

The deadlock results from "monologic argument," which Lamb classes as dualistic because she sees each side using the "thesis as a competitive act" (13). This impasse is the most difficult and most important situation for rhetoric to address, she says. She offers an elegant and useful method for mediating the standoff by redefining the opposed positions and discovering behind their pugnacious facades elements that may reveal shared values. The arbitrator who helps to negotiate this re-interpretation is the only pluralist in this situation. The opponents are both seen as stubbornly dualistic.

Such a situation, however, is already elevated to an extent. In the classic, evil case of authoritarianism, which Perry describes (51–79), there is only one strong opinion, against which no contrary opinion can stand. When a single opinion dominates, mediation is irrelevant. There must be a second strong voice, able to assert itself even under adverse conditions, in order for mediation to have the elements with which to work. This second voice (the voice, say, of a Thomas Jefferson, or of a Martin Luther King, Jr. — a voice that many find to be unreasonable or intemperate, a voice that because of the adversity in which it grows, perhaps, must exaggerate its own validity) is a sine qua non of successful mediation. Without the conflict created by such opposition, the mediator has nothing to work with, no material for the creative compromise. In plain terms, the pigheadedness of a single dominant voice is oppressive, but the pigheadedness of the opposing, insurgent voice is necessary and liberating.

Lamb's suggested mediation is certainly an enlightened view, because it is an alternative to force. But something must create the circumstances in which mediation can work. Every new idea, just because it is new, enters an unfamiliar world, parts of which are more and less disposed to make room for the newcomer. The unusual, the unlikely, the novel need a champion just to allow them to have a meaningful effect on their world. A new idea hardly arises except accompanied by a passion, even a rage, that would assert it, fight for it, create for it the conditions it needs to grow, and think of it, at least for a moment, as the only and the best idea in the world. Such a passion may easily be destructively authoritarian. But a *little* authoritarianism — a fierce loyalty to one belief — is part of a healthy intellectual climate. It creates the possibility of negotiation, of compromise — and with it the possibility of a broader field of choices.

Duality and Hostility

Hostility, the inevitable companion of authoritarianism, is also charged with shrinking rather than expanding the possibilities of thought. In "Beyond Literary Darwinism," Olivia Frey finds that published literary criticism betrays far too much hostility, attacking and discrediting other opinions needlessly. Critics consider themselves adversaries of each other, she says, and she faults "the adversary method" for the same quality for which Perry and Belenky et al. fault the dualist position: that it sets up a single omnipotent authority against which struggle is vain. "The scholar who attacks is usually sarcastic and condescending." The scholar's aim is "to establish cognitive authority . . . by demonstrating the weakness or error in the ideas of others. At the heart of the literary critical enterprise seems to be competition, not cooperation . . . [T]his is our business — to refute, repudiate, attack" (512). Instead of this unkind and unproductive aim, Frey praises prose that "weaves together the . . . voices" to which it refers, "disagreeing without a put-down" (521). Her description of a desirable writing strategy echoes Perry's and Belenky and her colleagues' definition of multiplicity: "Such a view of knowledge allows for two different views to be right, or partly right, or meaningful at the same time" (522).

But is the polarizing effect of criticism necessarily evil? As heartily as I applaud the virtue of kindness, I cannot help but relish how roundly Swift and Pope and Byron berate their opponents. I think of the celebrated wit of Gertrude Stein and Dorothy Parker, regularly unleashed to attack ignorance and pretense. Would we rather they had muted their sarcasm and expressed themselves more kindly? When we send our students to their writing groups to critique each other's papers, we tell them to be sensitive and constructive in their remarks. But a greater ill than unkindness in this context is easy tolerance. Writers want criticism of their work, even harsh criticism. Acerbity may be meanness, but as Benjamin Franklin said, "The sting of a reproach is the truth of it." The truth may be worth the sting.

A recent article by John Berendt describes salons, those soirees at which intelligentsia have gathered at all ages of history. Noted for the quality of their talk on art and politics, salons have brought together the brightest lights of their days, usually under the proprietorship of a vibrant hostess. "Salonistes" have been known not for pulling their punches, but for pronouncing their opinions pointedly. Berendt observes,

> Gatherings at which feelings are never hurt are not salons, they're tea parties. Gertrude Stein always spoke her mind. She let Matisse know when his work disappointed her, she disparaged Picasso's attempt to write poetry, and she told Hemingway he was 90 percent Rotarian . . . . Luba Harrington was likewise indifferent to the social cachet of her parties. She took delight in what each of her guests had to say, not in their reflected glory — which is why, in response to Timothy Leary's remark about the preeminence of her salon, she smiled and replied, "Dr. Leary, you are full of shit as usual." (71)

To remove the barb from the comment would subdue the spirit and curtail freedom of speech, which includes, if not slander, certainly insult. The freedom to attack an opponent is not really what we object to in dualism. Even when the atmosphere is less playful than in the salon, as in the "collision of mind with mind" (16) in John Henry Newman's university, contentious discourse can have a bracing, constructive life. If dualism means polarization by confrontation, or pointed criticism, even though it may lapse now and again into mere spleen, it is not an enemy but an avenue of constructive dialogue.

Rowdy, contentious discourse is useful when it occurs among people whose common interests bind them together so well that the centrifugal forces of debate do not threaten to overcome the participants' solidarity. In this atmosphere, the adversary method plows and aerates and fertilizes soil that otherwise might lose its vitality. The adversary method requires the earthy familiarity of *friends*. The place where we need a more conciliatory, placating, generous attitude, such as Frey recommends, is where we find ourselves in conflict with people with whom we hold little in common, adversaries whose allegiances and assumptions are so different from ours that they hardly bind us together. A *friendly* debate typically closes with a reassertion of camaraderie — not that opinions are forgotten, but that a sense of common interests prevails. So two athletes agree to box, and embrace afterwards; so a political party, after a heated primary election, closes ranks; so friends or lovers strengthen their relationship by letting fly from time to time with fiery accusations or demands. In each of these cases there is an attempt to assert one's own authority against all opposition — a reduction to "hostility," to pitched battle exercising the full strengths of each side. Ideally, the embracing agreement is stronger than the divisive force, but the regular recurrence of the no-holds-barred argument is necessary and healthy. As we did with authoritarianism, we must calibrate our disapproval of hostility. Extreme or prolonged or gratuitous hostility, as Frey warns, sours and impedes intellectual inquiry. But a seasoning of invective or of pointed wit, even if discomfiting, stimulates openness and earnestness in discussion.

Dualism itself, then — the tendency to advance a single view and reject alternatives — even with degrees of authoritarianism and hostility, has a place in critical discourse. Its narrowness sustains a particular idea and stimulates free processes of thought.

In arguing that dualism has its place within a broader context, I am accepting, in a way, the schemes of Perry and Belenky et al. Opponents who can set aside their disagreement and reassert shared values become pluralists in doing so. But just as disputants need to be good "pluralists" in order for their opposition to be constructive, they must be good "dualists" if their union is to be fruitful. The ability to focus an issue on one point to the exclusion of all else is an act of decisiveness, without which a world of possibilities is futile. At the moment that one performs this conceptual act, one is a dualist.

Rather than a selfish and stubborn authoritarianism, call it a healthy belief in oneself; rather than hostility, call it a skill at definition. These are both essential ingredients of a vital exchange of ideas.

Constructive Dualism

The undesirable qualities that we have come to associate with dualism are transitory, not natural to its operation. Duality polarizes and becomes hostile when it breaks down, when it loses its fine edge. Its positive state is more akin to our conception of multiplicity. When dualism breaks down, it becomes flat contradiction. This is its least subtle and most offensive expression. But as Walter Ong points out, dualism more constructively takes the form of "asymmetric opposition" (33), a somewhat oblique polarity in which conflicting views enhance each other. For example, the idea that "Experience is the best teacher" is flatly contradicted by the assertion "Experience is not the best teacher." But it is enhanced, rather than denied, by the challenge "Experience is also the worst teacher." Experience is the best teacher when we come to know something firsthand; but it is the worst teacher when that thing is deadly. In a flat contradiction, the dual members interact as opponents, needing to eclipse each other. In asymmetric opposition, the two parts interact as partners, correcting or qualifying each other. Currently educators tend to see all dual oppositions as flat contradictions; but this is not the whole of the nature of duality.

Nevertheless, duality has acquired an adverse reputation that in some sense it deserves. We are overly impressed with the accuracies of Newtonian physics and the successes of robotic technology. To free ourselves from the tyranny of mechanical processes (incidentally restoring duality's respectability) and to enjoy fully the expansion of creative and adventuresome thought, we need to encourage and explore ways of thinking pluralistically. We have too long dwelt near the edge of authoritarianism and hostility, too long labored, as Frey laments, in adversativeness, and we need to range far in the other direction, toward attitudes of kindness and speculative acceptance in order to reaffirm our footing there and replenish our wealth of free associations.

Excellent pedagogical tools for cultivating multiple perspectives are the mediation technique that Lamb outlines and Covino's dialogic approach to teaching writing (*Forms of Wondering*). The workshop I describe here is another such tool.

The Workshop

The Multiple Perspectives Workshop begins with a story. Browsing through a collection of African folktales, I came across some West African tales in which heroes performed incredible feats. What interested me particularly was that each story had three heroes who contended against each other, with no one winning. In fact, these stories flaunted their inconclusiveness. A typical ending was, "Now, among them, who was better off than another? If you do not know, there it is. Off with the rat's head!" (Courlander 59). There was no rat in the stories. No explanation was offered by the storyteller or by the editor of the collection. I asked some Nigerian acquaintances about the meaning of this closing formula, and they were as perplexed as I. I concluded that it was meant to leave listeners to their own devices, implying that there is no external standard for choosing among the three heroes — that each was great in a particular way. In other words, these stories were models of three-part form, the gangway of multiplicity.

The story I chose for the workshop is called "Three Friends Cross the Water." In it, three young men are walking along a forest path with three women companions when they come to a stream. The stream is too high to cross. The men decide that each will overcome this obstacle using his own particular skill. The three men are the King of Prayer, the King of Bowmen, and the King of Wrestlers. One at a time, in very different and marvelous ways, they cross the stream with their companions. And there the story ends: "Now among them who was better than another? If you do not know who was least, there you are. Off with the rat's head" (68).[1]

Other stories recount other impossibilities performed by three companions or rivals, building up their resourcefulness or prowess but declining to judge their comparative greatness. Relations among the heroes, rather than being authoritarian and hostile, are mutually tolerant. For while the stories do describe competition, they are playful in tone and imply that in fact no feat vanquishes or obscures another. Each story leaves all three performers proudly claiming glory.

In the workshop, the story's form becomes a template for the tripartite analysis of a literary text or other subject. The workshop leader tells the story, making it entertaining and suspenseful, exaggerating the characteristics of the heroes. The participants discuss the story briefly, identifying the heroes' qualities. Next, they address a new text or subject — an essay or story or poem, a puzzle or problem. Then, *adopting the attitude of one of the heroes*, each participant writes out an approach to the subject of analysis. When they have finished, they treat the same subject again from the viewpoint of a different hero, and then from the viewpoint of the third.[2] Finally, they discuss the different approaches to the topic that the three characters have suggested to them. In this process the participants practice and explore three different and equally productive ways of thinking.

Taking their analytical tools from a folktale gives their learning process authenticity. The story's history suggests that its heroes' traits are not arbitrary, but somehow fundamental to a worldview. These stories have woven themselves into cultural history (Courlander 1–5). Bruno Bettelheim says of traditional European "folk fairy tales" that they "offer new dimensions to the child's imagination" (7), and he adds that these stories have new meaning each time we read or hear them throughout our lives. In the stories' "basic human predicaments," Bettelheim finds the makings of a variety of archetypal situations — separation from a parent, death of a loved one, surmounting a great obstacle, entry into unknown territory, and so on. For the workshop, I assume that the African folktales have an archetypal appeal both in the human predicaments they present and in their tripartite form.

Equally important to its authenticity, the story as a medium allows each listener to make his or her own interpretation of each hero's character. Whatever triad of values forms in the listener's mind will be of the listener's own making. In this way the story is different from the usual academic medium, the lecture. A lecturer defines key terms explicitly. The storyteller, however, offers no analysis of the heroes' traits. In "The Storyteller," Walter Benjamin notes that it is crucial to the art that the storyteller not explain the tale, but allow its message to be absorbed almost physically (89). Bruno Bettelheim says that the parent reading a fairy tale to a child does not know what psychic use the child will make of the tale's substance, and so Bettelheim cautions the parent not to try to guide the child's interpretation (17–19). The story has its truest effect when it has an unmediated impact on the audience. As Petrosky contends, the ability to formulate one's own explanations is a hallmark of critical thinking. When the workshop participants interpret the heroes' traits for themselves, and then apply these in analyzing a text, the tool of analysis itself is a product of the participant's own mind.

Different groups of high school and college students and teachers who have done this workshop, for example, have attributed to the King of Archers skill in planning, strategy, ingenuity, resourcefulness, agility, imagination, balance, dexterity, craftsmanship, precision, intelligence, and good aim. They have not hesitated to interpret these qualities metaphorically. The King of Wrestlers has been credited with desire, strength, impulsiveness, perseverance, persistence, stubbornness, will, determination, passion, energy, impatience, coordination, flexibility, tenacity, and task diversity. The King of Prayer, according to his audience, displays faith, spiritual power, inner power, spiritual authority, positive thinking, will, divine intervention, and "mind over matter." These values seem to fall into a definable range for each character, confirming that the character's qualities are unified and his essential nature distinct from the others'. But when workshop participants apply their own words and meanings to the characters as encountered in the story, they feel an intimate ownership of the words they use. Owning their tools in this way, they are all the more likely to acknowledge and appreciate the products of their subsequent analyses.

The chief product, if the workshop is successful, is a sense that things may reasonably be divided into threes. No matter how the participant defines each hero's trait, the story establishes that the three heroes are all victorious and so their traits are all ratified. The subsequent three-way analysis of a literary text should show three fruitful and perhaps complementary angles of approach.

The groups who have participated in this workshop to date include high school students, college students, college teachers, and high school teachers, and naturally they display various degrees of sophistication and resourcefulness in applying the heroes' qualities to their own analyses.

One high school class was studying *Hamlet*. They turned their tripartite lenses on scenes or passages that they had been individually assigned. In the workshop that produced the analyses below, the leader led discussion toward "intellect," "passion," and "spirit" as the three heroes' qualities, and this coaching probably accounts for some uniformity in the students' responses. Nevertheless their responses show individual insights.

The Ghost Scene

Hamlet sees the ghost of his father. This scene uses spiritual belief to set the things that are to come. The plot of the play is created by Hamlet's belief in the ghost of his father. ... This is spiritual belief. It is faith in his (the ghost's) words that leads Hamlet to seek revenge on Claudius.

Now I believe Hamlet has a desire to seek out Claudius. He has a burning desire, as did the King of Wrestlers ... The King of Wrestlers used anger and pure will to accomplish his goal of crossing the river. I see this in Hamlet's desire to revenge his father.

The King of Archers is present in Hamlet's plot to take revenge on Claudius. He plans his revenge as the King of Archers plans skillfully and carefully.

Act I Scene V

I am the King of Wrestlers and I rule the ghost of Hamlet's father. I am mad at the murderous villain who poisoned me. ... I hate him.

I am the King of Archers. I let Hamlet know what really went on in my orchard and not what his uncle says happened. I saw what Claudius killed me with and how.

I am the King of Prayer. I believe in the superstition that ghosts can't stay out after dawn. I believe in witchcraft.

"O what a rogue and peasant slave am I"

Hamlet's desire for revenge is prompted by his belief in the spiritual power. He believes in eternal damnation and in heaven. His revengeful desire is driven by these beliefs and the fact that he wants to seek salvation for his father. Hamlet uses his own human quality, his intellect, to achieve such desire. He plans every detail out carefully, but yet, his impulses cause him to, seemingly, go mad at different parts in the play . . . . His intellect turns into impulses and then back again.

Besides discovering three basic qualities in the play, these responses show particular insights: the opinion that Hamlet's belief in the ghost drives the plot; the contrasting notion that it is intellect, not belief in ghosts, that tells Hamlet what really happened to his father; and the observation that Hamlet vacillates between his reason and his passion.

In other renditions of the workshop, the story characters are interpreted more liberally. In fact, the lightheartedness of the African tale evokes a fancifulness in some participants' responses. The comfortable, safe, imaginatively free ambience of story telling encourages each listener to relate the story's events to personal memories and scraps of thought. For example, in a workshop done in a college class, instead of a literary text, students analyzed problems in their lives. One student interpreted the three heroes as friends who put on a show to cure her of fighting with her roommate. It is apparent in her essay that each approach to the problem has its own fairly intimate effect. I reproduce her draft with its spelling and grammar unedited.

Our friends climbed upon the stage, and motioned for us to sit below in the seats. Katie walked to the front of the stage.

"There shall be no more fighting, by the end of the night you will be friends again," and with the last word still echoing in the air she pulled out two bibles and threw them our way. They landed on our laps.

"Annette," (my roommate), "teach her the ways of god." She began to tell me some of the stories from the bible. She was very religious, well very Catholic. I never understood her devotion, and it caused problems. But as she enlightened me, I began to understand.

Next Lorie walked up. She pointed to the sky and put out an arrow from out of know where. She shot one up into the stars. It flew higher and higher until it hit a star and exploded. Large flashes of light flew in front of us and landed on the stage. Two faint visions appeared, one looked like me, and the other like Annette. Both looked sad and gloomy, both ignoring each other, until they began to fight. We started laughing at the stupid visions, on how stupid they looked.

"Do we really look like that!" we were laughing like we used to.

"Now," Jan said come up here. Jan began to do cartwheels around us, faster and faster, faster and faster. A ring of light glowed around us until it was so bright we had to close our eyes. The light began to become hot and was getting closer and closer. We couldn't open our eyes, the ring of burning light was closer, and pushed Annette and I closer. If I didn't get closer to her we would get burned. Fear overcame me, Annette grabbed my hand in fear, and I hugged her. The light burned cool now, and we opened our eyes. The stars glistened and smiled down upon us. We were friends.

In this response, the three heroes seem to work as a team to bring about a desirable change. The King of Prayer is interpreted fairly literally, recommending the wisdom of the Bible to erring children. The Archer's quality is not named, but it gives the women a detached perspective of themselves, dissolving their differences in laughter. The Wrestler is seen as a cosmic force that overpowers personal animosities. All three of these approaches involve ways of minimizing a difficulty in the face of a larger consideration—a slant that clearly originates with the interpreter and not in the story. Observing her reading of the story and comparing it to others' readings could teach the participant a "lesson" beyond the scope of direct instruction.

Another workshop participant, a college teacher, assumed more creative license. She applied the story to her own imagined "search for the treasure of Time." To make their qualities fit her needs, she recast the three heroes as "a mother," "a siren," and "a nymph." Each had to get past a monster who ate Time, and each was accompanied by a small elf, which seemed to represent the work this participant hoped to accomplish if she only had enough time. In her writing, the mother "elbowed her way through with the elf in her arms." This image seemed easy enough to interpret. Next, the siren "lured the lion's attention away by the shadow of herself on the side of the cave." The nymph, "so light on her feet ... so fast ... put the elf behind her and stepped by ...." These last two images were harder to translate, but the participant accepted this task as her own creation.

After their first successful use of such a triad, students may use it freely in future analyses. I assume that as they use it, they will become more and more accustomed to treating any novel event as potentially having three aspects, rather than simply dividing it into "right" and "wrong" readings. One workshop participant noted, also, that the three-part analysis was confining. Why, he asked, among the three heroes, was the quality of *charisma* not represented? We concluded that the three heroes in the story did not represent the whole range of possible qualities of a hero, nor the whole range of approaches to a problem. This "deficiency" suggests, as I observe at the beginning of this chapter, that seeing things in threes is the threshold of seeing them in greater multiplicity.

The greatest multiplicity has the sense of crowds, bunches, tumultuous variety. There is no telling how many new ideas and unforeseen connections may occur in such "chaosmos." By limiting the field to three, we scale this riotous diversity down to the size of a laboratory experiment — or classroom exercise. But even this level of multiplicity retains its essential openness and free play. It is refreshingly non-dual. If we truly allow the interplay of three disparate elements, we do not just make conversation slightly more complicated; we remove it from the edge of opposed combat. With three distinct, equal agents comes an incipient sense of expanding, of exploring, of mixing and matching ideas experimentally, and of moving into full possession of whatever we discover.

The aim of the workshop is to make participants' future essays richer, more inclusive, more resourceful. The academy now chafes at its long habit of binary analysis. We are seeking new solutions to old and new problems. In Bakhtin's terms, we value centrifugal social and intellectual forces, forces that range outwards, more than centripetal ones, that retrace old ways. This workshop provides an avenue to such wide-ranging inquiry in the writing class.

We are at a moment of history when we loop outwards, like it or not. All social forms, including pedagogical ones, wear out, and the impulse to novelty forages freely again. No form, however intricate or flexible, can represent the living spirit for all ages. The best institutions we devise reach limits where we must acknowledge that we cannot encompass everything at once with our minds or with our contrivances. From time to time, we should be happy to start over again, looking out for new divisions and collections.

Appendix

The following African story appears in *A Treasury of African Folklore*, edited by Harold Courlander (New York: Crown, 1975).

Three Friends Cross the Water

A HAUSA STORY

This tale is about some youths. Certain young men went to an outlying village where some young girls were. They went on, and came to a stream. There was practically no water in the ford. The water came only up to their ankles. They passed on. They came to where the maidens were, and came and greeted them, and carried them off. They came to the stream and found it filled up with water. Then they said, "Ah, when we passed this water, it was not so." And they said, "How is this?" One among them said, "Let us turn back." The rest said, "No, we do not go back." Now they were three, the king of wrestlers, the king of bowmen, and the king of prayer.

And they said, "Let each try and get out of the difficulty by resorting to his own particular skill." They said, "Let the one who is strong in prayer commence." So he prostrated himself, spat on his staff, and struck the water; and the water opened and he with his maiden passed over. Then the water returned to where it was. Next the prince of bowmen drew out his arrows from his quiver, he set them in a line on the water, from one bank to another; he returned and lifted up his maiden. They stepped on the arrows and passed over. Then he came back and picked up his arrows. There remained the king of wrestlers. He too sought for what he should do; he could not find a way. He tried this way and failed, he made that plan and failed, until he was weary. Then he got in a rage, and seized his maiden and with a wrestling trick twisted his leg round hers and they jumped and rose in the air, and did not fall, except on the edge of the far bank. Now among them who was better than another? If you do not know who was least, there you are. Off with the rat's head.

Endnotes

1. Some workshop participants have wanted to work with female characters. There is one story in Courlander, "The Strong One," in which a woman surpasses all three male contestants. I have found no stories with three equal female heroes. One can, however, successfully revise "Three Friends" to make the heroes women.

2. It is possible to abbreviate the workshop by allowing each participant to write from only one hero's point of view, instead of all three. If each hero is chosen by one-third of the participants, then all may experience all three approaches by sharing the results of their writing among the group.

Works Cited

Anderson, Chris. "Dramatism and Deliberation." *Rhetoric Review* 4 (1985): 34–43.

Annas, Pamela J. "Style as Politics: A Feminist Approach to the Teaching of Writing." *College English* 47 (1985): 360–71.

Bakhtin, Mikhail. *The Dialectic Imagination: Four Essays*. Ed. Michael Holquist. Trans. Caryl Emerson and Michael Holquist. Austin: University of Texas Press, 1981.

Belenky, Mary Field, et al. *Women's Ways of Knowing: The Development of Self, Voice, and Mind.* New York: Basic, 1986.

Benjamin, Walter. "The Storyteller." In *Illuminations.* Ed. Hannah Arendt. Trans. Harry Zohn. New York: Harcourt, 1968.

Berendt, John, "The Salon." *Esquire* Nov. 1990. Rpt. in *Utne Reader* 44 (1991): 70–71.

Bettelheim, Bruno. *The Uses of Enchantment: The Meaning and Importance of Fairy Tales.* New York: Knopf, 1976.

Cixous, Hélène. "The Laugh of the Medusa." *New French Feminisms: An Anthology.* Eds. Elaine Marks and Isabelle de Courtivron. Cambridge: University of Massachusetts Press, 1980. 245–67.

Courlander, Harold, ed. *A Treasury of African Folklore.* New York: Crown, 1975.

Covino, William A. "Defining Advanced Composition." *Journal of Advanced Composition* 8 (1988): 113–22.

———. *Forms of Wondering: A Dialogue on Writing, for Writers.* Portsmouth, NH: Boynton/Cook, 1990.

Frey, Olivia. "Beyond Literary Darwinism: Women's Voices and Critical Discourse." *College English* 52 (1990): 507–27.

Heath, Shirley Brice. "Multiple Truths: Personal Responses to Texts." Conference on College Composition and Communication. Boston, 21 March 1991.

Juncker, Clara. "Writing (With) Cixous." *College English* 50 (1988): 424–37.

Lamb, Catherine E. "Beyond Argument in Feminist Composition." *College Composition and Communication* 42 (1991): 11–25.

Newkirk, Thomas. *Critical Thinking and Writing: Reclaiming the Essay.* Urbana, IL: NCTE, 1989.

Newman, John Henry. "What Is A University?" *University Sketches.* London: Scott, 1902.

Ong, Walter. *Fighting for Life: Contest, Sexuality, and Consciousness.* Ithaca: Cornell University Press, 1981.

Perry, William. *Forms of Intellectual and Ethical Development in the College Years.* New York: Holt Rinehart, 1970.

Petrosky, Anthony, "Critical Thinking: Qu'est-ce que c'est?" *The English Record* 37.3 (1986): 2–5.

Winterowd, W. Ross. "Rediscovering the Essay." *Journal of Advanced Composition* 8 (1988): 146–57.

Zeiger, William. "The Exploratory Essay: Enhancing the Spirit of Inquiry in College Composition." *College English* 47 (1985): 454–66.

Zukav, Gary. *The Dancing Wu-Li Masters: An Overview of the New Physics.* New York: William Morrow, 1979.

4

Using William Perry's Scheme to Encourage Critical Writing

Toni-Lee Capossela

In 1968, William Perry's *Forms of Intellectual and Ethical Development in the College Years: A Scheme* was published by the Harvard Bureau of Study Counsel. Republished in 1970 by Holt Rinehart, this book describes a developmental pattern extrapolated from a series of open-ended interviews with Harvard and Radcliffe undergraduates from the classes of 1958, 1962, and 1963.

The scheme describes a progression that in its broad contours was common to all of the students interviewed: the movement from dualism through multiplicity to committed relativism.

The beginning point in the sequence (although few students still held this worldview by the end of their freshman year, when they were first interviewed by Perry's staff), is that of basic duality: a dualist perceives life as a series of choices between right and wrong, correct and incorrect; authority is absolute, and truth is what authority says it is. Once a person finds dualism unrealistic or untenable, she begins moving toward multiplicity, the belief that there are no right or wrong answers, and so all answers are of equal value. Gradually one begins to discover figures of relativism on a dualistic ground, and then at some point the gestalt shifts, so that the ground becomes relativism, with rare isolated figures of dualism. Finally, some form of commitment occurs: in the absence of absolute answers, one consciously but tentatively selects answers of some kind, which are experienced as affirmations of self and necessary to a meaningful life.[1] For a fuller description of the scheme, see "Appendix 2: The Perry Scheme."

Perry's work has been a seminal force in developmental psychology: it was one of the first in a now-crowded field of adult developmental theories tracing cognitive maturity beyond Piaget's formal-operational stage (see Arlin, Basseches, Commons et al., King and Kitchener, Mines, Riegel, Sinnott). The Perry scheme has also had an enormous impact on teachers, administrators, and counselors who deal with college students and adult learners. But the model is not without its critics, and even proponents admit that it is in some ways problematic.

Objections to Perry's Scheme

The first question that arose in response to the study was the extent to which the scheme applies to a wider population. In the original study, Perry noted the selective nature of the test group, but hypothesized that "the implications for other colleges with a diverse student body and a pluralistic intellectual outlook seem obvious" (*Forms* 4). Studies on other liberal arts campuses have tested this hypothesis,[2] and invariably some version of the developmental pattern has emerged.

To test whether the continuum was peculiar to its time, Perry and his staff conducted similar interviews with students from the Harvard and Radcliffe classes of 1970–71. Although these students appeared to be more cognitively mature at the end of their freshman year than students from the earlier classes, in other respects the scheme held true. Perry concludes that these results, as well as interviews with members of the class of 1979–80, suggest that "the course of cognitive and ethical development outlined in our scheme appears to be a constant phenomenon of a pluralistic society" ("Cognitive" 98).

Some critics of the scheme see it as insensitive to gender differences, pointing out that of the 464 original interviews, only 28 involved women students. Perry notes that although the judges who evaluated the sample of four-year interviews found some differences based on gender, they decided that these differences were matters of content and manner rather than matters that affected the "forms" essential to the scheme (*Forms* 16).

Perry's scheme is the point of departure for *Women's Ways of Knowing* (Belenky et al.), the most frequently cited study of gender-based differences in epistemology (for a survey of other studies in this area, see Hays, "Intellectual"). At each stage in their model, the authors describe to what extent Perry's parallel position either does or does not reflect the attitude toward knowledge that they find in their women subjects.

The authors of *Women's Ways* find Perry's methodology "poorly designed to uncover those themes that might be more prominent among women",[3] and say that their own design can better focus "on what else women might have to say about the development of their minds and on alternative routes that are sketchy or missing in Perry's version" (9). This passage is often used to set up an either/or opposition between Perry's scheme and the scheme in *Women's Ways*. However, Hays describes the patterns traced in *Women's Ways* as "variations and elaborations of basic structures" identified by Perry rather than as an alternative model or a rejection of Perry's scheme (3). Both Hays ("Intellectual") and Kurfiss ("Knowing") combine the schemes of Perry and Belenky's group and use this synthesis to discuss possible applications to course design.

In addition to gender bias, the Perry scheme has also been accused of cultural bias and intellectual elitism. When Perry describes his model as relevant to "the intellectual and ethical development of late adolescence in a pluralistic society" (*Forms* 3), he implies that movement through the developmental scheme is inevitable in such a society. But critics disagree, claiming that the scheme presents as natural a sequence that is value-laden and culturally determined, and along which chosen initiates are guided by the gatekeepers of the academic tradition (Bizzell, "William").

Actually, Perry does not claim that his study is value-free; rather, he points out that the biological metaphor of growth implies the evaluative assumption that it is better to grow than not to grow (*Forms* 44). He also takes pains to identify the value system on which the scheme is built:

> The values built into our scheme are those we assume to be commonly held in significant areas of our culture, finding their most concentrated expression in such institutions as colleges of liberal arts, mental health movements and the like. We happen to subscribe to them ourselves. (45)

It is clear that Perry claims only limited applicability for the scheme, namely, within "significant areas of our culture".[4] Subsequent studies, which apply the scheme to other populations, suggest that the application may be broader than he originally claimed.[5] For instance, of the 135 women interviewed in the Belenky study, 45 were clients of family agencies dealing with parenting issues; the remaining 90 were recently or currently affiliated with a formal educational setting, only one out of the six kinds of which was a liberal arts college (12). Given the social and economic diversity represented by this population, it is remarkable that the resulting developmental sequence so closely resembles Perry's scheme in its general contours.

The Perry Scheme and Critical Thinking

Because the more advanced positions on Perry's continuum are parallel to the dispositions and attitudes characteristic of critical thinking, his work sheds light on the nature and difficulties of holistic critical thinking (see Brabeck; Fitch and Culver; King; and Van Hecke "Critical" for studies that link the Perry scheme and critical thinking).

First, Perry sees cognitive maturity as inextricably linked to matters of epistemology. The forms he identifies in his scheme are "those structures in which [the students] construe the nature and origins of knowledge, of value, and of responsibility" (*Forms* 1). An emphasis on epistemology is also central to holistic critical thinking.

Second, Perry's scheme deals with the moral and ethical dimensions of maturity as they converge with cognitive development. Whereas atomistic critical thinking deals with isolated cognitive skills and devalues affective or personal factors as contaminants in the reasoning process, for Perry the natural cap to cognitive maturity is personal commitment. Dewey, whose concept of reflection is the same as holistic critical thinking, reminds us that "with respect to education, no separation can be made between impersonal, abstract principles of logic and moral qualities of character" (34).

Third, Perry's scheme, like holistic critical thinking, is concerned with process as well as product, with how a student proceeds as well as with the outcome of the enterprise. There is a strong resemblance between McPeck's remark that critical thinking "is a function of the way a result is pursued, not the result itself" (44), and Perry's observation, "The development we trace takes place in the forms in which a person perceives his world rather than in the particulars or 'content' of his attitudes and concerns" (*Forms* ix).

A consequence of this emphasis on process is that in some ways critical thinking — and cognitive maturity — are never achieved once and for all. The reader will recall McPeck's observation that critical thinking does not require the successful completion of a task (13). For Perry, intellectual adulthood is marked by the ability to live with uncertainty and lack of closure. Perhaps the most challenging aspect of the Perry scheme is that it is by definition open-ended: commitment is meaningful only if it is undertaken with the understanding that it may have to be abandoned, adjusted, or transferred at any moment. In addition, as one enters new areas of inquiry, one can expect to travel the earlier stages all over again. As one student puts it, "Now I know I'll never know how many times I'm going to be confronted" (Perry, "Cognitive" 97). In retrospect, Perry regrets that the discursive journey metaphor in which the scheme is cast cannot accommodate this recursive quality—he proposes the helix as an image more suggestive of how cognitive maturity actually takes shape ("Cognitive" 97).

Finally, as might be expected from the fact that maturity develops independently in each area of one's life, Perry's scheme, like holistic critical thinking, is based on the importance of context and relationships. To quote Dewey, "All reflective thinking is a process of detecting relations" (77). The crucial nature of context lies at the heart of relativism, and the undeniable relevance of context is what finally forces one to abandon the comforting dualistic belief in permanent right answers to all the important questions.

The Perry Scheme and Teaching Critical Writing

Given the strong affinities between holistic critical thinking and the upper positions of Perry's scheme, and given the connections between writing and thinking, it is not surprising that writing teachers have found Perry's findings applicable to their work in many ways (see Haisty; Kiedaisch and Dinitz; Krupa; Oster; Reid; Van Hecke, "Re-Vision").

The Perry scheme helps all teachers, but especially teachers of writing, understand our students better, because it shows us how to identify students' epistemological assumptions. This identification can be done roughly, by following the chronological guidelines of upper- and lower-level courses: Hays says that most first-semester freshmen are dualists on the way to becoming multiplists ("Intellectual"). Or it can be done more discriminatingly, by taking note of how an individual's comments and writing are suggestive of her conceptions of knowledge. Even a pedestrian event like discussing the class syllabus is revelatory of epistemology, because students' questions are indicators of what they think knowledge is.

The Perry scheme also helps us read student writing more incisively and constructively. Problems such as poor organization, lack of audience awareness, and unsupported assertions—even technical errors such as tense shift and lack of agreement[6]—can be dealt with more effectively if they are seen as consequences of epistemological stance, rather than as signs of obtuseness, writers' block, or inability to follow a complex chain of reasoning.

Some teacher-researchers attempt to establish connections between specific levels of cognitive development and features of student writing. Hays's work here is the most detailed to date, including such features as content, organization, support, qualification, choice, diction, syntax, style, and preferred modes ("Intellectual") as well as an examination of argumentative writing for friendly and hostile audiences ("Socio-Cognitive"). Hanson uses an open-ended longitudinal interview format similar to Perry's to establish a developmental continuum tracing five kinds of voice in student writing. Beers claims that Perry's positions correspond to varying levels of sophistication in handling coherence and voice. Ryan investigates the connection between epistemological assumptions and conceptions of prose coherence. Shapiro examines the correlation between rhetorical maturity and position on the Perry scale.

If Perry's research helps us understand our students and their writing, then it should also help us teach them more effectively. There is much debate about the extent to which the scheme can, or should, be applied to curriculum. Perry was originally skeptical on this point, fearing that such applications would distort "a purely descriptive formulation of students' experience into a prescriptive program intended to 'get' students to develop." However, by 1981 he professed himself convinced that "our scheme of development can be of more practical use to educators than I first supposed" ("Cognitive" 107).

Developmental Instruction

One of the earliest and fullest curricular applications of Perry's findings was Knefelkamp's model of Developmental Instruction, illustrated by two University of Minnesota courses, one for dualists and one for relativists, on Themes of Human Development and Identity. Using Sanford's theory that effective teaching must balance support and challenge, Knefelkamp formulated different kinds of support and challenge to suit the cognitive levels of these two groups of students. Hays applies Knefelkamp's format to the design and methodology of writing courses ("Intellectual"; see also Quinn).

The greatest problem with developmental instruction on a curricular level is that it assumes students in a particular class are at approximately the same stage of cognitive development. This assumption, when based on age, is spurious: in his study Perry found a wide range of positions within any class year (*Forms* 215). The assumption is even more unwarranted in courses that draw from different classes, or that include adult learners.[7] Measurement and subsequent tracking — to control enrollment in a particular course so that all its students are on the same level — introduce another set of problems. The measurement issue is a thorny one; many admirers of Perry's work object that none of the current measuring devices are sensitive enough to reflect the richness of the scheme.[8] But the more troubling question is that of consequences and trade-offs: even if accurate measurement of cognitive maturity were possible, what would be the cost of tracking students in order to implement a developmental course? What would we — and they — be giving up? According to Perry and others, plenty.

Most importantly, we would be giving up the powerful ways in which students learn from each other's differences. This is particularly true in writing classes, where collaborative writing, peer review, and response groups successfully build upon the importance of audience and the social nature of writing (see Bruffee, Gere, LeFevre, Spear). Kurfiss points out that a student comprehends and seeks to emulate a level of cognitive maturity one level above her own ("Sequentiality" 569); in a heterogeneous class, students can model this behavior for each other.

Because Perry's scheme deals specifically with the recognition of alternatives and differences, it is essential for students to listen to peers as they express and justify differences of opinion. On all levels of the scheme, learning from peers is valuable. Dualistic students will observe that intelligent people disagree on important issues, a lesson that they often do not grasp from observing teachers disagree with each other: the dualist belief that authorities possess the right answer suggests that the phenomenon of two teachers disagreeing means that one teacher is a fraud or that the disagreement is fake.

Multiplists will learn from listening to peers that diversity is more complicated than the belief that everyone has a right to his or her own opinion, and they will begin to discriminate between well- and ill-supported opinions. Relativists will profit from peer models of commitment who can talk candidly about the costs of commitment, the questions they still have, and the ways they arrived at their decisions.

Finally, the centrality of community to the value system that supports Perry's scheme strongly argues for the importance of students learning from each other's differences. The pain and risk of abandoning earlier worldviews is too great to take on without help; according to Perry, that help must come from the group that first caused the student to question her attitudes.

> ... the community's substantive provision of worthwhile things to care about is not enough. Nor is the provision of an expectation that the student will care. The student finds his greatest sustenance, we feel, in a sense of community in the risks of caring. (*Forms* 200)

For most of the students interviewed, the strongest support for their development came from a sense of community, from "the realization that in the very risks, separateness and individuality of working out their commitments, they were in the same boat not only with each other but with their instructors as well" (*Forms* 213). It is clear from these remarks that homogeneous classes ignore the social framework of the Perry scheme, at the same time that they severely limit the use of important and effective writing strategies.

Teachers proposing developmental courses have also been accused of attempting to accelerate progress through a maturation sequence that students should travel at their own pace. Both Knefelkamp and Stephenson and Stephenson claim that developmental instruction leads to more rapid developmental progress as well as superior mastery of course material. Hays agrees, explaining that development is accelerated by the introduction of "calculated incongruities," to which the student responds by attempting to reconcile conflict and contradiction ("Development" 141). But Reinsmith questions the ethics of what he calls "educating for change," asking, "Does one have the right to orchestrate this kind of change, to set up materials in such a way as to insure that small, but violent, explosions will be set off in many students' minds?" (86). More to the point, Bizzell says that courses that claim to speed students' development are based on the naive belief that "we can get [students] to progress faster by forcing them to imitate more advanced positions until their brains kick on and hold these positions on their own" ("William" 452).

Both Piaget (*To Understand* 23) and Perry ("Cognitive" 107) disapprove of using education to speed up development. The teacher's most important role in fostering development, according to Perry, is not to accelerate it or "get it" to happen, but to offer kinship in the difficult enterprise it represents. A teacher must abandon the persona of infallible authority so cherished by dualists, and reveal herself as an authority within a relativistic context, whose credentials rest merely on "advanced experience and expertise in groping" (*Forms* 122).

Other Applications

One way to incorporate Perry's work into course design without tracking students or generalizing unnecessarily about their cognitive maturity is to design a flexible course that challenges and supports each student at her cognitive level. This can be as simple as offering a choice of writing assignments. Or it can be done with a combination of restriction and freedom — for instance, specifying an approach to a topic but allowing the student to select the subject itself. One-on-one contact, such as conferences, discussions, and written responses to student writing, can be adjusted to fit the teacher's observations of a particular student's epistemological assumptions.[9] Hays, in outlining her "developmental feminist pedagogy of writing," suggests many ways to accommodate students' varying cognitive levels within a developmental curriculum ("Intellectual").

Another way to incorporate the Perry scheme into course design is to use reading and writing assignments that require attitudes characteristic of Perry's more advanced positions. This approach is best embodied in Bartholomae and Petrosky's anthology, *Ways of Reading*, and its companion piece of theoretical essays, *Facts, Artifacts, and Counterfacts.*

The essays in *Ways of Reading*, rather than modeling the lucid windowpane prose enshrined in most student anthologies, are eccentric, thorny, and sometimes maddening pieces by authors such as John Berger, Paulo Freire, Clifford Geertz, and Walker Percy. These are works that, as the editors point out, leave lots of work for readers to do (9). Instead of trying to imitate the verbal clarity of E. B. White or George Orwell, students working with *Ways of Reading* write in self-defense: they must write something of their own, as they grapple with the gaps and inconsistencies of a particular text.

The writing assignments arising out of these difficult readings incorporate sequencing and revision, which build incrementally toward complex modes of thinking. As Salvatori points out, the assignments are arranged so that "they map out for the student the opening of a new critical perspective" (43). Assignments based on returning to a text and re-examining it through another author's conceptual framework require the same awareness of context that is essential to relativism. The final assignment of each writing sequence is recursive and meta-cognitive, asking students to "look back at, to assess, and to re-see what the process of thinking through, and articulating in writing, these various possibilities has contributed to his/her critical understanding of that particular issue" (Salvatori 45).

The intellectual challenge that is the greatest asset of a course based on *Ways of Reading* or a comparable text is also its greatest potential problem. If the demands of the course are pitched more than one stage beyond a student's current cognitive level, she is likely to become alienated and baffled.[10] In particular, dualistic students who fear that they are in over their heads become even more reliant on authorities' opinions and less likely to take risks in their writing. To reduce the potential for alienation, support is required in assorted forms and lavish amounts: a nonthreatening classroom atmosphere, many ungraded forms of writing, various kinds of collaboration and feedback, discussion of sample essays, and multiple opportunities to re-draft and revise. Another crucial form of support, particularly in the face of these difficult readings, is for teachers to practice what Perry calls "a certain openness — a visibility in their own thinking, groping, doubts, and styles of commitment" (*Forms* 213).

The Perry Scheme as Meta-Subject

In an effort to inform my teaching with Perry's findings but to avoid the problems of tracking, overgeneralizing, and artificial acceleration, I have developed a writing assignment sequence that uses the Perry scheme as its organizing principle and its implicit theme. Instead of prodding students through the continuum, it allows them to model for themselves a movement that they have already made, not necessarily through time, but while shifting from one context to another. With such a sequence, one need not measure students' cognitive maturity, arrange them into homogeneous groups, nor make gross generalizations about them. One can have the rich discussions that arise from diversity, at the same time that each student is challenged on the level that is appropriate for her.

The key to this sequence is the fact that cognitive maturity is achieved at different levels in different fields; one may be a dualist in one area and a relativist in another (Perry, "Cognitive" 97; Piaget "Intellectual"). Students are asked to consider, in three separate essays, three acts of interpretation which they recall themselves making (see "Appendix 3. Interpretation Writing Sequence"). The three acts represent increasingly complex kinds of interpretation, each requiring a more sophisticated epistemological stance than the one before it. Each essay, after describing and analyzing the interpretive act, must conclude with a definition of "interpretation" that can embrace the substance of the current essay and also of those preceding it. The sequence is thus developmental in the same sense that Perry's scheme is: earlier, simpler forms are subsumed in the more complex, later stages.[11]

The support in the sequence lies in the fact that the student describes acts of interpretation she has already accomplished; the challenge is that she must stand back and consider these acts from a metacognitive vantage point, figuring out what it means that she has constructed this kind of meaning. Perry sees this capacity for detachment as one of the essential qualities of intellectual maturity. "One must be able to stand back from oneself, have a look, and then go back in with a new sense of responsibility" (*Forms* 35). The definition section of each essay is the platform on which the student can stand back and achieve the necessary distance from herself.

Although I have taught this course exclusively to first-semester freshmen, who are usually assumed to be dualists on the way to multiplicity, each student has been able to recall and describe herself performing an interpretive act possessing some of the qualities of relativism. This fact suggests that we may still be underestimating the degree to which cognitive development is contextual, and that in assessing our students' maturity solely on the basis of their academic work we are overlooking areas where they are comfortable with more sophisticated epistemological positions.

A major strength of this sequence is that each student, regardless of her level of cognitive maturity, can account for the sequence in a way that makes sense to her—there is little danger of the alienation caused by a framework that is more than one step beyond the student's current level. Dualistic students accept the sequence as another set of rules from above—this particular authority figure wants it done this way. Multiplistic students see the sequence as proving the validity of their position: here comes yet another worldview, and this one refuses to see life in terms of black and white. Students in the early phases of relativism seize on the sequence as another pocket of relativism in a world that is still basically dualistic, and students approaching commitment make the sequence into a paradigm for the various ways that one can learn to live meaningfully in a complex world.

The sequence also supports Burnham's claim that the real impact of Perry's scheme on teaching writing is in the area of content rather than methodology. After reading Perry, he says, "Our writers and their views and beliefs become our content, the discovery of self in relationship to past and future becomes the dynamic of the course, and their writing becomes the text" (157).

Perry as a Mirror

In sharp contrast to the blizzard of enthusiasm that initially met Perry's study, a delayed and measured response comes from Patricia Bizzell. She opposes interpreting the Perry scheme as an inevitable developmental sequence, asserting that it is fundamentally and essentially culture-bound. She feels that basic writers in particular should not be evaluated within its terms, since many of them do not bring to college the mainstream cultural experience common to the Harvard students in Perry's study; instead, she calls for a similar study for basic writers ("What Happens" 300). This view of basic writers and their cognitive maturity is shared by Kogan, Martinez, and Rose.

Bizzell also takes issue with many of the specific applications of Perry's scheme discussed here. For instance, she warns against using features of student writing as an indication of cognitive maturity, pointing out the highly selective nature of Perry's sample and the absence of any developmental timetable in his scheme ("William" 451). She also finds the scheme unsuitable as a template for designing writing courses.

But after rigorously examining the many ways that Perry's scheme can be misused, Bizzell presents us with what is left: a distillation of the real value of Perry's work for college teachers, particularly those who teach writing. She credits Perry with documenting the confluence of cognitive development in the individual and the social forces that shape that development: "Perry's analysis describes the changes in student thinking that result from their socialization into the academic community" ("William" 452).

Moreover, Bizzell finds the Perry scheme an important source of information about ourselves, not just about our students. She sees

Perry's position of commitment through relativism as a good definition of academic discourse and a useful portrait of the kind of cultural literacy privileged by liberal arts teachers ("William" 453); as a cogent explanation of why the academic establishment values writing so highly (454); and as a constant reminder that what we do when we teach is not objective and value-neutral, but rather part and parcel of our discourse community's assumptions about knowledge and the communally accepted version of reality.

Endnotes

1. All attempts to summarize the scheme suffer to some degree from oversimplification. The scheme's richness and complexity can be best appreciated by reading interview excerpts from Perry's book, in which students speak for themselves. Perry describes the variety of ways in which students follow the scheme, and the many shapes that each position may take.

2. In a 1981 publication, Perry notes that the scheme has been applied in such diverse areas as admissions, placement, faculty evaluation, counseling, religious development, peer training, and courses in history, English drama, health, and counseling ("Cognitive" 98–102). For research after 1981, consult the Perry Network Bibliography and its quarterly additions, c/o coordinator William S. Moore, 1505 Farwell Ct. NW, Olympia, WA 98502. 206–786–5094.

3. Perry's research design is misrepresented by Belenky et al., since they say that the scheme is illustrated exclusively by interviews with men, and that interviews with women are interpreted to conform to the patterns thus established (9). In actuality, some interviews with women are used, although sparsely, to illustrate the scheme. This minor inaccuracy is troubling because throughout *Women's Ways of Knowing* there are references to "the men in Perry's study."

4. Perry carefully distinguishes between validation of the scheme in the original study, and his own thoughts on the significance of the study. Questioned about the degree to which the scheme is connected to the liberal arts experience, he said, "This development can be found in other places than a liberal arts college, and it is not always found in a liberal arts college. ... Some of the Harvard students [interviewed in the original study] learned their relativistic thinking someplace else. ... In liberal arts colleges there is an intensification of the experience, and in other places it may not be brought so forcefully to their attention" (telephone interview, August 4, 1991).

5. Clinchy and Zimmerman, two of the coauthors of *Women's Ways of Knowing*, conducted a study at Wellesley College and found such an orderly progression along the Perry continuum that they concluded his claims for the scheme are too narrow rather than too broad. For additional applications of the scheme in assorted contexts, see Perry ("Cognitive") and Moore.

6. Haswell uses developmental theory to make sense of the phenomenon of increased surface error among advanced students. Because development is multidimensional, Haswell asserts, a student struggling with new challenges

such as expressing complicated ideas or using a sophisticated vocabulary may commit more surface errors than in earlier, simpler work. These errors, he says, are "not so much stubbornness — fossils of previous more ignorant learning stages in need of clearing away to allow subsequent progress — as stumbles, wrong turns made when new tactics are attempted" (481).

7. Zachary questions the applicability of Perry's scheme to adult learners.

8. The most common measuring instruments are the Learning Context Questionnaire, the Learning Environment Preferences, and the Measure of Intellectual Development. Perry recommends that for a rough estimate of cognitive maturity, teachers ask students to write an essay about "How I Learn Best," and then have students grade two essays, one filled with discrete facts but no analysis, the other containing analysis but fewer facts ("Cognitive" 102).

9. Belenky points out that conferences are useful for identifying inaccurate assessments of a student's position, provided that the teacher makes generous use of the Rogerian identification prompt, "You seem to be saying . . .," at which point the student can respond, "No, what I meant was . . ." (qtd. in Ashton-Jones and Thomas 286).

10. The source of this response is explored in a study by Wispe and Allport (Wispe) in which students identified themselves as either "wanting more direction" or "wanting more permissiveness" from teachers. Students who wanted permissiveness and did not get it expressed frustration, but students who got less direction than they wanted exhibited intense anxiety and hostility. Perry's gloss on this study is that the students who wanted more freedom could understand an epistemological framework (dualism) that they had superseded, but that the dualistic students who wanted more direction were incapable of understanding an epistemological framework (relativism) too far beyond their current level ("Cognitive" 105).

11. The developmental nature of sequencing, and the concept of designing a series of what I. A. Richards calls "partially parallel tasks" is thoroughly developed by Coles.

Appendix 1: Suggestions for Perry Workshop Activities

I. Inductive Discovery of Perry's Scheme

Bring in a selection of student essays and have the participants form small groups and use the essays to extrapolate the writers' attitudes about learning. Ask them to arrange these attitudes in relationship to each other and account for the differences. Then briefly describe Perry's scheme and let participants discuss similarities and differences between Perry and the results of their group work. This exercise helps faculty see that students' epistemological assumptions differ dramatically. MacDonald gives a detailed account of this kind of workshop, and explains that it was judged useful by faculty who had previously been unimpressed by an expository presentation of Perry's findings.

II. Writing Sequence Design

Give a brief introduction to the Perry scheme, distribute the Interpretation Writing Sequence (see Appendix 3), then have workshop participants form small groups and design their own sequences.

III. Methodology

Have participants bring a past or current syllabus to the workshop. Give a brief introduction to the Perry scheme, suggest some of the possible applications, and have participants work in small groups to investigate ways of incorporating the developmental sequence into their syllabi.

IV. General Applications

Give a brief introduction to the Perry scheme and its applications (sequenced assignments, developmental instruction, Perry-scheme-as-structure, classroom techniques, etc.). Let the participants form groups, each of which will investigate the implications of one particular applications.

Appendix 2: The Perry Scheme*

1. Basic Duality. Authorities have the answers, and if I work hard and read every word, I will learn them too.

2. Multiplicity Prelegitimate. Good Authorities don't give me the Right Answer, which they possess; instead they give me problems that will show me how to find the Right Answer.

3. Multiplicity Legitimate but Subordinate. In certain areas, the Authorities disagree among themselves, but this is only because they are still working on getting the right answers.

4. (Sometimes these occur sequentially; sometimes only one occurs)
   a. Multiplicity (Diversity and Uncertainty) Coordinate. In situations where authorities don't know the Right Answer, all opinions are equally good.
   b. Relativism Subordinate. In certain areas, Authorities are less interested in having me come up with a Right Answer, than in my learning to think in a certain way, i.e., to support my opinion rather than merely asserting it.

* Adapted from William Perry, Jr., "Cognitive and Ethical Growth: The Making of Meaning," in *The Modern American College*, ed. A. W. Chickering, San Francisco: Jossey-Bass, 1981, pp. 76–116.

5. Relativism. Everything is relative; I have to understand the context; theories are not truths, but metaphors to interpret with; I have to think about my thinking.
6. Commitment Foreseen. I am going to have to make my own decisions in an uncertain world.

7–9. Evolving Commitments.

7. I've made my first commitment.
8. I've made several commitments, and now I will have to arrive at a balance. How many? Which are most important? How important?
9. This is how life is: I must commit at the same time that I continue to examine my commitments and be prepared to change or adjust them.

Deflections from growth can take the form of temporizing (a prolonged pause in one position), retreat to an earlier position, or escape (settling into a position while denying its implications for growth).

Appendix 3: Interpretation Writing Sequence

Assignment 1

Describe an incident in which you interpreted something in several ways, and then chose one of the ways as the "correct" interpretation. Describe the alternatives you considered, why you eliminated the ones you eliminated, and why you picked the one you picked. Work out a definition of interpretation based on this experience. For this first assignment, do not write about a piece of writing, art, or music that you interpreted; you can pick anything else.

Assignment 2

Recall and describe an incident when somebody helped you interpret something. What did they have that you didn't and that made them a better interpreter than you? Will you be able to interpret without them the next time? Explain what they gave you that will allow you to go it alone next time. Using both this incident and the one from the previous assignment, derive a new definition of interpreting.

Audience: Assume you are explaining this to someone who would have needed the same kind of help in the same situation.

Assignment 3

Recall and describe an incident in which you interpreted something in several ways, and then refused to select one way and refused to reject the others. Why did you decide not to choose? What did you gain by refusing? What did you lose? (You may find these questions easier to answer if you go back to Assignment 1, and try to figure out the differences and similarities between the two incidents). Using all three assignment incidents, derive a definition of interpretation that will cover all three; refer to the incidents in as much detail as you feel you need.

Audience: Someone who went through the same kind of experience and decided that only one interpretation was "correct"—his or her own.

Works Cited

Arlin, Patricia. "Cognitive Development in Adulthood: A Fifth Stage?" *Developmental Psychology* 11 (1975): 602−5.

Ashton-Jones, Evelyn, and Dene Kay Thomas. "Composition, Collaboration and Women's Ways of Knowing: A Conversation with Mary Belenky." *Journal of Advanced Composition* 10 (1990): 275−92.

Bartholomae, David, and Anthony Petrosky, eds. *Facts, Artifacts, and Counterfacts*. Portsmouth, NH: Boynton/Cook, 1986.

———. *Ways of Reading*. Boston: Bedford Books, 1990.

Basseches, Michael. *Dialectical Thinking and Adult Development*. Norwood, NJ: Albex, 1984.

Beers, Susan. "An Analysis of the Interaction Between Students' Epistemological Assumptions and the Composing Process." Conference on College Composition and Communication. New York, March 1984.

Belenky, Mary Field, et al. *Women's Ways of Knowing: The Development of Self, Voice and Mind*. New York: Basic Books, 1986.

Bizzell, Patricia. "William Perry and Liberal Education." *College English* 46 (1984): 447−54.

———."What Happens When Basic Writers Come to College?" *College Composition and Communication* 37 (1986): 294−301.

Brabeck, Mary M. "Critical Thinking Skills and Reflective Judgment Development: Redefining the Aims of Higher Education." *Journal of Applied Developmental Psychology* 4 (1983): 23−34.

Bruffee, Kenneth. "Collaborative Learning and the 'Conversation of Mankind.'" *College English* 41 (1984): 635−52.

Burnham, Christopher C. "The Perry Scheme and the Teaching of Writing." *Rhetoric Review* 4 (1986): 152−58.

Clinchy, Blythe, and Claire Zimmerman. "Epistemology and Agency in the Development of Undergraduate Women." *"The Undergraduate Woman: Issues in Educational Equity."* Ed. Pamela Perun. Lexington, MA: Lexington Books, 1982, 161–81.

Coles, Richard. *The Plural I: The Teaching of Writing.* New York: Holt Rinehart, 1978.

Commons Michael, Francis Richards, and Cheryl Armon, eds. *Beyond Formal Operations: Late Adolescent and Adult Cognitive Development.* New York: Praeger, 1984.

Dewey, John. *How We Think.* Boston: D.C. Heath, 1933.

Gere, Ann Ruggles. *Writing Groups: History, Theory, and Implications.* Carbondale: Southern Illinois University Press, 1987.

Fitch, Peggy, and Richard Culver. "Educational Activities To Stimulate Intellectual Development in Perry's Scheme." ASEE Annual Conference Proceedings, 1984.

Haisty, Donna Beth. *The Developmental Theories of Jean Piaget and William Perry: An Application to the Teaching of Writing.* Diss. Texas Christian U, 1984.

Hanson, Melanie. *"Developmental Concepts of Voice in Case Studies of College Students: The Owned Voice and Authoring."* Diss. Harvard School of Education, 1986.

Haswell, Richard. "Error and Change in College Student Writing." *Written Communication* 5 (1988): 479–99.

Hays, Janice. "The Development of Discursive Maturity in College Writers." *The Writer's Mind: Writing as a Mode of Learning.* Ed. Janice Hays et al. Urbana, IL: NCTE, 1983, 127–44.

———. "Socio-Cognitive Development and Argumentative Writing: Issues and Implications from One Research Project." *Journal of Basic Writing* 7.2 (1988): 42–67.

———. "Intellectual Parenting and a Developmental Feminist Pedagogy of Writing." *Feminine Principles and Women's Experience in American Composition and Rhetoric.* Ed. Janet Emig and Louise W. Phelps. Pittsburgh: Univ. of Pittsburgh Press, in press.

Kiedaisch, Jean, and Sue Dinitz. "Persuasion from the Students' "Persuasion from the Students' Perspective: Perry and Piaget." Conference on College Composition and Communication. Seattle, March 1991.

King, Patricia. "Thinking about Critical Thinking: Some New Developments." National Invitational Conference on Pedagogy and Practice for Student Intellectual Development. Davidson College, 20 June, 1985.

King, Patricia, and Karen Kitchener. "Development of Intellect and Character: A Longitudinal Sequential Study of Intellectual and Moral Development in Young Adults." *Moral Education Forum* 10 (1985): 1–13.

Knefelkamp, Lee. *Developmental Instruction: Fostering the Intellectual and Personal Growth of College Students.* Diss. U of Minnesota, 1974.

Kogan, Myra. "The Conventions of Expository Writing." *Journal of Basic Writing* 5.1 (1896): 24–37.

Krupa, Gene. "Perry's Model of Development and the Teaching of Freshman Writing." *Freshman English News* 11 (1982): 17–20.

Kurfiss, Joanne. "Sequentiality and Structure in a Cognitive Model of College Student Development." *Developmental Psychology* 13 (1977): 565–71.

———. "Developmental Perspectives on Writing and Intellectual Growth in College." *To Improve the Academy: Resources for Student, Faculty, and Institutional Development*, Vol. III. Ed. L. Wilson and L. Buhl. Pittsburgh, PA: Professional and Organizational Development Network in Higher Education, 1984, 136–47.

———. "Knowing, Learning, and Writing: Patterns in Students' Understanding of Academic Work." Annual Institute on Writing Across the Curriculum. Brainard, MN, August 1990.

LeFevre, Karen Burke. *Invention as a Social Act*. Carbondale, IL: Southern Illinois University Press, 1987.

MacDonald, Stephen C. "Critical Thinking: Grokking the Fullness." *College Teaching* 36.3 (1988): 91–93.

Martinez, Joseph, and Nancy Martin. "Are Basic Writers Cognitively Deficient?" Annual Meeting of Western College Reading and Learning Assn. April 1987. ERIC ED 285179.

McPeck, John. *Critical Thinking and Education*. New York: St. Martin's Press, 1981.

Mines, Robert, and Karen Kitchener, eds. *Adult Cognitive Development: Methods and Models*. New York: Praeger, 1986.

Moore, William. *Perry Network Cumulative Bibliography and Copy Service Catalogue*. Athens, GA: Perry Network, 1988.

Oster, Judith. "What ESL Students Can Teach Us About Perry and Iser." Conference on College Composition and Communication. Boston, MA, March 1991.

Perry, William, Jr. *Forms of Intellectual and Ethical Development in the College Years: A Scheme*. New York: Holt Rinehart, 1970.

———. "Cognitive and Ethical Growth: The Making of Meaning." *The Modern American College*. Ed. Arthur W. Chickering. San Francisco: Jossey Bass, 1981, 76–116.

Piaget, Jean. "Intellectual Evolution from Adolescence to Adulthood." *Human Development* 15 (1972): 1–12.

———. *To Understand Is To Invent: The Future of Education*. New York: Grossman, 1983.

Quinn, Mary. *Critical Thinking and Writing: An Approach to the Teaching of Composition*. Diss. U of Michigan, 1983.

Reid, Geneva Bryant. *The Use of the Perry Scheme in the Teaching of Freshman English*. Diss. Memphis State U., 1986.

Reinsmith, William. "Educating for Change: A Teacher Has Second Thoughts." *College Teaching* 35.3 (1987): 83–88.

Riegel, K.F. "Dialectical Operations: The Final Period of Cognitive Development." *Human Development* 16 (1973): 346–70.

Rose, Mike. "Narrowing the Mind and the Page: Remedial Writers and Cognitive Reductionism." *College Composition and Communication* 39 (1988): 267–302.

Ryan, Michael P. "Conceptions of Prose Coherence: Individual Differences in Epistemological Standards." *Journal of Educational Psychology* 76 (1984): 1226–38.

Salvatori, Mariolina. "The Teaching of Writing as Problematization." *Teacher Education Quarterly* 10 (1983): 38–57.

Sanford, Nevitt. *Self and Society.* New York: Atherton Press, 1966.

Shapiro, Nancy S. *Rhetorical Maturity and Perry's Model of Intellectual Development: Competence, Context, and Cognitive Complexity in College Student Writing.* Diss. U of Maryland, 1984.

Sinnott, Jan. "Everyday Thinking and Piagetian Operativity in Adults." *Human Development* 18 (1975): 430–43.

Spear, Karen. *Sharing Writing: Peer Response Groups in English Class.* Portsmouth, NH: Boynton/Cook, 1988.

Stephenson, Bud, and Christine Stephenson. "Intellectual and Ethical Development: A Dualistic Curriculum for College Students." *Counseling Psychologist* 6.4 (1977): 39–42.

Van Hecke, Madeleine. "Re-Vision: Student Writing and the Perry Scheme." *The Perry Network Newsletter* 11.1 (1989): 1–14.

———. "Critical Thinking and the Perry Scheme: Tangled Spirals." William Perry Conference. Washington, D.C., December 1990.

Wispe, L. G. "Evaluating Section Teaching Methods in an Introductory Course." *Journal of Educational Research* 45 (1951): 161–86.

Zachary, L. *An Analysis of the Relevance of the Perry Scheme of Intellectual and Ethical Development to the Practice of Adult Education.* Diss. Columbia U, 1985.

5

Sequencing Writing Assignments to Foster Critical Thinking

Betty P. Pytlik

That writing is a complex activity is readily acknowledged by writers, teachers, and researchers alike. Linda Flower and John Hayes, for instance, have demonstrated in numerous studies the complexity of the processes that writers go through to produce an organized set of ideas for an essay: from a vast body of knowledge, writers must select and manage ideas and relationships, and they must consider the demands of their audience and the purpose of their writing. Despite the general agreement that a great deal of thinking goes into producing an effective piece of writing, "what may not be so readily apparent," Carol Booth Olson points out, "is that writing is a learning tool for heightening and refining thinking" (30). Nancy Comley, in her *College English* review of five texts about critical thinking, summarizes current thought about the teaching of critical thinking in writing classes:

> Critical thinking is encouraged by an essentially interdisciplinary curriculum and by teachers who know how to encourage and coordinate reading, writing, and discussion. In such a setting, students and instructors "struggle with real problems and issues" [she quotes Chet Meyers 8], locating them in a social, historical, academic, or other context. (623)

A writing class, Joan Hunt reminds us, is an ideal context for encouraging students to consider a variety of sources of information and to develop skills in gathering and selecting information, recognizing relationships among ideas, reorganizing previously acquired knowledge for new purposes, and testing ideas in action.

In *Critical Thinking: Theory, Research, Practice and Possibilities*, Joanne Kurfiss's summary of the current literature about critical thinking and its development in college, the relationship between writing and the development of critical thinking skills is frequently documented. Generally, she concludes, composition teachers foster critical thinking by demonstrating how language reflects and shapes thinking. Citing the research of Flower and Hayes on defining rhetorical problems and Faigley and Witte on rivising, Kurfiss points out how analyses of written texts have demonstrated the link between writing and critical thinking. The connection is also confirmed by studies that show that writing short essays about texts (as opposed to taking notes or answering study questions) increases students' conceptual understanding of content. Kurfiss reports that "assignments that help students organize and develop the knowledge they are acquiring are likely to increase the quality of thinking they can do about the subject" (39).

The purpose of this chapter is to demonstrate to teachers in all disciplines the potential that writing classes have for fostering critical thinking. To that end, I provide a consciousness-raising exercise that is based on two assumptions. First, familiarity and experience with and interest in a subject are prerequisites for helping students think and write critically. As Frank Smith puts it (in a discussion about John McPeck's 1981 *Critical Thinking and Education*), " . . . thinking always has a subject — we always think about *something* — and . . . being unable to think about something in a particular manner indicates unfamiliarity with the subject matter rather than an underlying inadequacy itself" (49). Second, each assignment in a course should be connected with all that preceded it and all that will follow it, with writing tasks progressing from simple to complex.

To achieve my goal, I discuss the rationale for developing sequences of assignments around a theme. Then, using a sequence of eight writing tasks about family, I describe the rationale and procedure a colleague and I followed in designing the family sequence. Next, I offer some guidelines for developing sequences of writing tasks to foster critical thinking skills. Finally, I describe a faculty workshop structured around the family sequence.

Designing and Sequencing Writing Assignments

Too often, for whatever reasons, we plan our writing courses as we go, assigning writing tasks that do not connect to what came before and what will come after. In so doing, we divorce writing from learning. "There is," Gerard Cox reminds us, "a better way than this to give assignments. This better way consists simply of regarding assignments not as individual, isolated topics to be invented as necessity requires but as a coherent sequence designed to elicit responses appropriate for your course and, ideally, to build upon those responses" (88).

In the literature about designing sequences of writing assignments, the most frequently cited article is Richard Larson's "Teaching Before We Judge: Planning Assignments in Composition." Writing in *The Leaflet* more than twenty years ago, Larson praised the efforts of teachers and administrators who argued "that each assignment must fit into, and advance, the entire course, and that the composition course [at each level should] be part of a plan for the entire curriculum in composition" (210–11). He worried, though, that in their enthusiasm to sequence English courses and programs, planners would "neglect to advise teachers how to plan and present the individual assignments in their program" (211), that they wouldn't see an "arrangement of assignments . . . as a structure in which assignments are closely related to each other in service of the goals of the program" (212). "The goals of each assignment," Larson wrote, "should be to enlarge the student's powers of thinking, organizing, and expressing ideas so that he can cope with a more complex, more challenging problem in the next assignment" (212).

After reviewing the literature about designing writing assignments, I have come to believe that until perhaps ten years ago, Larson's recommendations were seldom reflected in discussions about assignment writing. Indeed, with a few exceptions, writing tasks were described as if they had been designed and assigned in a vacuum. Recently, however, the importance of sequencing assignments, as you can see from the bibliography for this chapter, has found its place in discussions about planning writing and reading courses and about creating assignments.

Those of us who have been teaching writing for decades have known intuitively that students benefit from writing about a series of tasks on a related subject. And if, like me, you taught business writing in an English department twenty or twenty-five years ago, you used texts that assigned a series of letters, memos, and reports based on transactions between a client and a businessman. I recall that twenty-five years ago there was something satisfying about a pedagogical approach that asked students to move from writing simple letters of inquiry to feasibility reports.

Today's interest in sequencing assignments can be described more specifically than "knowing intuitively that students would benefit from writing about a series of related subjects" or "there was something satisfying about that pedagogical approach." Here, for instance, are some of the instructional goals — many of them overlapping — that I found in the sources listed in Works Cited. Most of them, as you might suspect, evolve from ideas presented in James Moffett's *Teaching the Universe of Discourse* and William Coles's *The Plural I: The Teaching of Writing*.

Writing assignments, we know, should progressively distance the writer from her subject and her reader. As she is required to distance herself from her subject and reader, more complicated writing tasks are demanded of her. The ability to perform these tasks is related, we also know, to the student's level of cognitive development. Furthermore, as the distancing occurs, she learns more about herself, her world, and her language.

Of the writing course William Coles describes in *The Plural I*, Richard Larson says in his foreword that the program forces student writers to ask themselves, "Who is the writer in a given piece?" "Where does he stand in reference to his subject?" "To his readers?" "To himself?" (You may recall that Coles's first assignments require definitions of "professional" and "amateur.") Then Larson explains that Cole, coming at things slowly, "with a pattern of assignments that is deliberately both repetitive and incremental" (16), makes a series of assignments centered around the concepts of professional and amateur. The assignments require writers to examine, explore, discuss, write, and learn about these concepts, all tasks that become more complex as the course and the students move on.

One frequently identified goal of sequenced assignments is to move students beyond personal knowledge and personal responses to shared values and traditions. For instance, Katherine Adams explains that we can achieve this goal by incorporating expressive writing, observing, interviewing, revising, critiquing, editing, and literature into a "unified series that can overlap or be reordered and ... integrated into each writing assignment" (15).

Another frequently identified goal for sequenced assignments is to develop cognitive skills. To achieve this goal, Marilyn Sternglass recommends that we draw "on the insights of the psycholinguistic model of reading, a process-centered approach to writing, and a cognitive model integrating analysis and synthesis" to "prepare students to master educational and professional tasks at ever-higher developmental levels" (157).

A third goal is to help students see writing as a means of knowing and a means of coming to know. In a course that uses writing as a way of knowing, Ken Dowst says, "an assignment is part of a sequence of assignments that spiral around a central idea, progressing from relative simplicity to relative complexity of thought and expression" (78).

Some additional goals for sequencing assignments are

- to integrate the acts of reading and writing;

- to motivate students to write by encouraging a deep engagement with their material;
- to establish a community of shared knowledge;
- to prepare students for writing in their professions;
- to help students learn development of prose style and the vocabulary of, and method for, close reading of literary texts;
- to prepare students for academic writing; and finally,
- to build critical thinking skills.

Generally, the sequences themselves owe their structures — however loosely — to Moffett's discussions of distancing and development and to Coles's emphasis on the relationships among writers, readers, and subjects. Within that framework, David Foster points out, "The best sequence will bring together subject matter, writing purpose, and audience in clearly defined writing situations" (124), organized according to the writer's logical processes, topics, or different rhetorical situations. We would do well to follow Foster's criteria for designing effective assignment sequences: they should have some rhetorical context (i.e., a clear topic, a distinct audience, and an underlying purpose that determines structure and style), the possibility for the writer to use all elements of the writing process, and a genuine significance for the writer (128).

What I see in discussions about sequencing assignments is that in developing a series of related writing tasks, three movements help students achieve their goals. First, assignments are arranged linearly, from easiest to hardest in terms of cognitive and rhetorical demands — for example, from an expressive journal entry about a vivid childhood memory to an urge to action addressed to a general audience. Second, for each assignment, a subset of tasks leads students through the writing process, for example, from brainstorming to editing. Third, sequenced assignments are recursive, as Malcolm Kiniry and Ellen Strenski illustrate: "As students move on to more complex tasks, they find themselves increasingly capable of turning back profitably to those expository strategies they already have begun to master" (192). Of course, students draw not only from strategies used in previous assignments — such as summarizing — but also from information and situations in those assignments.

In "From Simple to Complex: Ideas of Order in Assignment Sequences," Elizabeth Rankin cites additional examples of assignment sequences: Macrorie's "I-Search Report" and the reading and writing course described in Bartholomae and Petrosky's *Facts, Artifacts and Counterfacts*, to name two. She expands my brief analysis of sequence design by classifying sequences into *formalist* and *epistemic* and reminding us that "the notion of sequence, like our various notions of simple and complex, is itself a social construct. It is a way of asserting order in the midst of chaos, a means by which we assure ourselves and our students that we are making 'progress.' To put it simply," she concludes, "an assignment sequence is a necessary fiction" (134).

The recursiveness in sequences is especially fostered when the class pursues one theme. Judith Langer and Arthur Applebee summarize this view: "Thinking skills are taught best when related to some content . . . and writing provides a particularly welcoming context" (2). It was, if fact, the goal of encouraging students to become engaged with their material that led me to design a sequenced course in the first place. Put simply, my freshman students have trouble believing that they know enough about any one subject to write effective papers. Family, my colleague Dave Bergdahl and I thought, was a subject about which they knew something, and designing a course around a theme seemed sensible. More specifically, as Deborah Brandt points out: "By pursuing one theme, a class can develop a set of concepts, a common vocabulary and common 'indexical expressions,' a body of shared experience, a collective frame of mind, to serve as a semantic reservoir for each writing assignment. Such continuity contributes to nearly every conceivable aspect of composing." Furthermore, "A thematic approach also provides opportunities . . . for a group to [use writing to] explore complex problems, conflicting viewpoints, and changes in understanding that occur with the acquisition of new knowledge" (123).

Mark Allister adds that ". . . writers, in gaining extensive knowledge of one subject, in delving more deeply than they would (or could) go in a single paper, explore rhetorical relationships and recognize improvements in their writing that wouldn't have been possible otherwise" (129). And, in a 1990 Conference on College Composition and Communication paper, Stephen Wilhoit argues that focusing on one theme provides "an explicit model of how knowledge, skills, and dispositions interact" when students analyze ideas and develop reasoned, informed judgments (12). Recursive assignments that ask students to reevaluate material as they learn more information put students "in a better position to compare perspectives on issues, to analyze different ideas, and perhaps to synthesize a position of their own" (7).

Although specifications for designing writing assignments have not been around for much more than fifteen years, discussions of using writing to promote critical thinking are even more recent, as Carol Booth Olson has pointed out in her *Educational Leadership* article mentioned earlier.

How does sequencing assignments that revolve around a single theme foster critical thinking? To answer that question briefly, let me first list some of the assumptions that are the bases of the sequence of assignments described in this chapter. Then, again for the sake of brevity, I will refer you to a recent collection of essays that argue eloquently for the connections between thinking and writing.

The eight assignments that serve here as an example of a sequence are arranged according to the degree of difficulty in the cognitive and rhetorical demands placed on student writers. The sequence is based on some assumptions about how writing can foster critical thinking; their practical implications are incorporated into the discussion of the workshop:

1. By developing assignments around one theme or topic, students use writing as a way for the class to, in Deborah Brandt's words, "explore complex problems, conflicting viewpoints, and changes in understanding that occur with the acquisition of new knowledge" (126).

2. Composing is thinking, as Ann Berthoff and others have observed. Berthoff argues that thinking and writing require us to see and to name relationships (71). Because discovering relations occurs most readily when students write about private experiences, each assignment in a sequence should draw to some extent on the writer's personal interests and experiences.

3. Berthoff also argues that when we establish relationships between information and between ideas, patterns emerge that help us to make sense of what we know and to discover new ideas (71).

4. Students need practice in analyzing the tasks they have completed. By building new assignments on previous tasks, a student must analyze the task and represent it to herself.

5. Theorists and practitioners of the rhetorical approach to teaching writing argue, as Janice Lauer does, that "writing, like all creating, begins with an exigency, a sense of discovery, an awareness of ambiguity, the urgency to know something unknown. It starts with questions, not answers" (56). In the case of the sequence discussed here, for example, the first question is, "What is a family?" The final question is, "How is family a political issue?"

The essays collected in Elaine Maimon, Barbara Nodine, and Fenbarr O'Connor's *Thinking, Reasoning, and Writing* support the connections between thinking and writing. In the essays, authors, whose academic disciplines are cognitive psychology, logic, and composition, "verify what [many writing teachers] have always felt: writing creates situations in which students can learn and think" (3). Developmental psychologists David Moshan and Bridget Franks remind us, for instance, that new knowledge is a product "of the active mind interacting with [a] complex and changing world." (Maimon et al. 13). The logicians tell us that formal and informal logic can help writers re-envision early drafts of persuasive writing. The philosophers encourage writing "in which the author detaches herself from the idea, claim, or argument put forward and seems to join with the reader in assessing its worth" (Maimon et al. 154). This kind of writing, Jerry Cederblom argues, draws "the reader into the stream of thought of the author" and reflects "the identification of the self as a belief-forming process rather than as a particular set of beliefs" (Maimon et al. 154). Composition scholars and teachers, the editors tell us, have in the past twenty-five years "shifted attention [from surface features in texts] back to composition, the creative act of forming and arranging linguistic elements that generate and express thought" (161).

A Sequence About Family

The eight assignments described below are offered as an example of a sequence of assignments developed around one theme. I revised these assignments the next quarter, using friendship as the theme, making the exploratory paper into a prewriting assignment for the proposal, and adding a unit on writing definitions. Nevertheless, I use the sequence here and in faculty workshops because the flaws inherent in the assignments promote lively, productive discussions.

Paper 1. In-class Diagnostic Essay

Purpose: The purpose of this essay is to help your instructor determine some of your strengths and weaknesses in writing. Therefore, the essay will be read carefully but will not receive a grade. Nor will it affect your final grade.

Assignment: Family is a subject about which we all have something to say. Relying on either your own experience or someone else's, write an essay that answers the question, "What is a family?" Your audience is college students.

Paper 2. A Personal Account (Adapted from Donald Daiker's assignment in Coles and Vopat's *What Makes Writing Good?*)

Take any family-related event, however trivial it seems, that you still remember from your childhood. That you still remember it is one sign of its importance to you. In a paper of approximately 500 words (two to two and a half typed pages), narrate and describe the event so that your readers — our class — come to feel and understand why it was (is?) important.

Narration aims not to tell us about an event but to give us the event. Description aims not to tell us about an object but to give us the object. Because your aim in both narration and description is to show rather than tell, you will want to use specific details, especially sensory details, details that appeal to your reader's sense of taste, touch, sound, sight, and smell.

Try to make your readers experience what you experienced.

Paper 3. Ghost Writing

Exchange papers with your assigned partner and rewrite your partner's story, continuing to use "I".

The purpose of telling your partner's story is to interpret the childhood event described in his or her paper 2. That is, you need to help us understand what and how your partner learned from the incident. To achieve that purpose, begin your story with this sentence: This is a story about when I was _____ and I learned that _____. Keep only those details that help achieve your purpose and add new ones if they help us understand. (You will need to interview your partner to elicit additional details.)

Paper 4. Summary

From a recent periodical, select an article about some aspect of family. Summarize the article, assuming that the summary will be sufficient for the reader, that she will not need to go back to the article.

Paper 5. Developing a Thesis

Identify a family relationship that emerges from your reading of the four short stories discussed in class. Formulate a thesis about that relationship and develop an essay based on your thesis. (The class had discussed Cheever's "Goodbye, My Brother," Lawrence's "The Rocking-Horse Winner," Olsen's "I Stand Here Ironing," and a story of their choice.)

Paper 6. An Exploratory Essay

Political rhetoric of both the right and the left (e.g., President Bush, Governor Cuomo) claims to be Pro-Family. In an exploratory essay of approximately 1,000 words (four double-spaced typed pages), consider what it means for a political program to be pro-family. Since an exploratory essay does not come to a conclusion and is not, therefore, thesis-driven, we would like you to begin your essay in a special way. Rather than beginning with a thesis, we would like you to begin with an anecdote or a narrative that exemplifies or embodies a pro-family stance. Develop your paper by clarifying or explaining the implications of your opening, and then follow the question wherever it leads you.

Paper 7. A Proposal

The previous paper explores the government's impact on one aspect of the family, for example, divorce, student financial aid, Medicare, AIDS. This paper calls for you to perform several writing tasks:

1. Define the problem that you identified in the previous paper.
2. Identify the causes of the problem.
3. Identify the solution(s) to the problem. These will be solutions only a government agency (national, state, local) can provide.
4. Identify an audience who can act on your proposal or who can persuade that person or agency to act on your proposal.
5. Present a proposal in which you discuss your solutions.

Paper 8. Final In-class Paper

Purpose: The purpose of this essay is to help your instructor to determine if, in what ways, and how much your writing skills have improved over the quarter.

Assignment: Family is a subject about which you know a great deal. Relying on either your own experiences or someone else's, write an essay that answers the question, "What is a family?" Your audience is college students.

When my colleague and I developed the sequence of assignments about family, we assumed that assignments in a sequence should move linearly, progressively within the linear sequence (i.e., following steps in the writing process), and recursively. To arrange the assignments linearly, we designed the last assignment first, asking ourselves, "What knowledge of family and what writing skills do students need in order to urge a specified reader to take some action on a family issue?" We developed the assignments, then, with these two considerations: First, what methods for gathering information about families should they know how to use? We asked them to interview each other about their families; to reminisce; to investigate library sources; to analyze and discuss periodical articles on a wide range of family-related topics; to analyze and discuss family dynamics in four short stories, a poem, and a film; to respond in their journals to class activities and their own family dynamics. Second, what kinds of writing skills must our students practice before they leave our classes, the scene of the only formal writing instruction they will have for two years? We wanted them to be able to summarize for a purpose and a reader, to frame their own theses, to explore a subject without taking a stance.

I can't discuss all of the assignments we gave to prepare our students to write the major papers in the sequence, of course, so I have begrudgingly omitted a discussion of the formal summary assignment; "begrudgingly," I say, because summary writing is an important skill that fosters critical thinking, that calls for a clear sense of purpose and audience, that requires a minimal effort in responding to it, and that serves the students well at various stages in a set of assignments. And I have omitted a discussion of the diagnostic and final essays (the definition papers), although later I will comment briefly on how the pre- and post-essays compared. About the "free thesis" assignment, I will simply say that students need to take away from a writing class the ability to create their own theses, and that the assignment is placed, as you can see, in the middle of the sequence. By then, we assumed, the earlier papers and the frequent class and written discussions of family would help them identify a thesis in the literature selections and provide them with supporting frameworks for their papers. That distancing, cognitive difficulty, and knowledge of the subject influenced our order of assignments will be even more obvious later, when you read workshop participants' discussions of the assignments.

To illustrate how we incorporated the second movement, the stages of the writing-as-process — a progressive movement within a linear assignment sequence — I will describe some of the writing activities that made up the second and third assignments. In prewriting exercises, students discussed a summary of Eric Erickson's theory of the life cycle of the family, responding in their journals to ideas in the article and then responding to a classmate's journal response. They also wrote in their journals a brief account of a childhood incident they recalled vividly, one that had something to do with their family. Using the incident they had written about in their journals, they drafted paper 1, written with the class as the audience. They did a round-robin reading of those papers to establish criteria for revising. After small-group peer evaluations, they expanded their scoring guide for their revisions and for their grades. Before they submitted their final versions, two classmates helped them edit. Indeed, there were many occasions for us to intervene in the students' writing processes.

In the third assignment, which evolved from the second, each student rewrote a classmate's paper, this time making explicit in the paper the moral that was implicit in the first account. First, two students asked of each paper the question, "What did the writer learn from this incident?" After interviewing the writer of the original account, each student added and deleted details to make her point explicit. Peer revisions, the revision of the scoring guide, and peer editing followed, as did individual conferences about both papers.

While I described the steps in the evolution of those two papers to illustrate the movement of writing as a process, you can also see the recursiveness — the third movement in a sequence of assignments — built into those two sets of writing activities. Nevertheless, I want to illustrate an important advantage to sequencing by describing the recursiveness in papers 6 and 7, the exploratory essay and the urge-to-action paper. For one thing, both papers called for a great deal of information about one aspect of government intervention in the family, so for the exploratory papers, students were forced to locate facts about the issues they selected to study (surrogacy, incest, divorce, single-parenting, care for the elderly, AIDS, social security, welfare, sex education) — information that they would use selectively in the next paper. Second, their library searches also required them to summarize material. Third, for the first of the two related assignments — to present two sides to a family issue without taking a stand — we discussed their original narratives and required that the students capture in a narrative introduction the nature of the problem. We discussed many examples of opening anecdotes in popular magazines. Fourth, in the meantime, students reacted to their issue informally in their journals, discussed their issues in class, and developed a scoring guide, all tasks that had recurred during the quarter.

The next assignment required students to consider who in the government or what local, state, or national agency could do something to solve the problem they had identified for the previous paper. This complicated assignment was broken into discrete tasks, all of which they had performed before. For the students, the most perplexing part of the assignment was the audience. Although they had written to a variety of audiences — to themselves, to their classmates, to me, to a general audience — they had problems identifying an appropriate audience for their paper. To help them focus on the needs of their audience, I asked them to write the reader of their paper a telegram in which they could have only five sentences: one establishing a context for the telegram, another stating the problem, one identifying the cause or causes of the problem, another suggesting a solution, and a final one stating what action the reader should take. In other words, they had to write a summary of their drafts.

The papers arising from assignment 6 were somewhat disappointing, although they satisfied the requirements of the assignment. Students wrote effective anecdotal introductions, explored the issue (albeit cursorily, since we had specified only 1,000 words), and came to no conclusion about their issue. Finding a structure for the paper was easy for them. Nearly all writers settled on an introduction, a brief discussion of one side of the issue, a transitional paragraph, a brief discussion of the other side of the issue, a conclusion reiterating the problem and the need for a solution. In short, we got what we had asked for — lifeless, formulaic essays — and not what we had wanted — lively explorations of possibilities, like those that evolve from freewriting and discovery drafts. So, although the assignment prepared students for writing proposals (paper 7), as essays they were disappointing. In subsequent uses of the sequence, therefore, I asked students to explore an issue through free writing, eliminating the formal exploratory paper from the sequence.

A few words about papers 1 and 8. Although we had half expected the underdeveloped, generalized definitions of family elicited from assignment 1 — extended definitions are difficult to write, we knew — we were surprised to find the final essays equally underdeveloped and generalized. So much for conventional wisdom, we thought: students' writing does not necessarily improve as their knowledge of a subject increases. But the proposals that had preceded the in-class definitions had been outstanding, reflecting the writers' experience in analyzing audiences, in selecting appropriate material, in finding effective structures and the like, and their knowledge of the subject.

To improve the results of this closing assignment, I adjusted later sequences — using friendship rather than family as the central theme — to include prewriting activities focusing on definition. For the final paper, students submitted five to six typed pages of well-developed definitions that reflected their sense of audience and their familiarity with the subject of friendship.

To summarize: sequencing writing assignments linearly, progressively within that movement, and recursively allows teachers to incorporate into writing courses much of what we have come to understand about writing processes and about learning. It is an approach that is sound theoretically, pedagogically, and practically. It offers students frequent opportunities to write and to acquire writing skills through repetition, progressively more complicated cognitive and rhetorical demands, and a diversity of learning activities. Planning sequences around a theme such as family offers students a chance to become deeply engaged in their material, to use writing as a way of discovering what they already know about a subject.

Guidelines for Designing and Sequencing Writing Assignments on a Theme

Here, I would like to recommend two essays that can help instructors plan activities that foster critical thinking. Linda Flower's "Taking Thought: The Role of Conscious Processing in the Making of Meaning" summarizes what is known about cognition and writing and offers a sequence of journal assignments used in the freshman program at Carnegie-Mellon. As Flower explains, the journal assignments "ask the students to analyze a problem, then to rewrite the analysis either for a different reader or from the perspective of a different discourse community. In parallel with this sequence, the student is doing a self-analysis and using the problem analysis assignments as a window on his or her own writing process" (207).

The second essay is Peter Elbow's "Teaching Two Kinds of Thinking by Teaching Writing." Elbow describes these two kinds of thinking as "careless," first-order thinking, and "careful," second-order thinking. He explains:

> There is an obvious link between the writing process and these two kinds of thinking. I link first-order intuitive or creative thinking with freewriting and first-draft exploratory writing in which one defers planning, control, organizing, and censoring. I link second-order thinking with slow, thoughtful rewriting where one constantly subjects everything to critical scrutiny. (57–8)

Excellence in writing and thinking, Elbow says, involves "finding some way to be both abundantly inventive yet toughmindedly critical" (60).

Here is a heuristic for designing a set of assignments that encourage students to practice thinking skills. Each step requires some brainstorming, clustering, looping, or whatever invention strategy you prefer.

1. Select a topic that builds on knowledge students share, about which students can find new information from a variety of sources, and that will not make students uncomfortable when they share their writing with peers.

2. What skills do you want the students to practice during the term? Summarizing? Defining? Synthesizing? Developing theses? Analyzing? Persuading? Analyzing audiences? Editing?

3. What information-gathering and -sharing techniques do you want the students to master? Interviewing? Free writing? Library search? Peer responses to discovery drafts?

4. Considering the skills and strategies you want your students to practice during the term, formulate a question about the topic.

The question is crucial to the effectiveness of a sequence: it drives all the writing assignments and class activities, and it is the basis for the final writing assignment, a rhetorically and cognitively complex task.

5. Relying on your notes about question 2, arrange the major assignments according to some principle, such as the difficulty of assessing audience and purpose or the skills that require reinforcement throughout the term, like using narrative for a purpose, summarizing for a specific audience, and the like.

6. Relying on your notes about question 3, list the in-class activities and out-of-class assignments that will be required to connect and complete each assignment.

A Faculty Workshop on Designing Sequenced Writing Assignments

Step 1

Before I begin the main business of the workshop, I want to find out what assumptions the participants hold about writing and the teaching of writing. Here is an activity I have used in orientations for new graduate teaching assistants, in-service programs for elementary high school teachers and administrators, workshops with faculty from disciplines other than English, and convention workshops for secondary and college writing instructors. As an opening exercise, the cooperative assignment, the purposes of which are listed below, has always helped to achieve my goals for workshops on assignment design:

- To elicit from workshop participants standards by which a writing assignment can be assessed.

- To introduce the workshop format to the participants, emphasizing collaboration and a participant-centered environment.

- To demonstrate through their critiquing of a writing assignment that participants share criteria for good assignment design and, by implication, for effective writing.

- To set the context for critical thinking among the participants.

- To emphasize that the demands of a writing assignment help to determine the quality of the writing that the assignment will elicit from students.

To illustrate this point, I ask participants to spend fifteen or twenty minutes identifying the assumptions about writing and the teaching of writing that underlie this essay assignment:

Essay 2. Typed, 3 to 5 pages. Due Friday. Discuss the implications of the recent [breakup of the Baltic states, confirmation hearings of Clarence Thomas, anti-abortion demonstrations, or any headline item]. As usual, spelling, punctuation, grammar, and usage will be taken into account when your paper is graded.

Step 2

Workshop participants never fail to point out some assumptions as we move around the circle sharing our notes. The assignment assumes that student writers are interested in the topic and care about its resolution, whereas participants observe that their own students would see the topic as having little impact on their lives. Another general comment about the assignment is that half of the space is devoted to an admonition about correctness, leaving student writers with the impression that for their instructor form is more important than content. Participants focus on the individual elements of the assignment and discuss the assumptions implicit in them:

"Essay 2" Someone always points out that an Essay 1 has preceded this assignment. However, given how unhelpful the current writing assignment is, no one has ever argued that Essay 1 probably prepared the students for all of the instructions that the current phrase "as usual" entails. Nor has anyone argued that Essay 1 instructions about the meanings of "discuss" and "implications" were probably discussed adequately and therefore do not need to be discussed in detail in preparation for Essay 2. (Here it is interesting to pause and ask participants to define the term *essay*.)

"Typed" This requirement implies that the essay due Friday is a final product since it is to be typed. It also assumes that all students have access to typewriters or word processors, can type, or know someone who will type the paper for them.

"Friday" The due date—in this exercise, I name a due date that is three days from the distribution of the assignment—indicates that little peer or teacher intervention will take place with drafts, that the paper is a one-shot deal. In addition, it assumes that the students can generate information about the topic in a short time—that they either know enough about the topic to brainstorm sufficient information or will have enough time to study library resources, conduct interviews, and so on.

"3 to 5 pages" As it is worded, the assignment merits a book-length manuscript. This prompt assumes that students know how to narrow a general topic so that they can treat it adequately in the assigned number of pages.

"Discuss"   What tasks does "discuss" involve? The topic assumes the writer will be able to choose among comparing, contrasting, summarizing, arguing, persuading, narrating, reporting, critiquing, and so on. It also assumes that the writer can impose a purpose on the general directions given in the topic.

"Implications"   For whom? The assignment assumes students are sophisticated enough to select one implication to focus on and one audience on whom to concentrate.

"As usual"   How can expectations be "as usual" when only one essay has preceded this assignment? Nevertheless, the assignment assumes that students will know the standards by which the conventions in their papers will be judged.

"Will be taken into account"   By whom? The passive voice verb indicates that the teacher is not accepting the responsibility for "grading" the essay. Ironically, the assignment specifies no audience, so here is one more example of the teacher as evaluator, despite the teacher's unwillingness to acknowledge that fact.

"When the paper is graded"   Since there is no mention of revising, students can assume that the primary concern of the teacher is the product, the finished essay. We can also assumes that the teacher's emphasis will be on judging rather than critiquing the paper.

Step 3

The participants read the eight sequenced assignments silently.

Step 4

For five to ten minutes participants in pairs analyze the relationships between two paper assignments that I assign to them. How much direction I give the teachers depends on their teaching experience. Sometimes I simply tell them to consider why their two assignments have been placed beside each other in the sequence. Other times I ask them to look especially at the audiences specified in the assignments, the skills required, the purposes of the assignments, the sources of information required for the assignment.

Step 5

The two participants who discussed the same paper assignment then switch partners to share what they had learned from their previous discussion. That is, the person who had discussed papers 1 and 2 discusses paper 2 with the person who had looked at papers 2 and 3, and so forth.

Step 6

The whole group then listens to the analyses, adding their observations and raising questions. Here are some relationships noted by faculty.

Papers 1 and 2

- While in 1 the writer is anonymous to her peers and to the teacher, the writer of 2 is known to the teacher and peers.
- Although the audience in 1 is ostensibly the writer's peers, the teacher is the "real" reader; the audience in 2 is the writer's peers.
- The purpose of writing 1 is twofold: to define a term through personal knowledge of the subject and to provide a sample of writing for "diagnosis" by the teacher; the purpose of writing 2 is to explore a personal experience, selecting and shaping the details so the reader can feel its importance to the writer.
- Both 1 and 2 call for some degree of personal experience, although the writer of paper 1 could distance himself from the material.
- The kind of prose called for in 1 is expository: the writer is to inform the reader; the kind of writing called for in 2 is expressive, specifically a personal account.
- The mode called for in 1 is definition, although students could use narration and description in defining; the genres called for in 2 are narration and description in the service of a personal account.
- 1 asks for a more general level of response to the task than 2 does; 2 requires specific details from the point of view of the writer.

Papers 2 and 3

- Students don't have as much personal investment in 3 as they have in 2; in 3, the writer has more distance from the material.
- The purpose for 2 is to recount a significant childhood event, making the reader sense why the event was significant; in 3 the writer is asked to offer an explicit interpretation of the event.
- This pair of assignments is excellent for practice in revision. First, in 3 the thesis is clear, so students must select details more judiciously, saving only those that support the thesis and eliciting additional details from the author of 2. Second, rewriting 2 gives students a chance to practice changing points of view about material.
- Both papers draw on students' own experiences, thus validating the writer's experiences and knowledge.

Papers 3 and 4

- In both assignments, the writer uses another writer's material.
- 3 is told in the first person; 4 is told in the third person.

- 3 is based on a peer's writing.
- In 3 the reader won't necessarily make use of the material or its interpretation in another paper; the reader will use the material in 4 in a later paper.
- Both 3 and 4 foster collaboration, in 3 through interviewing, in 4 through providing peers with additional information about some aspect of family.
- Both require students to analyze information in support of a thesis and a purpose.

Papers 4 and 5

- Both papers connect reading and writing.
- Theses from 4 (summaries) provide ideas for theses for 5.
- Both 4 and 5 require students to support a thesis.
- Both require students to make use of information, not personal experience.
- In order to write 5, students must be able to summarize (4).
- 5 requires a greater range of skills then 4 does; whereas a summary requires students to identify a thesis and select the important details that support it, 5 requires those skills plus interpretation.

Papers 5 and 6

- For support of the thesis, 5 requires interpretation of fiction; 6 requires analysis and interpretation of facts, plus practice in maintaining objectivity.
- The introduction for 6 requires a review of narrative skills. Students will have seen this kind of introduction in the articles they summarized in 4.
- 6 proves to students that they have something valuable to say.

Papers 6 and 7

- 6 collects information for use in 7.
- Previous expressive writing helps generate material for 7.
- 6 helps students clarify the issues and consider opponents' position.
- 7 requires students to analyze their audience more thoroughly than they have had to analyze earlier audiences for their papers.
- 7 requires a solution to the problem identified and explored in 6.

Papers 1 through 7 and 8

- While having to gather additional information, students review all the skills they have worked on: summarizing, developing a thesis, selecting material to support a thesis, analyzing their audiences, using personal experience as support of the thesis, introducing the thesis through a short narrative.

- Assignments 2 through 7 require an increasing need for secondary materials, and students are asked to recognize relationships and reorganize previously acquired knowledge for new purposes.

Step 7

If I have several hours for these activities, I ask groups of three or four teachers to create guidelines for developing sequences of assignments and to share with the whole group the guidelines they have created. If pressed for time, I distribute the guidelines mentioned above and omit the group development of guidelines.

Time and again, these workshop exercises have demonstrated to new and veteran teachers the complexity of writers' processes. They reinforce the notion that writing helps heighten and refine thinking, and they demonstrate that sequencing writing assignments around a common theme helps foster critical thinking.

Works Cited

Adams, Katherine H. "From James Britton: The Rhetoric of Spectating." *Freshman English News* 13.3 (1984): 15−17.

Allister, Mark. "A Marriage of Pedagogy and Theory: Sequencing and the Pentad." *The Writing Instructor* 2 (1983): 129−36.

Bartholomae, David, and Anthony Petrosky. *Facts, Artifacts and Counterfacts: Theory and Method for a Reading and Writing Course.* Portsmouth, NH: Boynton/Cook, 1986.

Berthoff, Ann. *Forming/Thinking/Writing.* Portsmouth, NH: Boynton/Cook, 1978.

Brandt, Deborah. "Social Foundations of Reading and Writing." *Convergences: Transactions in Reading and Writing.* Ed. B. T. Peterson, Urbana. IL: NCTE, 1986. 115−26.

Coles, William E. *The Plural I: The Teaching of Writing.* New York: Holt, Rinehart and Winston, 1978.

Coles, William E., Jr., and James Vopat. "Donald Daiker's Assignment." *What Makes Writing Good: A Multiperspective.* Lexington, MA: D. C. Heath, 1985. 47−51.

Comley, Nancy R. "Review: Critical Thinking/Critical Teaching." *College English* 51 (1989): 623−27.

Cox, Gerard H. "Designing Essay Assignments." *Teaching Prose: A Guide for Writing Instructors.* Ed. F. V. Bogel and K. K. Gottschalk. NY: W. W. Norton and Company, 1984. 87−113.

Dowst, Kenneth. "The Epistemic Approach: Writing, Knowing, and Learning." *Eight Approaches to Teaching Composition.* Ed. T. Donovan and B. McClelland. Urbana, IL: NCTE, 1980. 65−85.

Elbow, Peter. "Teaching Two Kinds of Thinking by Teaching Writing." *Embracing Contraries: Explorations in Learning and Teaching.* New York: Oxford UP, 1986. 55−63.

Faigley, Lester, and Stephen Witte. "Analyzing Revision." *College Composition and Communication* 32 (1981): 400−14.

Flower, Linda. "Taking Thought: The Role of Conscious Processing in the Making of Meaning." Maimon et al. 185−212.

Flower, Linda, and John R. Hayes. "The Cognition of Discovery: Defining a Rhetorical Problem." *College Composition and Communication* 31 (1980): 21−32.

———. "A Cognitive Process Theory of Writing." *College Composition and Communication* 32 (1981): 365−87.

Foster, David. "Planning the Course: Six Key Questions." *A Primer for Writing Teachers: Theories, Theorists, Issues, Problems.* Portsmouth, NH: Boynton/Cook, 1983. 116−38.

Hunt, F. Joan. *Let's Teach Students to Think.* ERIC, 1975. ED 096 294.

Kiniry, Malcolm, and Ellen Strenski. "Sequencing Expository Writing: A Recursive Approach." *College Composition and Communication* 36 (1985): 191−202.

Kurfiss, Joanne G. *Critical Thinking: Theory, Research, Practice, and Possibilities.* ASHE-ERIC Higher Education Report No 2. Washington, DC: Association for the Study of Higher Education, 1988.

Langer, Judith, A., and Arthur N. Applebee. *How Writing Shapes Thinking: A Study of Teaching and Learning.* NCTE Research Report No. 22. Urbana, IL: NCTE, 1987.

Larson, Richard. "Teaching Before We Judge: Planning Assignments in Composition." *The Leaflet* 66 (1967): 3−15. Rpt. in *The Writing Teacher's Sourcebook.* Ed. G. Tate and E. P. J. Corbett. NY: Oxford UP, 1981. 208−19.

Lauer, Janice. "The Rhetorical Approach: Stages of Writing and Strategies for Writers." *Eight Approaches to Teaching Composition.* Ed. T. Donovan and B. McClelland. Urbana, IL: NCTE, 1980. 53−64.

Macrorie, Ken. *Searching Writing.* Rochelle Park, NJ: Hayden, 1980.

Maimon, Elaine P., Barbara F. Nodine, and Finbarr W. O'Connor. *Thinking, Reasoning, and Writing.* New York: Longman, 1989.

McPeck, John. *Critical Thinking and Education.* New York: St. Martin's Press, 1981.

Meyers, Chet. *Teaching Students to Think Critically: A Guide for Faculty in All Disciplines.* San Francisco: Jossey-Bass, 1986.

Moffett, James. *Teaching the Universe of Discourse.* Boston: Houghton Mifflin, 1968.

Olson, Carol Booth. "Fostering Critical Thinking Skills Through Writing." *Educational Leadership*. 42.3 (1984): 28–39.

Rankin, Elizabeth. "From Simple to Complex: Ideas of Order in Assignment Sequences." *Journal of Advanced Composition*. 10 (1990): 126–35.

Smith, Frank. "Learning to Be a Critical Thinker." *Joining the Literacy Club*. Portsmouth, NH: Heinemann Educational Books, Inc, 1988. 47–63.

Sternglass, Marilyn. "Integrating Instruction in Reading, Writing, and Reasoning." *The Writer's Mind: Writing as a Mode of Thinking*. Ed. J. H. Hays et al. Urbana, IL: NCTE, 1983. 153–58.

Wilhoit, Stephen. *Critical Thinking and the Thematic Writing Course*. ERIC, 1990. ED 321 254.

Additional Works Consulted

Beene, Lynn Diane. "Assignment Making." *Research in Composition and Rhetoric*. Ed. M. G. Moran and R. F. Lunsford. Westport, CT: Greenwood, 1984. 239–62.

Cochran, Janet F. "The Interview: Combining Humanities and Cognitive Value in the Teaching of Composition." *Activating the Passive Student*. The Committee of Classroom Practices. Urbana, IL: NCTE, 1979. 60–64.

Coles, William E. *Composing: Writing as a Self-Creating Process*. Upper Montclair, NJ: Boynton/Cook, 1983.

———. *Seeing Through Writing*. NY: Harper & Row, 1988.

Comprone, Joseph. "Integrating the Acts of Reading and Writing About Literature: A Sequence of Assignments Based on James Joyce's 'Counterparts.'" *Convergences: Transactions in Reading and Writing*. Ed. B. T. Petersen. Urbana, IL: NCTE, 1986. 215–30.

Cunningham, Frank J. "Writing Philosophy: Sequential Essays and Objective Tests." *College Composition and Communication* 36 (1985): 166–72.

Dellinger, Dixie G. *Out of the Heart: How to Design Writing Assignments for High School Courses*. Berkeley, CA: The National Writing Project, 1982.

Fulwiler, Toby, and Robert Jones. "Assigning and Evaluating Transactional Writing." *Language Connections: Writing and Reading Across the Curriculum*. Ed. T. Fulwiler and A. Young. Urbana, IL: NCTE, 1982. 45–55.

Haisty, Donna. "Sequencing Then and Now." *The Writing Instructor* 3 (1984): 169–76.

Johannessen, Larry R., Elizabeth A. Kahn, and Carolyn C. Walter. *Designing and Sequencing Prewriting Activities*. Urbana, IL: ERIC/NCTE, 1982.

Katz, Marilyn. "From Self-Analysis to Academic Analysis." *College English* 40 (1978): 288–99.

Laughlin, James S. *When Students Confront the Experts: Toward Critical Thinking in the Classroom*. ERIC, 1990. ED 322 516.

Lindemann, Erika. "Making and Evaluating Writing Assignments." *A Rhetoric for Writing Teachers.* 2nd. ed. NY: Oxford UP, 1987. 191–223.

Lunsford, Andrea A. "Assignments for Basic Writers: Unresolved Issues and Needed Research." *Journal of Basic Writing* 5 (1986): 87–99.

Moffett, James. "I, You, and It." *College Composition and Communication* 16 (1965): 243–87. Rpt. in *Active Voice: A Writing Program Across the Curriculum.* J. Moffett. Portsmouth, NH: Boynton/Cook, 1981. 140–48.

Moran, Charles. "Teaching Writing/Teaching Literature." *College Composition and Communication* 32 (1981): 21–29.

Petersen, Bruce. "In Search of Meaning: Reader and Expressive Language." *Language Connections: Writing and Reading Across the Curriculum.* Ed. T. Fulwiler and A. Young. Urbana, IL: NCTE, 1982. 107–22.

Scanlon, Leone. "Invention and the Writing Sequence." *The Writer's Mind: Writing as a Mode of Thinking.* Ed. J. H. Hays et al. Urbana, IL: NCTE, 1983. 95–101.

Schuster, Charles. "Situational Sequencing." *The Writing Instructor* 3 (1984): 177–84.

Soven, Margot. "Helping Students Generalize, Specify, Clarify: A Sequence for Writing Assignments." *Structuring for Success in the English Classroom: Classroom Practices in Teaching English 1981–1982.* Committee on Classroom Practices. Urbana, IL: NCTE, 1982. 102–6.

Tremblay, Paula Y. "Writing Assignments for Cognitive Development." *College Composition and Communication* 37 (1983): 342–43.

Walter, Otis M. "Plato's Idea of Rhetoric for Contemporary Students: Theory and Composition Assignments." *College Composition and Communication* 35 (1984): 20–30.

Wilhoit, Stephen. "Moffett and Point of View: A Creative Writing Assignment Sequence." *Journal of Teaching Writing.* 5 (1986): 297–305.

6

Improving Critical Thinking Through Problem Analysis

Lois Rubin

Many educators believe today that American students lack the higher-order reasoning skills they need to function well in the complicated society of the late twentieth century. The following gloomy assessment from *The Nation's Report Card* is typical of many such reports: "Only small percentages of children and young adults can reason effectively about what they are reading or writing" (Applebee, Langer, and Mullis 11). Young adults still seem to be relying on what Scardamalia and Bereiter call "knowledge telling," writing down content in much the same manner in which it was stored in memory—the thinking strategy characteristic of young children (13). Indeed, some college teachers report that their students have difficulty moving from "summarizing to synthesizing, from retelling to drawing original conclusions," that they still rely on "chronology" as their organizing structure (Freisinger 8).

If students are entering college without the higher-order thinking skills that they need to do college work and to function in the complex, technological workplace of the twenty-first century, then those of us who teach on the college level have a clear mission: to help them improve their thinking skills. In particular, those of us who teach composition have the opportunity of using writing, widely considered to be an aid to thinking and learning (Emig, Fulwiler, and Young), to help them reach that goal. One college composition teacher, Mike Rose, has done just that; he designed a basic writing course with the goal of preparing students to do the complex, analytical writing required in the academic world. In place of the simple, personal, narrative and descriptive assignments that appear in many traditional basic writing courses (but nowhere else in the university), he offers assignments that require students to "select and order information, and to see and re-see data and events in various contexts" (111). In particular, he creates assignments that enable students to learn the various organizational patterns (schemata) widely used in college writing (122−23).

Another way to promote higher-order thinking in students is through the problem-analysis approach created by Young, Becker, and Pike and described fully in *Rhetoric: Discovery and Change*.[1] Problem analysis starts by developing students' metacognitive knowledge, that is, "knowledge about one's own cognitive processes and products or anything related to them ..." (Flavell, "Metacognitive Aspects" 232).[2] In particular, problem analysis teaches the student to become sensitive to a particular kind of metacognitive experience, the sense of unease a person feels

> when features of the image are perceived to be inconsistent with one another ... when a person becomes aware that two beliefs to which he is deeply committed are incompatible ... when he discovers something in the nature of the world that doesn't "fit" his conception of it, when he has a desire or a need that he finds he cannot fulfill. (Young, Becker, and Pike 90)

According to Young, developing sensitivity to the "problematic situation" is crucial, for this unease is what motivates people to solve problems, to make discoveries. For a writer it is the motive for writing; he begins to gain control over his problem through "its analysis and articulation" (Young 62).

Flavell observes that frequently "metacognitive experiences can activate [cognitive] strategies" ("Metacognition" 908). Just so with problem analysis. Once the problem has been discovered, problem analysis provides the writer with a set of sophisticated cognitive strategies for analyzing and resolving it. Students are taught to find and state the problem (to distinguish the clashing elements, to pose a question whose answer will resolve the clash), then to explore and resolve the problem (to find the necessary information, to form hypotheses from this information, to test and evaluate them). In essence this system teaches the student reflective thinking, according to the model Dewey describes in *How We Think* (106−7).

At the same time that problem analysis improves students' thinking skills, it works on the affective level as well. Because the writing topic grows out of students' own problems—what surprises or disturbs them, what clashes with their expectations—the assignment is intrinsically engaging to them. As Young puts it,

> Thus problems are important motivations to action; none of us needs to be prodded to solve a real problem any more than we need to be urged to eat when we are hungry. Much could be done to solve the teacher's perennial problem of student motivation if our methods were rooted in these facts of human behavior. (65)

Classroom Application

My experience using problem analysis in the classroom has demonstrated to me that the affective and cognitive benefits of the approach claimed in theory are true in practice. In this section I will describe the way that I use problem analysis in my writing classroom.

To develop students' sensitivity to the problematic situation, I start with examples from their personal lives. To that end, I ask them to write down on a slip of paper what "bugs" them — that is, what things in their lives disturb or bother them, are other than they would like them to be. Needless to say, students have a lot to say on this subject; some even offer to write a book in answer to this question. As they write, I walk around the class looking for good examples to put on the board. Here is one of these:

> I keep my room neat. I spend time vacuuming and straightening up. Then my brother comes in and in two minutes undoes my work, throwing clothes all around, dropping food on the floor, etc.

Once we have a few problematic situations at hand, we work on shaping the anecdotal accounts, as above, into clearly formed problem statements. To do this, students must first distinguish the two parts of the problem. That is, a student may find that one of his beliefs or values conflicts with a reality; two values that a student holds may be in conflict; or a student may have a need or desire that he cannot fulfill. The two elements that are in conflict, incompatible, or unfulfilled are then labelled A and B. For instance, in the first problem above, the A and B would be as follows:

A. I like to keep things neat and orderly, with everything in its place.

B. But my brother is just the opposite; he continually makes a mess of the bedroom we share.

Sometimes one of the elements, usually the student's belief, is so obvious that the student doesn't name it. Note the following: "What bugs me is Professor X. He just gave us a test that had nothing to do with anything we studied in the text or talked about in class." To make a complete problem statement, the student must be taught to articulate the assumption that underlies his discontent: "I think professors should only test students on what they have taught or assigned them." With that assumption as his A, he can then present as his B the reality that conflicts with his assumption: "Professor X tests us on things we never learned."

Once the A and B have been identified, the next task is to state the unknown; that is, to raise the question whose answer will resolve the problem. With the "messy room" problem above, the question that jumps out of the conflict in living styles is, "What can I do about it?" This is the question the students needs to know the answer to in order to solve his problem.

For more practice in forming situations, I provide samples of problematic situations extracted from their "personal problem papers," written earlier in the term:

> My problem is my shyness and how it affects me. There is just something inside of me that keeps me from talking to people. I would love to talk to people I know and meet new people. There are not many people who can understand how it is to want to talk to somebody, but just not be able to.

This situation can be expressed as follows:

A. I would like to be friendly and talk to people.

B. I'm shy and can't talk to people.

? How can I overcome my shyness and become friendly?

> I started dating Jim at the beginning of the summer. I always wanted to be with him and enjoyed his company. Well, the problem arose when school started in the fall. As usual, I was happy to see all of my friends since I had not seen them that often during the summer. We made plans to go dancing that Saturday night. I could not wait to get together with my friends again. When I told him about my plans, he hit the ceiling. Everytime I wanted to go out with my friends, Jim would get mad.

This situation can be expressed as follows:

A. I like to spend time with my friends.

B. I like my boyfriend and want to stay on good terms with him, but he objects to my spending time with my friends.

? How can I stay on good terms with my boyfriend and still see my friends?

? Whom should I choose — my boyfriend or my friends?

These two examples illustrate two different types of problems: the first, the incompleteness problem (I would like to be here, but I'm not); the second, the inconsistency problem (I like two things that are in conflict).

The next step is to move from exploring personal problems to exploring those found in literature. Reading a piece of literature is itself a complicated mental act, as Louise Rosenblatt points out:

> As the reader submits himself to the guidance of the text, he must engage in a most demanding kind of activity. Out of his past experience, he must select appropriate responses to the individual words, he must

sense their interplay upon one another, he must respond to clues of tone and attitude and movement. He must focus his attention on what he is structuring through these means. He must try to see it as an organized whole, its parts interrelated as fully as the text and his own capacities permit. (633)

And so, in being asked to apply problem analysis to their reading of a book, students are being asked to perform a doubly challenging mental task. As a way into the process, students are asked to keep a journal of their responses to the reading, noting in particular aspects of the book that puzzled and surprised them or clashed with their expectations.[3] In so doing, they can be "reflecting" on their reading as Louise Rosenblatt advises (671), and at the same time establishing the personal connection with the problem that they will later investigate. For "problems do not exist independent of men. There are no problems floating around in the world out there waiting to be discovered; there are only problems for someone" (Young, Becker, and Pike 90). For that reason, students must include a statement of value as either the A or B of their problem statement: "I would expect . . ." or "I don't understand why . . ." Note the following:

Dinner at the Homesick Restaurant

A. I'd expect a married couple who had lived apart and had no contact for many years to get a divorce.

B. But Pearl and Beck lived apart for thirty years, but remained married.

? Why didn't Pearl and Beck ever get a divorce?

A. I would expect a writer to have a reason for the imagery she uses in a work of literature.

B. Tyler uses a huge amount of food imagery in the book, and I'm not sure why.

? Why does Tyler use so much food imagery in *Homesick Restaurant*? What purpose does this food imagery serve?

We have Always Lived in the Castle

A. I would expect to find a person who murdered her family evil and hateful.

B. Merricat murdered her family, but I don't find her hateful or evil. In some ways she is likeable and sympathetic.

? Why do I find Merricat likeable rather then hateful?

A. Normally I expect a cat to be just a pet.

B. But in this book Jonas the cat is an important character.

? Why has the author gone to the trouble of making Jonas an important character in this book? What is his purpose or significance?

To increase our stock of problems that can serve as topics for the papers, we then collaborate. I divide the class into groups according to aspects of the book: characters, setting, imagery, and so on. In their groups students work on formulating several interesting problem statements. When they have successfully formulated one, it is entered in black ink on a page that will be duplicated at the end of the session for all the members of the class to have. At the end of this session, we all have copies of several pages of problems (a total of fifteen to twenty) on a variety of subjects, all of which are possible paper topics.

Students now select the topics they will write their paper on, choosing one from our list or finding another. At the next session each student presents his or her topic (problem and question) for evaluation according to the following criteria. One, is the question answerable? That is, is there enough evidence in the book with which to answer it? For instance, a question about how Pearl's childhood years affected her personality, while interesting, could not be answered with the information available in the book. Two, is the question worth answering? That is, does it concern an important aspect of the book, something that is not too obvious or has not been overly discussed? For instance, the question from *We Have Always Lived in the Castle*, "Why does Constance call Mary Catherine Merricat?" is too minor, and the question from *Homesick Restaurant*, "Why does Cody hate Ezra?" too obvious to be worth writing papers on. All members of the class participate in the judging, recording their judgments on a chart; several students acting as judges lead the discussion. As a result of the feedback they get at this session, some students revise or switch their questions.

With their questions approved, students now move to answer them. The process involves basic reasoning skills: moving from evidence to generalization, moving from generalization to supporting evidence. Sometimes the possible answers (hypotheses) come to mind first, and the supporting evidence follows. In the "Why I Don't Hate Merricat" paper the hypotheses ("strong," "caring," "imaginative") came first, and the evidence for each followed. Sometimes the evidence comes to mind first, and hypotheses are induced from it. For instance, in answering the question, "What is the significance of the cat Jonas in the book?" the writer came up with the assorted examples of interaction between the cat and the character Merricat. Looking them over, he perceived that they grouped themselves in two categories: "a friend whom she talks to and who understands her" and "someone she can have fun with and care about." These became his two hypotheses.

Once students have formulated hypotheses, they go on to evaluate them on the basis of support, plausibility, and originality. For instance, in answering the question, "Why do I like Merricat?" the third hypothesis of the writer ("She is imaginative") was judged the most original and best supported. Whereas most students had regarded Merricat's fantasies as negative (a sign of her mental unbalance or weirdness), this student had found them to be "creative." He had also gathered from the book many examples of Merricat's imaginative behavior as support.

In writing up the hypotheses in draft form, students are urged to do a thorough exploration, openly admitting the existence of opposing evidence or other weaknesses in the hypotheses where they exist. The idea is to inquire and explore, not to prove the merits of all solutions. For instance, the above student had to admit to some counterarguments for even his strongest hypothesis:

> Some conflicting evidence was that her imagination would sometimes become brutal or disturbing. An example was when she imagined, "I would have liked to ... see them all, even the Elberts and the children, lying there crying with pain and dying" [Jackson 12]. I think this was from her sickness which, as I said before, exaggerated her feelings.

After discussing the hypotheses throughout the paper, students make their final evaluation of them in their conclusion. The above student, after weighing all the factors, still found his third hypothesis to be the strongest: "Her most appealing feature is her imagination." On the other hand, another student writing to answer the same question came to a different conclusion: "Merricat's major appeal to me undoubtedly was her childlike behavior and how she dealt with Charles."

In my view, the results of the problem analysis assignment are good. Problem analysis both engages students and develops their cognitive skills; papers written by this method are valued by both student and teacher. When students select at the end of the semester the paper they are most satisfied with, the problem analysis paper always receives a high rating. For instance, the three classes who wrote papers on *The Clock Winder* in fall 1989 gave it more positive ratings and fewer negative ratings than any other paper of the semester. Students valued the assignment because it was challenging and gave them the chance to explore characters and motifs in the book, to choose their own questions and include their own ideas. Papers produced for this assignment are valued by the teacher as well. I have always found the problem analysis papers to be among the strongest produced by my students over the semester. Colleagues of mine who have tried out the assignment have felt the same way, finding the papers well documented, original, and generally strong.

Looking more closely at the finished papers, I was able to identify the elements that had made me regard them so highly. First and most striking was the originality—of problems or topics, hypotheses, and evaluations. Because the topic for the paper was a problem the student had found—something in the text that puzzled, disturbed, or surprised him—and because people are puzzled, disturbed, or surprised by different things, the students had written on a variety of subjects. There were about thirty different problems that served as subjects for papers on *Homesick Restaurant*, fifteen of which were new to me. With the tagmemic assignment on *We Have Always Lived in the Castle*, of the thirty-five papers I received, twenty-one different topics were represented, a number of which were new to me. One student noticed and explored a truly puzzling element that I had overlooked: "Throughout the book a bizarre relationship exists between Uncle Julian and Merricat. What makes this relationship so strange is the total lack of recognition shown to each other during the entire story, especially on Uncle Julian's part." In his conclusion, he explained his motivation to write on this problem:

> I suppose to the average reader this strange situation is ignored because of its relative insignificance to the story. However, to myself it presented a seemingly impossible question to answer dealing with a very abnormal set of circumstances. I feel that I now partially can understand the fundamental reasons for this lack of interaction.

The papers on *The Clock Winder*, written by sixty-five students, represented thirty-five different topics, some of which were quite original: "Why was there a chapter 13 in the book when the action seemed to be concluded at the end of Chapter 12?" "Why, after so many years of separation, did Jimmy Joe come back to haunt Margaret late in the book?" "Why in such a character-oriented book does the author spend so much time describing houses?"

Secondly, students brought in original material from their own knowledge of life and values in discussing their hypotheses. As the student above discussed one possible reason ("mental unbalance") for Uncle Julian's failure to recognize Merricat, he made this interesting, contemporary analogy:

> All these symptoms of living in the past point to Uncle Julian's being in some type of permanent shock which he cannot escape. It reminds one of combat flashbacks experienced by soldiers who went through traumatic battlefield experiences, never able to escape those terrible minutes or hours of shock. Uncle Julian is probably in a similar condition, never able to see reality and always reliving the most traumatic experience a person could live through.

In explaining why she didn't like the character Elizabeth in *The Clock Winder*, one writer moved back and forth between the behavior of the character as presented in the book and her own values;

> Another thing that I didn't like about Elizabeth was the way she kept
> herself. She was plain, almost shabby. She wore jeans almost all the
> time, she never fussed with her hair, and she didn't wear makeup. . . .
> I guess her appearance bothered me because I have been taught to
> always look presentable and to take pride in my appearance. I try to
> wear immaculately ironed clothes, styled hair, and polished shoes.
> Elizabeth didn't have to spend hours getting ready every morning,
> but she could have taken a bit more pride in her appearance.

The complexity and depth of the papers were two other factors
that caused me to regard them highly. The elaborate prewriting procedures for the assignment that I have described push students to use
many of the intellectual skills named in Bloom's *Taxonomy of Educational Objectives*: interpretation, extrapolation, application, analysis,
synthesis, evaluation (204–7). Because of this, a measure of complexity
in the final product is assured; if they have done the prewriting properly
(and it is checked at every point), their final paper cannot be simply
plot summary or "knowledge telling" (Scardamalia and Bereiter 13).
The final paragraph of a paper shows one student in the act of analyzing
and evaluating:

> Cody's continuous jealousy of Ezra can be seen as the effect of
> several influences. Ruth and Ezra in their own ways cause his jealousy
> even though the relationship between them that Cody is afraid of is a
> figment of his imagination. His son, Luke, can also be seen as a factor
> which furthers this jealousy since Cody sees Ezra in Luke. However,
> the dominant reason for Cody's jealousy is the way Pearl had favored
> Ezra over him throughout their lives. She engraves this jealousy so
> deeply in him that Cody cannot be satisfied even after he has married
> Ruth.

At the same time, in doing all these things — in creating, supporting,
and evaluating hypotheses — students should produce papers that are
adequately rather than poorly developed. Because they are eager to
give each hypothesis fair consideration, students gather numerous quotes
and other references from the book. As a result, their discussions are
not skimpy and undeveloped, but full and well-documented paragraphs.
Papers written for this assignment were on the average a full page
longer than those written for other assignments. As one student put it,
"I got into detail in this paper, and, whereas I usually stretch my
writing out to make two pages, this assignment smoothly made it to
three."

Workshop Application

For faculty workshops in this problem-analysis approach, participants
take the role of students and simulate the classroom procedures described above. In one such workshop, I asked participants to begin by

reading the story "The Use of Force" by William Carlos Williams (Howe and Howe), noting down problematic elements: aspects of the story that puzzled or disturbed them. Then, following the method outlined on a handout, they presented their "problems," which were recorded by me on the blackboard. We selected one problem to work with and formed it into a problem statement, consisting of an A, a B, and a question. Participants then offered hypotheses or possible answers to the question they had raised, which were examined and evaluated by the group according to the specific criteria of support, plausibility, and originality. With the formal part of the session complete, we spent the remainder of the time discussing participants' concerns about the method—concerns both practical (classroom management) and theoretical (the issue of closure, relevance to a history course).

In the following description of the workshop conversation, *L* indicates the leader, *S1* is the first speaker, *S2* the second speaker, and so on. The participants read "The Use of Force" and make notes of their reactions,

L: What struck you as strange or unusual or different in this story?

S1: I don't know that it's strange, but it was interesting that this doctor moves from an interest in saving the girl and saving society from a plague like diphtheria to an interest in overpowering her. It becomes a sort of brute interest.

L(*writing on board*): Doctor moves from interest in the girl herself to interest in winning the ...

S1: Battle.

L: That's the word for it.

S2: I think he initially thinks he needs to do this, to save the girl and the people she is going to come in contact with.

L: And then it becomes something else.

S2: Yeah, then he loses sight of that.

S3: He starts seeing her as a normal patient, and then he says he's fallen in love with her. In other words, part of the violence grows out of his increasing affection for her.

L: Could that interrelationship be called something strange or curious?

S3: Yeah, exactly.

L: What would you call that?

S3: He calls it love.

L(*writing on board*): The doctor has some sort of attachment to the girl ...

S3: Empathy.

L: Attraction?

S3: Probably.

L: Anything else on the girl's part, in her behavior that you noticed?

S1: The fierceness with which she resists her parents and the doctor was surprising [*L* writes this on the board] with this array of authority figures against her. I don't know why she's resisting so much. It's just a simple thing.

S2: She knows he'll find something that will mean hospitalization.

Now I intercede. I don't want the discussion truncated; that is, I don't want them to explain away the problems before they've considered and explored them. Here's my attempt to slow down the process.

L: OK, I like that—even if you will ultimately try to explain it. But what I want you to do now is just stick with the things you notice that are strange. Don't try to explain them too fast because that is what your students may try to do, and what I want to do instead is stretch out the process a little bit. Eventually you may come back to the very same explanation you had initially, but I want you to do more exploring and I want them to do more exploring first.

S1: We expect this to be a story of a poor, sick, little girl and the doctor caring for her, but in the end we've lost that totally, and the focus is off the girl and instead of the doctor caring, he's exactly the opposite.

L: Terrific. (*writes on the board*) Instead of caring relationship, the focus of attention shifts; it's all turned upside down.

Actually there are *two* problems here: the doctor's unexpected attitude toward the girl, and the shift in focus from the girl to the doctor's point of view. The participant merged them, and so did I.

S1: The story ends surprisingly, instead of ending with the recognition of what the disease is.

L: Other groups noticed this. What is this paragraph there for? You would expect the story to end with discovery of the disease.

S1(*disagreeing vehemently*): That's what the story's *about*. She's defeated. The story's a clash of wills and he's won.

When explained this way, I have to agree. What seemed problematic before, to other people, is shown to be quite logical by these participants. This one ("the strange ending") does not get written on the board.

Now that we have collected a few good problematic elements, it's time to take the next step of turning them into formal problem statements, so that we can then move to explore and resolve them.

L: "Almost any one of these problems listed on the board—doctor's change from interest in saving the girl to winning the battle, girl's fierce resistance to the doctor and her parents, shift of focus from girl to doctor, change of doctor from caring to not caring—will take you into the story. Let's work with one of them. Do you want to work with the girl's fierceness of rejection or the doctor's change from caring to not caring—the doctor or the girl?"

S1: The girl.

L: Now with your students, you want to get them to notice some of these same problematic things that we've noticed, and then you want to teach them how to more precisely form that sense of unease you talked about into what I call a problem statement, with an A, a B, and a question. You want to move them from sensing something strange in the story to trying to form that strange thing a little more. Let's take the girl's fierceness of rejection. In what way is that surprising—what would you normally expect of a child in that situation?

S1: To do what the doctor says; if not what the doctor says, then you would do what your father says.

At this point I show them how to distinguish the A, a statement of value or expectation ("I would expect a child patient to submit to the doctor or her parents"), from the B, opposition between what was expected and what happened ("But, in this story, the girl does not submit; instead she fiercely rejects treatment"), and finally to raise the relevant question ("Why does the girl not submit?"). I then show them how to move to try to answer the question, with "hypotheses," possible answers to the question.

L: OK, let's try to come up with some "hypotheses." Why does the girl act this way?

S1: Other people in the school have died, and she wants to die.

Although this first hypothesis seems farfetched to me, I try to give it full consideration.

L: Interesting. At this point you want to entertain everything possible, although you could reject it later.

S2: She certainly feels her bodily integrity is being violated or going to be.

This one seems strong to me.

L: Good, what gave you that idea?

S2: Because she's fighting off every attempt of his to touch her.

S3: Denial, two kids in the school have died and she doesn't want to die.

L: That's ironic, of course, for the way not to die is to let herself be examined, but in her childlike mind . . .

S3: If it isn't confirmed, then it doesn't exist.

S4: It's an abusive family and she's used to keeping secrets. The family didn't tell the truth.

L(*trying to see the logic of this*): Let me see if I understand you: her parents don't share their feelings and she doesn't want to share hers.

S4: Yes, or the truth of what happens in the family is concealed.

L(*trying to make the idea more plausible*): "OK, so let's not call the family abusive, but rather secretive or withholding. She's learned from them to hide vulnerability, perhaps. Oh boy, terrific."

Again I am amazed by the imaginative hypotheses of the group. A participant, as amazed by these speculations as I, argues for a common sense explanation.

S5: Couldn't she just be stubborn? I have seen kids do this. With people on both sides of a conflict, it becomes, "I'm not going to do it because you want me to.

L: OK, that's the battle of the wills again, the battle between her and the doctor, and she is going to win. (*L writes that on the board*)

S5: And children at the right age are very good at that.

L: You don't know how many people, how many of my students felt that way. Not one of my students was sympathetic to the girl; they were all angry with her. This struck me as very strange, but maybe it comes back to what you're saying: people evidently have strong experiences with stubborn children that they remember.

S5: They all have little brothers and sisters.

S6: The mother has made the hospital into this horrible, fearful place, so she wants to avoid the pain of the hospital, all of which she associates with the doctor discovering what's wrong with her.

Now that we've collected some hypotheses, it's time to take a closer look at them, as I now move to do. At this point I direct them to the page of the handout that gives criteria for judging hypotheses.

L: OK, we have a bunch of hypotheses here. You want to get them all out, not excluding any in the beginning, and *then* go back and judge them. And the first point of judgement is, "Is there any support for the hypothesis in the story?" Someone in one of the other groups had a marvellous hypothesis that the doctor was just burned out from treating the diphtheria, and that was why he acted as he did. That was a great idea, but we all made the point that you have to go outside the story to get much evidence for that. I tried to find out if there was anything in William Carlos Williams's practice as a doctor that might explain the behavior of the doctor in the story, but I couldn't find anything. So some hypotheses are better supported than others in the story, and that's what you want to train your students to figure out. Can we support any of these? Let's see. Could you find any support for the "stubborn, wanting to win" hypothesis in this story?

S1: Sure, the details of the way in which she fought.

L: How about, "that her bodily integrity is being violated and she is afraid of that." Can you find anything in the story to give reason to this fear on her part?

S2: You could give a Freudian reading of it.

L: Can you find that in the language of the story?

S2: Yes, the story's full of sexual imagery and violent imagery. For instance, the "muscular release."

S3: The original description of her, "an unusually attractive little thing, a heifer in appearance, face was flushed, breathing rapidly."

L: There you go. I think there would be a lot of proof for this one, that she senses her bodily integrity is being violated, that this doctor's interest in her has some other basis besides just curing her, and that is making her even stronger in her resistance. (*Shifting*) Are there any hypotheses that we would have trouble proving, finding any proof for in the story?

S1: That she wants to die.

S2: Right, the two children who died were not even identified as being in the same school.

S3: But we've already said that she's resisting the very thing that will help her to get well, and you could see that as a form of death wish. She's fighting help, and if she really has diphtheria, whatever the deeper reason is (fear or whatever), she would be bringing on her own death.

L: So you think you could make a case for it.

S3: I think I could make a case for it.

L: But it'd be a little harder than the others. (*Moving on*) Another criterion for judging is "originality." Any of these strike you as being original, a little different maybe from what everyone would think of?

S1: That she wants to die.

L: Yes, this one didn't come up in any other group. So, if a student were writing a paper dealing with this problem, "Why does the girl react so fiercely?" he would then take each of his hypotheses and discuss them. Now, I think that these two ("her stubborness, her determination to win"; "fearing her bodily integrity is being violated") are the strongest of the ones you have here. They have the most evidence. This one ("that she wants to die") I would tell the student to put in, even though you can't prove it, but I would have him say that in his discussion. So the students would write them up discussing each one, and then finally in the conclusion come to some sort of resolution, which one or ones best seemed to explain the problematic aspect.

At this point, we've run through the essentials of the method. Now the discussion moves to participants' concerns, most of which focus on the openness of the method, its lack of a single thesis or definite resolution.

One person expresses the need for the group to come to a definite conclusion about the story.

S1: I was wondering what we think the theme of the story is, if the theme of the story is the contest of the wills.

L: Well, I guess some people might see it that way, and some might see it another way.

S2: Which is one of the nice things about this method.

L: Exactly, and one of the good things about this method is the variety of viewpoints it allows. This story is short, so there aren't that many questions, but when you use the method with a novel, you can imagine how many questions you can generate — twenty — thirty good questions. And even if you have students working on the same question, what they come up with may be entirely different. For one the power struggle or determination to win may be the answer. But for someone else, the sexual thing will be the answer, and she can convincingly portray it.

S2: What's unusual about the method is that there are a number of hypotheses at the same level. Usually if there's more than one hypothesis, they're subordinate to one another; there's a central one.

L: You're right, it's different from the central thesis paper, because the hypotheses are as you say somewhat equal, coordinate in some respects. However, the student can still emphasize some more than others. Some will be much longer than others because there is a lot more to say; some will turn out to be more like opposing evidence rather than full hypotheses in their own right. But you're right; it's not a paper with one thesis; it's a paper that explores several.

S2: What would be interesting is if all the hypotheses work together, and the student could go from this listing to a paper where he or she is subordinating and putting them together.

L: Well, remember, he doesn't have to follow the list the way it is set up here. If I were writing the paper I would rearrange it, and you could do it in a superordinate/subordinate way. You could perhaps start out with your strongest one or start out with your weakest one and build up, and spend half of your paper on the one that you thought was the strongest. So they don't all have to be equal, even though they may look that way in the notes.

S2: It seems to me that what was said is that this kind of paper is the way to get to a paper with a thesis, a step to a paper with a thesis. A prewriting kind of thing.

L: That's true; it could be thought of that way.

These ideas strike me as creative modifications of the method. Linking the various hypotheses is a sophisticated variation, and using the method as prewriting, a way of getting to a central thesis, seems a good solution for those uncomfortable with multiple theses.

The "central thesis" discussion deepens into the larger issue of openness versus closure in thinking and writing.

S1: I was trying to transpose this. It seems to me wonderful in terms of getting students to work with hypotheses. But it remains at the level of hypothesis, so it never gets to the level of meaning or establishing a point of view. For a content piece you really want them ultimately to make a decision so that the whole piece takes on meaning, and takes on a recognition of the point of view that they feel to be most appropriate.

L: Well, I think it can. For instance, I had a student who did a paper on child abuse, "Why do people abuse children?" And she came up with seven hypotheses, a whole bunch of different reasons, each of which she investigated. She used facts and readings and reasoning and illustrations. Then she was able to judge which hypotheses she thought were the strongest. It's true you might want more closure in a paper than isn't about fiction (like the story we worked with), that's about a real life situation. But then again, maybe you wouldn't. Maybe you would want the student to say, "Gee, I can't really say why people do this; it's partly this and partly that, but I'm still not entirely sure."

S1: But then it never reaches closure, the piece never takes on meaning.

L: But sometimes maybe that's the way things are. I'm not saying that you would always want that to be, but in some circumstances maybe we really don't know the answer.

S2: I'm pulled. On the one hand, I think it's important for students to learn not to reach closure; that's an important skill for them to have. But I was wondering if students would get as involved in a paper where they're not able to have a thesis, where they have instead a number of hypotheses.

L: But they do, because they very often will have one that is stronger than another and they put their hearts into that one. For instance, often they do a paper on "Why I liked a character that nobody else liked." There will be one reason that catches their fancy in particular, and that's the one they will *put the most* into, and it will turn out to be the strongest one. Students generally do tend to lean toward one or the other, and the cases where they say there's no closure are rare.

S3(making the best case for multiplicity): I think I really like your willingness to let people be less than singular in closing everything up. I feel it [one answer] is basically unrealistic. I've encountered in teaching and in other things so few situations where there is a single cause or a single motive. Even if students are satisfied with one answer, I'm not sure that that's good. Maybe it's satisfying because they like that one, simple resolution, but I'm not sure it's necessarily good.

L: Although people could argue that eventually you do have to act.

S3: That's different from saying there's only one cause.

S1: I'd like to hear some more from our history professor here because I think what we're saying is true in a literature class. We all these days have that concern of allowing students to create their own meaning. But I'd be interested in hearing what your thoughts about this process are and if it can be useful in learning history.

S2(the history professor): I think this is an excellent process for getting kids to identify hypotheses, but in one book I'm using, the author has a definite point of view, that European technological inventiveness led Europeans to take over the world. That's the dominant theme in the book — there are many other hypotheses out there — but unless students ultimately come to identify that one as the author's point of view in the book, then the book loses significance.

S3: This method might be helpful toward that. Sometimes students will miss the main point simply because they haven't gone through the process of seeing what is the evidence. If they could map it out in this way, they could say, "My gosh, look at all the evidence for this one point, this obviously must be the main point."

L: What you're saying is that it could be used not only for writing but for reading a book, to find out what the author's major hypothesis is, as a technique for analyzing what someone is presenting to you.

S4(noticing that this idea is not really new at all): That's what we were doing here with the Williams story, wasn't it, except that we didn't know for certain what the author was getting at, but in a piece of nonfiction, presumably you could.

S5(trying to pull together the whole discussion): What we are saying then, the important lesson that you're teaching is that how you hold an idea is more important than the conclusion itself. It's not important to come away with that particular conclusion (European world dominance through technology) but instead to understand the conclusion, what evidence is given for it, and still hold it tentative. Is that right?"

L: Exactly, it's the *process* more than the end result that's important here.

As the session draws to a close we stumble unexpectedly on a problematic aspect of the story that hadn't yet been mentioned. In disputing the "death wish" theory that one participant continues to advance, another participant comments that the intricate planning that this theory presupposes would be inconsistent with the proposed youth of the girl. And so I raise the new issue.

L: How old is the child? That is the best question of all.

S1: I picture someone older, in her fierceness and the way they were holding her and the sexual way they were describing her — like at puberty.

L: Would she be sitting on her father's lap? I think of her as a very stubborn six-year-old.

S2: But look at what she says. At one point she says, "You're killing me," and that seemed to me too old for a six-year-old: "Stop it! Stop it! You're killing me!" [178] Would a six-year-old say that?

S3: We don't know whether she has older brothers or sisters, no siblings here. My feeling is that she was slightly older even though they described her as an "attractive little thing" [175]. I saw her as slightly older, but big enough to cause that many problems.

S4: A little kid can cause problems.

L: But I think it's the sexual thing that makes you think that she is older. That's another evidence for that thesis.

S5: I like it better if she is too young to be consciously aware and is instinctively fighting off the violation. The violation is symbolic and the reaction is instinctive, so it's all going on under the conscious level and probably at both ends of the stick, or the doctor wouldn't talk about it the way he does. It is so self-incriminating from the doctor's point of view that he has either got to be confessing or unaware, and it's apparently instinctive and almost an animal defense from the girl's point of view.

L: I think that is perfect, an animal defense, which goes along with our earlier hypothesis of "fierce resistance."

We had actually, without realizing it, been playing out the problem analysis technique: raising a question (her age); formulating various hypotheses (teenager, six-year-old); testing them out (note participants' references to the text to support their theories); and, in my case, coming to a conclusion (choosing the young child hypothesis because the supporting argument of "animal defense" so well complemented the "fierce resistance" hypothesis that we had discussed earlier). Our unconscious dramatization of the technique shows its naturalness, how closely it stimulates the problem-solving nature of the mind. Problem analysis makes this natural process conscious, and thereby more usable and controllable.

The variety and interest of the questions and hypotheses formed both by teachers in the workshop and by students in the classroom testify to the power of problem analysis to generate ideas. Clearly, teachers and students were not just summarizing or "knowledge telling" but thinking critically — analyzing, evaluating, synthesizing. Further, the excitement displayed by teachers and students as they devised and defended their questions and hypotheses suggests that the approach is not only fruitful but enjoyable. Participants took pleasure in the process, I believe, because they were investigating questions of personal interest to them, were discovering original answers to their questions, and, finally, were working collaboratively — helping others come up with new ideas and evidence, debating and supporting their favorite hypotheses.

Acknowledgment

I gratefully acknowledge the assistance of Dr. Anita Brostoff, whose work and support enabled me and many other teachers to use Young, Becker, and Pike's problem analysis in our classrooms.

Endnotes

1. The discussion that follows contains some material that was published in my article entitled "A Tagmemic Approach to Writing About Literature."

2. In support of this premise, I cite the following statement of Ann Brown: "My bias is that the processes described as metacognitive are the important aspects of knowledge, that what is of major interest is knowledge about one's own cognitions rather than the cognitions themselves ... [that] in the domain of deliberate learning and problem-solving situations, conscious executive control of the routines available to the system is the essence of intelligent activity — the underlying force that the observed routines reflect, are symptomatic of, and are epiphenomenal to" (79). See also the following research: memory (Wellman, Ritter, Flavell); comprehension (Markman); reading (Hare and Pulliam).

3. To move into problem analysis of literature, I sometimes give students the opportunity to practice the method on a short story that we read and work with together in class. For a really short story, I recommend the selections in *Short Shorts: An Anthology of the Shortest Stories*, (Howe and Howe). In particular, I suggest "The Use of Force," by William Carlos Williams; "Eveline," by James Joyce, and "The Untold Lie" by Sherwood Anderson. A longer short story that is rich in problematic situations is Mordecai Richler's "The Summer My Grandmother Was Supposed to Die." The full-fledged application of the method on a novel — including reading, analysis, and writing of the paper — takes four to five weeks. The novel selected should be complex enough to offer a number of problematic elements to work with. At the same time, because my students are first-generation college students who do not have rich literary backgrounds, I try to select novels that are contemporary and accessible — books that they might pick up and read for enjoyment, not distant or extremely difficult works. The works of Anne Tyler (*Dinner at the Homesick Restaurant, Earthly Possessions, A Slipping Down Life, The Accidental Tourist, The Clock Winder*) and Shirley Jackson (*We Have Always Lived in the Castle, The Sundial*) fit these criteria well.

Works Cited

Applebee, Arthur N., Judith A. Langer, and Ina V. S. Mullis, *The Nation's Report Card: Learning to Be Literate in America: Reading, Writing, and Reasoning*. Princeton, NJ: Educational Testing Service, 1987.

Bloom, Benjamin S., ed. *Taxonomy of Educational Objectives, Handbook I: Cognitive Domain*. New York: David McKay Company, 1956.

Brown, Ann L. "Knowing When, Where, and How to Remember: A Problem of Metacognition." *Advances in Instructional Psychology*, Vol. I. Ed. Robert Glaser, Hillsdale, NJ: Erlbaum, 1978, 77–165.

Dewey, John. *How We Think*. Boston: D.C. Heath, 1933.

Emig, Janet. "Writing as a Mode of Learning." *College Composition and Communication* 28 (1977): 122–27.

Flavell, John J. "Metacognitive Aspects of Problem Solving." *The Nature of Intelligence*. Ed. Lauren B. Resnick. Hillsdale, NY: Erlbaum, 1976.

———. "Metacognition and Cognitive Monitoring: A New Area of Cognitive-Developmental Inquiry." *American Psychologist* 34 (1979): 906–11.

Freisinger, Randall. "Cross-Disciplinary Writing Programs: Beginnings" *Language Connections: Writing and Reading across the Curriculum*. Ed. Toby Fulwiler and Art Young. Urbana, IL: NCTE, 1982, 3–13.

Fulwiler, Toby and Art Young, eds. *Language Connections: Writing and Reading Across the Curriculum*. Urbana IL: NCTE, 1982.

Hare, Victoria C., and Cynthia A. Pulliam. "College Students' Metacognitive Awareness of Reading Behaviors." National Reading Conference. San Antonio, TX, Nov.–Dec., 1979.

Howe, Irving, and Elana Wiener Howe, eds. *Short Stories: An Anthology of the Shortest Stories*. Boston, David R. Godine, 1982.

Jackson, Shirley. *We Have Always Lived in the Castle*. New York: Penguin Books, 1984.

Markman, Ellen M. "Realizing That You Don't Understand: A Preliminary Investigation." *Child Development* 48 (1977): 986–92.

Rose, Mike. "Remedial Writing Courses: A Critique and a Proposal." *College English* 45 (1983): 109–29.

Rosenblatt, Louise M. "Coda: A Performing Art." Reprinted in *English Education Today*. Ed. L. S. Josephs and E. R. Steinberg. New York: Noble and Noble, 1970. 661–72.

Rubin, Lois. "A Tagmemic Approach to Writing About Literature." *The English Record* 38.2 (1987): 12–19.

Scardamalia, Marlene, and Carl Bereiter. *The Psychology of Written Composition*. Hillsdale, NJ: Erlbaum, 1987.

Tyler, Ann. *Dinner at the Homesick Restaurant*. New York: Berkley Books, 1983.

———. *The Clock Winder*. New York: Berkley Books, 1983.

Wellman, Henry M., Kenneth Ritter, and John H. Flavell. "Deliberate Memory Behavior in the Delayed Reaction of Very Young Children." *Developmental Psychology* 11 (1976): 780–87.

Young, Richard. "Problems and the Composing Process." *Writing: The Nature, Development and Teaching of Written Communication*, Vol. 2, Ed. Carl Frederiksen and Joseph Dominic. Hillsdale, NJ: Erlbaum, 1981, 59–66.

Young, Richard E., Alton L. Becker, and Kenneth L. Pike. *Rhetoric: Discovery and Change*. New York: Harcourt, Brace, 1970.

7

A Dialogue Across the Disciplines: Two Voices on Problem Solving

Anne C. Coon and Marcia Birken

We bring to the study and teaching of problem solving, and to this dialogue, two very different backgrounds, Marcia Birken's in mathematics and Anne Coon's in literature. Several years ago we began a collaboration that resulted in our developing and teaching an interdisciplinary problem-solving course for students who were placed on probation or suspended from Rochester Institute of Technology, a highly technical four-year institution. The course was eventually adopted as part of the core curriculum in an academic "restoration" program and although we no longer teach the course, it is team taught by two other faculty members and remains an important component of the program. We have written elsewhere about the benefits of collaboration (Coon and Birken) and the specific advantages to teaching mathematical problem solving when interdisciplinary linkages are established (Birken and Coon). Since we both teach exclusively within our own disciplines now, we have begun to explore ways in which our experiences in team teaching, along with our collaborative research and writing, have affected the way we now teach our respective courses in mathematics and English.

The more we become involved in the research in problem solving, the clearer it becomes that there are several underlying concepts that are reiterated by most authors, whether their backgrounds are in mathematics, psychology, English, or engineering. We have chosen to highlight five of these concepts: following steps, defining the problem, selecting and following procedures, representing the problem in new ways, and going beyond the answer. We will show how we integrated these concepts into the curriculum of an interdisciplinary problem-solving course and how each of us now applies them in her own teaching.

Although the terms *problem solving* and *critical thinking* are used in many contexts, and sometimes interchangeably, for the purposes of our joint course we adopted a distinction made clear by James Kinney, who described critical thinking as an "expanding, exploratory process," and problem solving as a "progressively narrowing process" (5). By breaking problems into smaller component parts, we can see, and demonstrate, how individual problem-solving tasks may contribute to the larger process of critical thinking. Although we encouraged our students to be aware of their critical-thinking activities, the emphasis in our team taught course was on the solving or understanding of particular problems, tasks, or texts that were in most cases capable of being discretely defined.

Here, we will be using the term *problem solving* more generally, to refer to a self-conscious, structured approach to completing assignments. The fact that the term needs to be defined for a specific context is typical of the somewhat controversial history of this field. Not only is the definition of terms sometimes problematical, but serious questions have been raised over how — and even if — critical thinking or problem solving could be taught and who should do such teaching, "thinking teachers" or content instructors. Similarly, others have questioned whether a problem-solving model that originated in the sciences is applicable outside the sciences. We maintain that thinking skills *can* be taught, that such instruction is best done *in* the context of a specific curriculum, and that broadly applicable approaches to problem solving *can* be developed from the early scientific models.

Following Steps

The first concept we are examining from problem-solving theory — *following a series of logical steps to solve problems* — can be illustrated by an early model that is still used today.

Polya's Steps to Problem Solving

1. Understanding the problem
2. Devising a plan
3. Carrying out the plan
4. Looking back (Polya xvi–xvii)

The idea of using steps to take a problem from beginning to end pervades the problem-solving literature. Although Polya's original treatise on the subject was published in 1945 and was aimed specifically at teaching students to be better *mathematical* problem solvers, he is quoted extensively today and is accepted as an authority by social scientists, psychologists, and others in the liberal arts, as well as mathematicians and scientists.

The necessity of breaking the process up into steps appears in all problem-solving theory, although the names of the steps, the number of steps, and the order of steps may vary. Underlying all models, however, is the need to be self-conscious, to be directed and yet reflective. The reflection must precede the "execution" of problem solving and yet must continue to be part of the execution.

The concept of breaking a problem into steps or discrete tasks has always underpinned mathematics, but Polya also emphasizes the related concepts of decomposing and recombining. Before decomposing, we must understand the problem as a whole in order to know which parts are essential (Polya 75−76). It is only then that we can break it apart and attempt to recombine the parts into something more accessible and helpful for devising a plan of solution.

In our interdisciplinary course we used a General Problem-Solving Worksheet with five steps modeled after Polya's. In the early weeks of the course, students were required to fill in the steps when working on problems and to hand the sheets in with their homework. Later we had the students make oral presentations on their problem-solving steps. Throughout the course we often referred to these steps, and even though the students worked independently from the worksheet by the end of the quarter, we frequently asked them to articulate the steps they used in approaching a problem.

Birken

Polya's steps 3 and 4 (carrying out the plan and looking back) have always been important in mathematics classes. Traditionally, students are given a problem to solve and then asked to apply the appropriate algorithm and check their answer. As a result of our collaboration in the problem-solving class and after seeing the successes from backing up to steps 1 and 2, I now ask my mathematics students to think about a given problem, ask questions about the problem, and contemplate relationships between this problem and past problems before tackling the "execution" in step 3. I also often require my students to write about what they are doing, ask them questions about the process they are using both in homework and on tests, and have them apply their answers in "practical" situations to test for validity. Writing about what they are doing forces students to see relationships, make decisions, voice an opinion, and stop doing rote manipulations.

Coon

As in mathematics, having students start at the beginning — understanding the problem, rather than jumping to step 3 — is essential in an English class. This is especially true for first-year students, who may be accustomed to very different types of assignments, expressed in very different language, from what they experience in the college classroom. For basic writers, understanding the problem is easier if we place it in a context of other, familiar assignments or encourage the students to read or paraphrase the assignment itself carefully, visually or verbally "highlighting" the key words. For literature students, understanding the problem is a twofold process: First, they must be able to place the work in context, identifying the genre and its features, as well as the author and the relevant historical, social, and critical material. Then they must understand the assignment — whether it be, for example, an oral presentation, character analysis, or comparison/contrast between two pieces — and decide how to organize and present their ideas.

Defining the Problem

Although most academics would be comfortable using the term *problem* to refer to an assignment or investigation in mathematics or science, some of us might balk at using the same term in the liberal arts. The second problem-solving concept we have chosen to examine, *defining the problem*, not only attempts to decide what constitutes a "problem," but also places problems into two broad categories, *well-structured* and *ill-structured*. This terminology, first developed by cognitive psychologists, places various kinds of intellectual tasks along a continuum, as Norman Frederiksen describes:

> Instruction in problem solving generally emphasizes well-structured problems — the kind of problem which is clearly presented with all the information needed at hand and with an appropriate algorithm available that guarantees a correct answer, such as long division, areas of triangles, Ohm's law, and linear equations. But many of the problems we face in real life, and all the important social, political, economic and scientific problems in the world are ill-structured. (363)

In our problem-solving course, we deliberately defined the term *problem* broadly enough to include mathematics, literature, and logic assignments, as well as the preparation and staging of a formal debate. Furthermore, we gave students problems that fell all along the continuum, from well structured to ill structured. The range of mathematics assignments included problems of direct and indirect proportion, logic problems, and math word problems. The assignments from English ranged from outlining and summarizing to creating metaphors and writing parody.

One-third of the class time was devoted to the debate, itself an ill-structured problem that included several well-structured problems. We chose to include a debate in the course as a way of emphasizing and developing logical thinking skills, which we see as a bridge between literature and mathematics. The pedagogical advantages to using such an assignment have been explored by Green and Klug, who used class debates and found some evidence of improvement in writing and critical-thinking skills, as well as an increase in "students' participation in and enthusiasm for class discussions" (469).

Coon

In addressing the objections raised to the application of a "mechanistic or scientific" model of problem solving to the process of writing, Michael Carter asserts that a pluralistic definition of *problem* will lead to a broader view of *problem solving*, which could appropriately include various writing assignments. Going beyond the ill- and well-structured problem distinctions, Carter proposes a continuum of problems with "simple information-processing problems on one end and complex epistemic problems on the other" (558). In the first type of problem, the method of solution is clear, an answer is attainable, and the emphasis is on the individual process of the problem solver. By contrast, the second type of problem is "defined by an incongruity" which provides the "impetus" for solution. With this type of problem, Carter continues, problem solving is "an epistemic act, a way of learning," and "both problem and problem solving are social concepts" (553–54).

Whether using the term *ill-structured problems* or *epistemic problems*, we are in either case expanding the range of problem-solving activity to include assignments from writing and literature courses in which the student defines a problem and both creates knowledge and imparts knowledge in its solution.

Birken

Most people have no difficulty identifying what constitutes a problem in mathematics, and in fact, we usually view mathematics as a series of well-structured problems. Too often, these are the only kind of problems we present as learning tools to our students. In actuality, the field of mathematics is made up of both types of problems, and the professional mathematician working in industry is often confronted with ill-structured problems. For example, we teach many techniques for solving differential equations and ask our students to solve many well-structured problems. In applied mathematics or engineering, one can often show that a problem requiring differential equations is solvable, but that the exact solution itself is unattainable by algorithms carried out by hand. In the past few years, the development of a new generation of computer programs known as computer algebra systems, such as Mathematica and Maple, allows students to see almost instantaneous solutions to previously "unsolvable" problems. The students need not understand either the algorithm or how the computer performs approximations to a solution. The distinction between well-structured and ill-structured problems blurs when a machine produces answers without regard for the type of problem being entered.

Some mathematics problems that students readily label as ill structured are word problems. Although not all word problems are ill structured, clearly the translation from English words to mathematical symbols provides the greatest ambiguity for students. As Donald Trismen reports, students may be extremely sensitive to distinctions in the wording of problems. These distinctions may not be noticeable to the expert problem solver and yet may throw the amateur completely off track (361). Frequently, students can read the words but cannot define the problem or place it in a category. They may also be unable to distinguish between a word problem that provides clear information for a single solution, and a problem that provides insufficient data or has multiple solutions.

Selecting and Following Procedures

The third underlying concept of problem-solving theory we are examining helps students to understand and define the problems they are working on as well as to carry out the steps they are following. This is the concept of purposefully *selecting and following procedures*.

Almost all current problem-solving theory lists general procedures that apply to solving problems, both well structured and ill structured, across the disciplines. Sometimes these general procedures are referred to as heuristics, sometimes as strategies or plans. These heuristics or procedures are practiced unconsciously or subconsciously by successful problem solvers, and are often overlooked or only dimly recognized by weak problem solvers. As Alan Schoenfeld points out, it is our obligation as teachers to make these procedures explicit.

> Mathematical thinking is logical and precise, and the techniques we use for attacking problems are broadly applicable. But students are not likely to get a feel for "understanding" or to profit from these techniques, unless they are made explicit; they are unlikely to develop their mathematical thinking after instruction unless we serve as the catalysts for their doing so. (*Problem Solving* 7)

Although the list is hardly exhaustive, some common problem-solving procedures include using analogy, breaking problems into components or subproblems, restating the problem, checking to see if all data is used, drawing diagrams, visually imaging, guessing, generalizing, categorizing, sequencing, trying a variation of the problem or a simpler problem, outlining, summarizing, and patterning.

Schoenfeld further explains that the procedures by themselves are not helpful without an organizational scheme. He likens haphazard application of these procedures to trying to open a door with a huge ring of keys. Even if one of the keys fits in the lock, without a system for trying them one may never unlock the door ("Heuristics" 9–15). Further, Rosemary Schmalz warns that we should not give students "the impression that problem solving is a bag of tricks we apply at the right time and place. It is important that we discuss with them that our attitude toward our work is just as important as the strategies we use." Schmalz goes on to describe a "mathematical disposition" that leads to productive use of problem-solving heuristics (685–86).

Turning to one particular type of heuristic or procedure, we believe a complete understanding of analogy is crucial in problem solving, and we explored the use of analogy in traditional and nontraditional contexts for several classes of our problem-solving course. We found it was essential to discuss analogy as having two distinct applications in problem solving. The first application of analogy is used when describing a unique or unanticipated similarity between two phenomena. For example, the effectiveness of any poetic metaphor relies on the poet's identification of an inherent, and perhaps subtle, similarity between two apparently dissimilar phenomena. Similarly, much of our educational, political, and religious language relies on this use of analogy. (Some common examples include the "K-turn" as taught in driver's education manuals; the "Iron Curtain" and "domino theory" identified by political scientists; and the "Star Wars" defense system.) The second application of analogy involves the reasoning process employed when we first observe that two things are similar in some respects and then infer that they must share other similarities. It is this application we use most often in logic, mathematics, or the sciences.

In order to provide experience with both applications, we required that students complete and explain analogies and that they construct analogies of their own. After alternating lectures on the applications of analogy in mathematics and literature, we gave the students a series of class activities and homework assignments that provided them with many different experiences in thinking analogously. They completed standard Miller analogies and explained the relationships that were operating in the analogies; then they undertook the mathematical counterpart, direct and indirect proportions, and a series of progressively more difficult exercises that relied on an analogous application of mathematics principles. Finally the students analyzed literary applications of metaphor and simile and composed descriptive figurative language of their own.

Birken

In mathematics, students see the parts of mathematical study — arithmetic, algebra, geometry, trigonometry, calculus, differential equations, statistics, and so on — as discrete, with few relationships between the subjects. One cannot understand mathematics however, until one sees the analogous relationships. Without analogy, mathematics is a long list of formulas, theorems, and algorithms. A simple example of learning mathematics through analogous reasoning occurs in algebra. We expect students to understand how to add arithmetic fractions and then apply this knowledge to adding algebraic fractions. It is important to emphasize and make explicit the analogy between the two fractional forms:

$$\frac{1}{3} + \frac{1}{5} \text{ and } \frac{1}{x} + \frac{1}{y}$$

Often the relationship is so clear to us that we fail to make the mathematical analogy clear to our students.

Coon

Although so much education relies on referring the unknown to the known, we sometimes overlook the power of analogy in examining or explaining. I've asked basic composition students, who may never have considered how or why to improve their writing skills, to consider how people go about improving their skill at a sport, such as basketball, and then to consider how some of the same principles — practicing, watching others, learning rules — may or may not be helpful in improving writing skills.

Just as constructing analogies is useful, recognizing and explaining — actually exploring — analogies is vital, especially in literature classes. Burns's simile "O my luve is like a red, red rose" can be rescued from triteness if one first takes the time to list and discuss the features of a "red, red rose" before discussing the analogous features of "my luve." Further, exploring the use of analogy can lead students to important discoveries about the denotative and connotative natures of language, as the limits of literal meaning are transcended by the simile or metaphor.

Another procedure that is very useful in English instruction is the opposite of constructing or exploring analogy; that is, constructing or exploring anomaly, or to use Michael Carter's term again, *incongruity*

(554). Using this approach in literature can lead students beyond superficial analysis of the text to more involved questions. For example, one might consider the development of the English sonnet as an anomaly, and then not only look for explanations for the changes in rhyme scheme and form from the Italian sonnet, but also ask how these changes affected poetic expression.

Birken

Similarly, the development of polar coordinates in mathematics can be considered an anomaly. After investigating why Cartesian coordinates were unsatisfactory for describing spirals (Eves 288), one can ask what other mathematical developments resulted from this anomaly.

Representing the Problem in New Ways

The fourth major concept of problem-solving theory, that is, *representing the problem* in new ways, not only makes problem solving more interesting, but often provides insight into a problem.

> There are, of course, situations where quick action is required, but in most cases it is possible to spend some time structuring the problem, presenting it and re-presenting it, each time allowing the new perspective to reveal new elements. Allowing sufficient time for representation is conceptually similar to inspecting an object as one walks around it. (Rubenstein and Firstenberg 29)

In our problem-solving class we used many techniques to encourage multiple representation of problems. Before discussing Jonathan Swift's satire on cannibalism, "A Modest Proposal," we asked students to prepare a formal outline of the essay, thus focusing their attention on structure and encouraging a close reading before addressing the content. In order to help them organize information in complicated logic problems, we asked students to represent the problems in a matrix grid or other diagram of their own design. In preparing for the debate, the students had to research and outline their opponents' point of view and potential fallacies, as well as their own.

Coon

In introductory literature courses, this concept of "re-presenting" has led to some very interesting and successful assignments. Although writing outlines is common practice, I've asked students to go further and create their own visual representations of short story plots. The resulting drawings, graphs, and charts have been imaginative and detailed; further, the assignment allowed each student to grapple with and represent the story according to his or her own experiences and interpretation.

Reading aloud to students and asking them to visualize a scene can be very powerful, especially when studying a short story such as Faulkner's "The Bear," which students may initially find inaccessible because of the vocabulary.

> It ran in his knowledge before he ever saw it. It loomed and towered in his dreams before he even saw the unaxed woods where it left its crooked print, shaggy, huge, red-eyed, not malevolent but just big — too big for the dogs which tried to bay it, for the horses which tried to ride it down, for the men and the bullets they fired into it ... an anachronism, indomitable and invincible, out of an old dead time, a phantom, epitome, and apotheosis of the old wild life ... (Faulkner 68)

If we ask students to concentrate and imagine the "huge, red-eyed" bear while listening to the passage, the results can be dramatic. Visualizing a powerful physical image seems to make it easier for students to apprehend the metaphysical powerfulness described in the last lines in the passage, where the bear is seen as an "indomitable" and "invincible ... apotheosis." If we connect the concrete details of the bear's description to the abstractions embodied in the bear we can bring Faulkner's theme, and his language, more easily in reach of the students. This process is much like asking students to watch a film of a short story and then using the visual images from the film to help explicate the story.

Another new way to present problems from the English curriculum is to assign "persona narratives" (Coon), in which students are asked to write in the first person, pretending to be someone else. This technique is especially effective when writing about controversial issues or ethical questions, since it demands that students examine their topics from alternative points of view.

Other techniques generally adaptable to literature or writing classes include using oral presentations, in which the students pose a problem and lead the class discussion; and requiring "original" research as well as library research, in which students must devise a questionnaire or survey or conduct an interview on the research topic, thus collecting information from many perspectives.

Birken

Math teachers often ask students to represent problems by graphs, charts, and other illustrations. In the primary grades we encourage learning through the use of tactiles, such as colored rods of various gradations and circles that break apart into fractional pieces. But at the college level, we have moved away from being able to touch and manipulate a math problem. Today, however, we can use the computer to present three-dimensional diagrams that were previously inaccessible to students (and faculty) who could not draw. I often ask my students to represent math problems in another way, through writing. I've assigned comparison/contrast essays, used essay questions on tests, worked with expressive writing in class, and assigned technical reports in many math classes (Birken).

In another attempt at representation, I have asked students to look at mathematical symmetry by examining slides and tessellations, and by coming up with original creations. I have assigned projects in which students create their own tessellations and then explain in writing the process they used and the symmetries that resulted. In a lecture class, I have even asked one row of students to pose in front of the room and then asked a second row of students to use their bodies to demonstrate the appropriate translation or reflection symmetry. My goal is to make students do more than rote learning and mechanical manipulation, and to go beyond answers as a key to understanding what they are doing.

Going Beyond the Answer

This brings us to the final underlying concept of problem solving: *going beyond the answer*. One of our goals in team teaching was to encourage our students to go beyond giving answers and instead to ask more questions. This is a difficult task, especially in our highly technical educational system, in which it is assumed every question has an answer—and only one answer. Roger Shank of Yale University has explored questioning in his work on creativity. In Shank's words, "Teaching people to think means teaching people to ask questions, not coercing them into memorizing answers. A questions that has a stock answer to it is always the wrong question" (35).

In our problem-solving course some assignments specifically prohibited giving a solution and simply asked for the *methods* of solution, a very difficult task for our students. Our first assignment, for example, asked students to give five methods of adding up the first 1,000 positive integers. Instead of handing in different methods, many students simply gave us the total of the integers; these students were understandably frustrated when they failed the assignment.

Birken

We need to ask the right questions of our students in order to get them to ask questions in return. For instance, I've posed problems to my students that appear at first glance to require application of a clear set of mathematical procedures. The answer resulting from the mathematical manipulations, however, may make no sense in the context of the original problem. The following is an example.

> Sue is ten years older than Bob. The product of their ages is 600. How old are Bob and Sue?
>
> Let x = Bob's age
> $x + 10$ = Sue's age
>
> $x (x + 10) = 600$
> $x^2 + 10 x - 600 = 0$
> $(x + 30) (x - 20) = 0$
> $x = -30 \quad x = +20$

If x is Bob's age, how can there be two answers? Do both answers make sense? How many students would answer the question with "-30 and 20" without looking back to remember that they were solving for ages? Mathematically, the problem yields two sets of answers:

> Set 1: $x = -30$ and $x + 10 = -20$
> (Bob is -30 years old and Sue is -20.)
>
> Set 2: $x = 20$ and $x + 10 = 30$
> (Bob is 20 years old and Sue is 30.)

Had the problem read: "One integer is 10 more than another integer. The product of the two integers is 600. What are the two integers?" both sets of answers could be correct. But for an age problem, only the second set makes sense. Students must learn to ask themselves appropriate questions after employing a mathematical formula to ensure that the numeric values obtained are indeed the correct answer.

Coon

There are several ways to encourage students to look beyond the answer in English courses. In writing classes, especially for freshmen, going beyond the answer often means encouraging students to see writing as more than the mechanical activity of creating five-paragraph essays. McGlinn and McGlinn discuss the importance of prewriting activities, such as brainteasers, verbal reasoning problems, free writing and dialoguing as means of developing students' creativity, confidence, and reasoning skills (4). Through these types of activities, the creative and explorative aspects of the writing process are emphasized over the more formulaic.

Another approach to going beyond the answer is to shift the emphasis away from single answer/single grade term papers and include several graded or ungraded component assignments, such as multiple drafts and revisions, outlines, oral presentations, or article summaries on a topic. Although the term paper may still be a major assignment, and a significant part of the grade, we can recognize the importance of the pieces or steps involved in its production. We can also ask students to pose and answer their own questions, especially for research assignments. Given adequate guidelines, students can bring valuable insights back to the class, in research presentations and class discussions, if they are encouraged to "go beyond" the questions posed in their textbooks or even by their professors. We should also encourage out-of-classroom experiences and multiple experiences with course material by making students aware of lectures, films, plays, readings, and exhibits that could augment their study, and when possible, integrating these activities into class assignments.

Throughout our collaboration, we have struggled with these five concepts ourselves. In fact, the curriculum development of our course has illustrated each of these principles of problem solving in turn. From the beginning we followed steps, constantly planning, outlining, and checking our work. We worked hard to define our problem, asking ourselves what we are doing and why we were doing it. We experimented with dozens of pedagogical approaches, assignments, classroom "routines," and even authorial voices. And we searched continually for the best way to frame a problem for our students or to convey our ideas to our colleagues. Like good problem solvers, we have learned as much about the process as about the subjects we are teaching.

Most importantly, we have continued to ask questions. We question our students, ourselves, and each other, firm in the belief that questions force us to reexamine basic assumptions about knowledge and about ourselves.

Works Cited

Birken, Marcia, "Using Writing to Assist Learning in Mathematics Classes." *The Role of Writing in Learning Mathematics and Science*. Ed. Paul Connolly. New York: Teachers College Press, 1989.

Birken, Marcia, and Anne C. Coon "Enriching Mathematical Problem Solving: Interdisciplinary Linkages," *1988 American Society for Engineering Education Annual Conference Proceedings*, Vol. 5, 2089–90.

Carter, Michael. "Problem Solving Reconsidered: A Pluralistic Theory of Problems." *College English* 50 (1988): 551–65.

Coon, Anne C. "Using Ethical Questions to Develop Autonomy in Student Researchers," *College Composition and Communication* 40 (1989): 85–89.

Coon, Anne C., and Marcia Birken. "The Common Denominators: A Collaborative Approach to Teaching Reasoning Skills Through Literature and Mathematics." *Innovative Higher Education* 12 (1988): 91–100.

Eves, Howard. *An Introduction to the History of Mathematics*. Rev. Ed. New York: Holt, Rinehart and Winston, 1964.

Faulkner, William. "The Bear." *An Introduction to Literature*, 8th ed. Ed. Sylvan Barnet, M. Berman, and W. Burto. Boston: Little, Brown, 1989.

Frederiksen, Norman. "Implications of Cognitive Theory for Instruction in Problem Solving." *Review of Educational Research* 54 (1984): 363–407.

Green, Charles S. III, and Hadley G. Klug. "Teaching Critical Thinking and Writing Through Debates: An Experimental Evaluation." *Teaching Sociology* 18 (1990): 462–71.

Kinney, James. "Why Bother? The Importance of Critical Thinking." *Fostering Critical Thinking*. Ed. Robert E. Young. New Directions for Teaching and Learning Series, No. 3. San Francisco: Jossey-Bass, (1980): 1–10.

McGlinn, James E., and Jeanne M. McGlinn. "Problem Solving and Prewriting: Mental Play in the Writing Class." *CEA Forum* 20.3/4 (1990): 4–6.

Polya, G. *How to Solve It: A New Aspect of Mathematical Method* 2nd ed. Princeton: Princeton University Press, 1945.

Rubenstein, Moshe F., and Iris R. Firstenberg. "Tools for Thinking." *Developing Critical Thinking and Problem Solving Abilities*. Ed. J. E. Stice. New Directions for Teaching and Learning Series, No. 30. San Francisco: Jossey-Bass, Summer 1987. 33–36.

Schmalz, Rosemary. "Problem Solving—An Attitude As Well As a Strategy." *Mathematics Teacher* 82 (1989): 685–87.

Schoenfeld, Alan H. "Heuristics in the Classroom," *Problem Solving in School Mathematics 1980 Yearbook*. Ed. Stephen Krulik. Reston, VA: National Council of Teachers of Mathematics, Inc.

———. *Problem Solving in the Mathematics Curriculum: A Report, Recommendations, and an Annotated Bibliography*. MAA Notes Series No. 1, The Mathematical Association of America Committee on the Teaching of Undergraduate Mathematics, 1983, No. 1.

Shank, Roger (with Peter Childers). *The Creative Attitude: Learning to Ask and Answer the Right Questions*, NY: Macmillan, 1988.

Trismen, Donald A. "Hints: An Aid to Diagnosis in Mathematical Problem Solving." *Journal for Research in Mathematics Education* 19 (1988): 358–61.

8

Seeing, Composing, Knowing: Critical Thinking and the Epistemic Approach to Composition

Richard Jenseth

> If we once start thinking no one can guarantee where we shall come out, except that many objects, ends and institutions are surely doomed.
>
> John Dewey, *Experience and Nature*

Writing teachers have long cared about the relations between language, experience, and knowing, but in recent years two provocative approaches to the teaching of composition have redefined these relations and have made them the center of their work: the *social-epistemic* and the *critical-thinking* approaches. In this essay, I will outline what I see as important theoretical and pedagogical parallels between these two approaches. I will also describe in detail two social-epistemic assignment sequences that attempt to enact these common concerns as they introduce my composition students to questions about the nature of interpretation, understanding, and composing.

My task is complicated by the general befuddlement within composition studies about these basic terms, *epistemic* and *critical thinking*, both of which mean many things to many people, and each of which remains a center of theoretical contention. I cannot take time here to discuss these matters in any great detail, but I can try to make clear at least what I mean by the terms.

What Is (Are) Critical Thinking(s)?

"Do we know what we mean by critical thinking?" asks Marilyn Wilson in her 1988 *Language Arts* article, "Critical Thinking: Repackaging or Revolution?" (544). She suspects we do not, and after my own trek through ERIC's 1,600 entries on critical thinking, few of which appeared to be about the same thing, I agree. True, most of the articles agreed that, whatever it is, critical thinking opposes rote learning, the passive memorization of facts, fiddling with workbooks or exercises, and a reliance on the old-fashioned, teacher-centered lecture. Beyond that, however, agreement was hard to come by. My notion of critical thinking is best made clear by saying what it is not, that is, by differentiating the reflective, dialectical pedagogy I have in mind from the more systematized critical thinking pedagogies whose theoretical and epistemological foundations are in formal logic or problem solving.

This problem-solving view of critical thinking, which my ERIC tour suggests dominates the education and composition literature, sees critical thinking as a response to what Tracey Baker calls "the crisis of simplistic and illogical thinking in our students' essays" (37). Its various manifestations of formal and informal logic provide students with strategies or formal heuristics meant to help them analyze or construct logical arguments. As Kathleen McCormick explains, critical thinking can teach students to "recognize an illogical, poorly written essay," and to appreciate that "there is frequently another side to an issue" (141).

The critical-thinking approach I have in mind is little interested in teaching formal heuristics, or in simply critiquing poorly written essays. Neither is it willing to settle for the unexceptional premise that *some* issues have another side. Instead, this version of critical thinking prefers what Anthony Petrosky calls "ill-structured tasks" that present "meaningful problems for which there are no clear solutions or algorithms" (3). This approach sees knowledge as "something people make" and therefore something "subject to change and revision" (Petrosky 2).

In fact, Mariolina Salvatori, who like Petrosky shows the influence of Paulo Freire and Henry Giroux, calls critical thinking "the antithesis of the technocrat's 'problem solving' stance," where an expert "takes some distance from reality, analyses it into component parts ... then dictates a strategy or policy" (42). In the critical-thinking classroom, Salvatori asserts, knowledge, "both for the teacher and the student, is always tentative, always approximate" (43). Barry Beyer makes much the same point when he says, "A critical thinker approaches information, assertions and experiences with a healthy skepticism about what is *really* true or accurate or real" (272).

Of course, in practice there exist any number of ideological variations of this reflective critical-thinking pedagogy — *liberatory education, radical pedagogy, critical literacy*. Yet, whatever their particular emphasis or degree of healthy skepticism, all certainly share the aims Henry Giroux and Roger Simon claim for their *critical pedagogy*:

> To understand why things are the way they are and how they got that way; to critically appropriate forms of knowledge that exist outside [a student's] immediate experience; to make the familiar strange and the strange familiar; to take risks and struggle with ongoing relations of power ... to envisage versions of a world which is "not yet" in order to be able to alter the grounds upon which life is lived. (3)

The Epistemic Approach(es)

As for the epistemic approach to the teaching of composition, it too represents a variety of pedagogies championed by a variety of theorists, from Walker Gibson to Ann Berthoff, from William Coles to James Berlin. Yet here again one finds important theoretical predispositions common to all. To begin with, these epistemic pedagogies share what Berlin has called an "orientation to language." In several important articles and in the 1987 NCTE monograph *Rhetoric and Reality*, Berlin has effectively argued that what truly distinguishes one approach to teaching writing from another is not simply individual assignments or classroom techniques, but how they define the elements of the composing process — writer, reader, language, reality — and how they conceive the relations between those elements.

Finally, argues Berlin, competing approaches to the teaching of writing present a "different world with different rules about what can be known, how it is known, and how it can be communicated" ("Contemporary Composition" 766). What distinguishes the epistemic approach is its emphasis on the relations between writer, language, and reality, and most important, its understanding of these relations as dynamic and dialectical, not fixed and unproblematic. In an epistemic pedagogy, as in a critical-thinking one, reality and truth, far from being "pre-existent and waiting to be discovered" are the result of human activity, what Berlin calls "a dialectical interplay between the individual and the world," the center of which is language ("Contemporary Composition" 774).

Put simply, the significance of the interplay is this: language is not a transparent or neutral mirror of the real world, nor is it simply a convenient way to talk about the world. Rather, language is seen as a primary means by which worlds and selves are created. Language creates the world, says Berlin, "by organizing it, by determining what will be perceived and not perceived, by indicating what has meaning and what is meaningless" ("Contemporary Composition" 775). If we know the world only indirectly, through the filters of symbol and sign, it follows that the way we represent the world to ourselves affects the nature of the world we can know, which in turn determines how we can act in that world.

As the name implies, then, the primary subject of an epistemic composition course is not informal logic or problem-solving strategies, but the character and quality of knowledge making, our own as well as that claimed by others. And here, I think, lies the essential similarity between the epistemic and critical thinking pedagogies: a view of knowledge as "a product of social relations," and an insistence on what Giroux has called "the active nature of human agents in its construction" (26).

Naturally, such assumptions about language and knowledge alter the view of writing and writers in some interesting ways. For one thing, the writer is seen as "a creator of meaning, a shaper of reality, rather than a passive receptor of the immutably given" (Berlin, "Contemporary Composition" 776). For another, attention is given to the importance of writing to the writer, not just its effect on a reader. Given their creative role, it makes sense for writers to reflect critically upon what William Coles calls "the various arrangements of terminologies or names or symbols (whatever you wish to call them) with which each of us frames and organizes the world he lives in" (1). Such views of language and knowing transform the idea of revision in the composition classroom. Revising prose becomes an invitation to experiment with new ways of knowing, to see the world and our roles in it differently, perhaps more honestly, or more completely, and thereby make possible a new itinerary of action.

This experimenting with new ways of seeing and knowing is, I think, the aim of the epistemic sequences presented in textbooks like Coles's *Composing*, Walker Gibson's *Seeing and Writing*, Ann Berthoff's *Forming/Thinking/Writing*, and James Miller and Stephen Tchudi's *Writing and Reality*. It is worth noting, however, that some of these epistemic pedagogies—the best example being Miller and Tchudi's—make personal introspection and self-discovery the focus of the course. In recent years, James Berlin has deliberately distanced what he calls "social epistemic" rhetoric from the "psychological" or "expressionist" epistemic pedagogies. Berlin worries that these introspective pedagogies neglect, among other things, the social and dialectical dimensions of knowledge making, conceiving the individual rhetor as flying solo, that is, "shaping private rather than social versions of knowledge" (*Rhetoric* 115).

In general, if not always in specifics, Berlin's criticisms are well taken, and it is this less ideologically naive, and more fully rhetorical, social-epistemic rhetoric that I believe most closely parallels the views of Giroux, Petrosky, and Salvatori, all of whom insist on knowledge as "something people make as they work and write together" (Petrosky 2). Thus, the theoretical formulations that underlie the epistemic and critical-thinking approaches run not just through neo-Kantian philosophy (Cassirer, Langer) and cognitive psychology (Piaget, Bruner, Vygotsky), but through contemporary cultural studies, social psychology, and, most important, through poststructuralist views of language, text, and knowledge.

One clue to the extent of this poststructuralist influence can be seen, I believe, in how much the critical-thinking and epistemic approaches have in common with the deconstructive pedagogies outlined in Atkins and Johnson's 1985 *Writing and Reading Differently: Deconstruction and the Teaching of Composition and Literature*. Consider, for example, Barbara Johnson's description of deconstructive practice as a "way of paying attention to what a text is doing, how it means, not just what it means" (145). Equally interesting is her refutation of the charge that deconstruction is a kind of cynical textual vandalism, "designed to prove that meaning is impossible." the kind of charge critics have leveled at both the epistemic and the critical-thinking pedagogies (144).

Consider also Paul Northam's characterization of deconstruction as not a set of skills or a heuristic, but "an attitude toward the texts surrounding us" (126), or David Kaufer and Gary Waller's description of deconstructive practice as "an initiation into the ways in which language really functions." To read a text deconstructively, Kaufer and Waller argue, is to be "thrown into language, into its flow and surprises, and to recognize that we are part of that flow" (83). Finally, there is Vincent Leitch's call for a deconstructive pedagogy that would instill in students a "vigilance about language." Students and teachers work together to defamiliarize and denaturalize the structures of a world that presents itself to us as inevitable and unalterable. "Everything is susceptible to critique and transformation," Leitch concludes (23).

Two Social-Epistemic Sequences

This vigilance about language and unrelenting critical reflection are exactly the aims of the two social-epistemic sequences I will discuss here. Before I describe these activities in detail, however, let me mention four specific ways that the theoretical assumptions I have been discussing shape classroom practice. To begin with, these sequences rely upon open-ended dialogue to accomplish much of their work.

Such dialogue assumes a willingness to "let classroom discourse float, fragment, digress," as Leitch puts it, which means relinquishing the authority of teacher-centered discussion (21).

Second, these sequences assume that writing is a way to create new knowledge as well as a way to communicate what is already known. Throughout the sequence students write in a variety of modes for a variety of aims and audiences, but ungraded exploratory writing, done in class and out, plays an especially important role. All writing is kept in a course portfolio to be turned in at semester's end. Third, throughout the sequence, students engage in the sustained, tough-minded interpretation of texts, the kind of contextualized, aggressive reading that opposes what Nancy Comley has called "reading for information," that is, reading in which language is "considered to be transparent, revealing content that is accepted, not questioned; memorized, not interpreted" (130).

Finally, there is the importance of assignment sequencing, that is, the deliberate arrangement of related writing, reading, and speaking activities around some intellectual issue or social problem worthy of sustained critical attention. Though the teacher has an important and active role in the classroom, deciding the exact direction of the sequence is a collaborative activity, as each new task grows out of the group's sense of what is important and what needs to be pursued.

Sequence 1: Why (And How) Does Sexist Language Matter?

One issue or problem that has often become the focus of an assignment sequence in my first year composition courses is sexist language and sexual stereotyping. The sequence I want to describe for you here began when I brought into class a sampling of the guidelines on sexist language one finds in composition rhetorics and handbooks, or in the official handouts from organizations like the National Council of Teachers of English.

Most such guidelines present two columns of words:

NO: fireman	YES: firefighter
DON'T: the average American loves his coffee	DO: the average American loves coffee

I asked everyone to read the guidelines carefully, then respond to them in a piece of informal writing. I had guessed that most students would greet these official recommendations with amused indifference; instead, they reacted with anger and hostility. "Come on! How does *chairman* hurt anybody?" demanded one male student. "It's too picky," insisted a female student. "If a woman wants to be a fireman, who's stopping her? Who worries about a word?" They were particularly angry with what they saw as the pushy and dismissive tone of the guidelines. "Personally, I take offense when someone tells me my language is wrong, and that my common everyday nonsexist words offend them," said one male writer. "It makes you want to use the wrong word," offered a female writer.

After some discussion, we agreed it would be worth our time to explore the resentment and hostility these guidelines had evoked. What exactly had made them so angry? Why do so many people take this fussing over *fireman* or *man made* so seriously? What gives hand-books, or teachers, or feminists the authority to decide what words others can and cannot use? Fairly quickly, we discovered that beneath their anger about those "pushy" language guidelines lay a deeper anger about "pushy" feminists and liberal college professors, who always seem to be making demands about one social issue or another. Through discussion and exploratory writing we probed this anger, speculating about its origins and its consequences. A subsequent writing assignment asked them to revise the guidelines, making whatever changes they felt appropriate.

As writers shared their revisions in small groups, we noticed a number of telling similarities. The first thing most writers had changed, for example, was the didactic voice of the opening paragraph. Most had also eliminated the YES/NO, DO/DON'T format. "Not so naggy," one writer said of her revision. As for the content of the guidelines, most writers had dropped all but the most blatant examples of sexist language. As one female student said of her decision to ignore more subtle forms of sexism, "Today when people say 'businessman' or 'fireman' we know they mean man or woman, even if they don't say it."

After we had discussed their dramatic revisions, I asked, "So, there is no problem here at all? Is it all a figment of a publisher's imagination?" They agreed not, and so we worked to reformulate our questions. What *is* sexist about sexist language? Who really gets hurt by words, and how? How are sexist language and sexual stereotyping like or unlike other ways that symbols affect our lives?

For the next few weeks we read and discussed articles on sexual stereotyping and the media (see Katha Pollitt's "The Smurfette Prin-ciple"); on gender and childhood (see Amy Sheldon's "'Kings Are Royaler Than Queens': Language and Socialization" and Letty Cottin Pogrebin's *Growing Up Free*); and on sexism in the workplace (see Amott and Matthaei's "Comparable Worth, Incomparable Pay" and Susan Fraker's "Why Women Aren't Getting to the Top"). We also analyzed persistent images of women in popular television shows and films: the unflappable June Cleaver and Donna Reed, dizzy but lovable Lucy, the tough-skinned yet vulnerable women on "L.A. Law" and

"China Beach." My students quickly pointed out the often dismal images of men portrayed on television, from the one-dimensional tough-guy cop to the hapless sitcom father.

After our close reading of familiar cultural texts, we returned to our original questions: What difference might these symbols actually make to us, to the way we think and the way we act? Do such images, does language itself, mostly reflect our world, or somehow shape that world? The next few assignments examined specific ways that sexual stereotypes might actually affect our own lives. This part of the sequence began with a simple questionnaire:

Because I am a man, I must _____.
If I were a woman, I could _____.
Because I am a woman, I must _____.
If I were a man, I could _____.

Students responded to a dozen such prompts, then wrote an informal essay that summarized and reflected critically upon the results. In a sense, each student had composed a kind of gender-role self-portrait, and our far-reaching, often hilarious workshops allowed us to speculate further on the origins and the power of these cultural conventions. Why can't men cry in public? Why are women expected to? Why are men expected to be brave? Why do "aggressive" women make men nervous?

Eventually our focus shifted to the role of language in other forms of discrimination or stereotyping. Prohibitions against less subtle forms of racial bias—words like *nigger* or *colored*—have become part of our unconscious cultural makeup. Yet, about a third of my students were surprised to hear that many blacks also find *negro* demeaning. How do we explain the sanctions against *negro*? Why do some blacks now prefer *African American*, or *person of color*? And here again, exactly how do such things get decided? What are the social and political forces that make people comply with these preferences, or forget to comply, or deliberately refuse?

For the rest of the semester, we continued to move between the text of our own experience and the larger texts of cultural practice. For example, one assignment had students list and analyze all the labels, good or bad, used to refer to themselves: *freshman, nerd, Christian, jock*. "Which have the most power for you, or over you? Which are assigned but not gladly accepted?" The final assignment of the sequence sent us back to revise the revisions of the handbook guidelines. More discussion, more questions, more debate, all aimed at what Henry Giroux calls "breaking apart or deconstructing the ideas or structuring principles in a cultural artifact and then placing them in a different framework" (26).

Sequence 2: "Can You Believe Your Eyes?"

Next I want to describe an extended assignment sequence that makes newspapers and television news the target of critical reflection. Since one aim of a social-epistemic pedagogy is to help students see themselves as active composers and interpreters of far more than freshman themes or college textbooks, this sequence began by asking students to interpret the text of their own experience. They were asked to write a reflective essay about a significant event in their own lives: a memorable journey, an especially good or bad job, some moment of crisis.

Through the early stages of composing, as they worked with drafts in small groups, I stressed that to be useful these essays had to be more than lists of facts, no matter how accurate, and more than a venting of feeling, no matter how genuinely expressed. Writers had to weigh the experience, to see and re-see events in the larger context of their lives. In our final workshop we indirectly approached epistemic concerns: the complex relation between word and world, the importance of *how* writers refer to the world around them.

We then began to examine the way newspapers and news magazines bring us the world in words and pictures. For several days we carefully studied the layout of a variety of newspapers — *USA Today*, the *New York Times*, the *Christian Science Monitor*. How carefully is "hard news" differentiated from analysis or commentary? How much space is given to entertainment, sports, and other non-news features? How do they use color, startling pictures, and headlines to present news stories?

Fairly quickly our discussion shifted to questions about the accuracy and objectivity of the reporting. An informal assignment asked, "If there is bias or slanting in newspapers, where is it?" What does it look like?" Another asked, "If purely objective reporting were possible, what would it look or sound like?" We went out to scour newspapers and news magazines for examples of this ideal news. As we analyzed what we found, we discovered our next question. If totally accurate, objective news is *not* possible, what do we call the stuff that fills our newspapers?

At that point, since we had been so tough on newspapers and newspaper reporters, we decided to try our hand at reporting. Students scattered around town and campus to observe people and events, then tried to compose an absolutely objective, accurate description of what they had seen. "No opinion, no slanting, just the facts," the assignment warned. Our workshops let us playfully expose even the slightest hints of bias or slanting, intentional or otherwise. As a follow-up, I asked them to go back and reread and revise the experiential essays they had done several weeks earlier. Had they somehow been able to report the whole truth of events in that account?

We then turned to the matter of how television affects the way we see and know the world. Obviously, most of them were eager consumers of television's products, but I quickly discovered they also knew what psychologists, educators, and social critics had been saying about the evils of television. Through discussion and in-class writings we fleshed out the details of these persistent complaints: television causes violence in children; it's to blame for declining test scores and the disintegration of the family; it perpetuates racist and sexist stereotypes. We discussed the relative merits of such charges, then tried to ground these abstract concepts in our personal experiences with television. The writing assignment, "TV Confessions," asked:

> How would you describe your own viewing profile? Frequent social watcher? Heavy user? Hopeless addict? How do you think television has affected you personally, for better or worse?

Their sometimes poignant, sometimes startling responses provided several days of lively discussion. The majority confessed that television had indeed affected their lives, in some cases to the detriment of social life, family relationships, and school work. A few argued that, despite periods of abuse (what one writer called "my summer of 'soaps' addiction"), television had never been a problem, had even helped them develop emotionally or intellectually. We followed these personal observations with a more formal analysis of television and individual development, Maurine Doerken's "What's Left After Violence and Advertising?" Among other things, Doerken charges that television isolates individuals, encourages violence, and creates within its heaviest users a "narcotic dysfunction" that leaves them dangerously suspended between fantasy and reality. My students laughed at what they saw as Doerken's gloomy extremism; yet how, I asked, could they reconcile that laughter with their own ambivalence towards television?

Finally, we turned to television news. Much as we had with newspapers, we began by examining the basic layout of the network news shows. How is time divided between hard news, entertainment, sports, and "human interest" stories? How clearly are analysis and commentary differentiated from news? We also performed a detailed semiotic analysis of several news broadcasts. Why all those blinking lights and people on telephones behind Peter Jennings? Why do reporters stand in front of the White House to read their reports? How are film, colorful graphics, and music used in the presentation of news events?

To help our analysis along, we read Henry Fairlie's "Can You Believe Your Eyes?" a fascinating discussion of television news which begins by asking, "Can television, by its nature, ever tell the truth?" Fairlie says it cannot, arguing convincingly that the problem is not so much the intentional bias of producers or reporters as it is the limitations of the medium itself. Television distorts events in the very act of reporting them. The presence of cameras alters what people do and say; moving pictures and sound create the illusion that viewers are actually present, that they have in fact witnessed events as they happened. Fairlie worries, too, that the reporter's affectations of objectivity — the deadpan expression, the confident voice — create an ethos of authenticity and authority.

Perhaps most pertinent to our epistemic concerns is Fairlie's contention that, by its very nature, the camera imposes its own vision of the world on the viewer. As it necessarily chooses to show some things and exclude others, the camera comments on what it represents; it never can offer unmediated access to the world *as it really is*. With these concerns in mind, we decided to try composing our own television news report. Working in teams, students gathered information, wrote a three- to four-minute script, decided how to use pictures, film, interviews, music, and so on. After several revisions, each group performed their spot for the rest of the class, then turned in a self-critique that explained how they had attempted to meet the standards for accuracy and honesty we had agreed upon.

The point of all this was not to insist that "meaning is impossible," as Barbara Johnson puts it, or that newspapers or television news are so filled with lies and distortions we should stop reading or watching them. Rather, the aim was to "incrementally problematize" our taken-for-granted understanding of these familiar media, to expose the myth of the neutral observer, or the notion of a transparent, innocent language with which we can talk about the world around us. Students had come to appreciate that all knowing — even the official-sounding knowing of the *New York Times*, or CBS News, or the Modern Language Association guidelines on language and gender — is a human construction. "To admit this inventive human element in knowledge," argues John Soltis, "does not mean that we do not know things or cannot come to know things or that knowledge is a figment of the imagination." It means, Soltis concludes, that "knowing is a human intersubjective activity and that we are not infallible" (508).

Works Cited

Amott, Teresa, and Julie Matthaei. "Comparable Worth, Incomparable Pay." Ashton-Jones and Olson, 393–401.

Ashton-Jones, Evelyn, and Gary Olson, eds. *The Gender Reader*. Boston: Allyn and Bacon, 1991.

Atkins, C. Douglas, and Michael L. Johnson, eds. *Writing and Reading Differently: Deconstruction and the Teaching of Composition and Literature*. Lawrence: UP of Kansas, 1985.

Baker, Tracey. "Critical Thinking and the Writing Center: Possibilities." *The Writing Center Journal* 8.2 (1988): 37–41.

Berlin, James. "Contemporary Composition: The Major Pedagogical Theories." *College English* 44 (1982): 765–77.

———. *Rhetoric and Reality: Writing Instruction in American Colleges, 1900–1985.* Urbana: NCTE, 1987.

Berthoff, Ann. *Forming/Thinking/Writing: The Composing Imagination.* Portsmouth, NH: Boynton/Cook, 1982.

Beyer, Barry. "Critical Thinking: What Is It?" *Social Education* 49 (1985): 270–76.

Coles, William. *Composing: Writing as a Self-Creating Process.* Rochelle Park, NJ: Hayden Books, 1974.

Comley, Nancy. "A Release from Weak Specifications: Liberating the Student Reader." Atkins and Johnson 129–38.

Dewey, John. *Experience and Nature.* Chicago: Open Court Publishing, 1926.

Doerken, Maurine. *Classroom Combat, Teaching and Television.* Englewood Cliffs, NJ: Educational Technology Publications, 1983.

Fairlie, Henry. "Can You Believe Your Eyes?" *Horizon* 9 Spring (1967): 24–7.

Fraker, Susan. "Why Women Aren't Getting to the Top." Ashton-Jones and Olson 473–82.

Gibson, Walker. *Seeing and Writing: Fifteen Exercises in Composing Experience.* New York: David McKay, 1974.

Giroux, Henry. "Ideology and Agency in the Process of Schooling." *Journal of Education* 169.2 (1987): 112–29.

Giroux, Henry, and Roger Simon. "Ideology, Popular Culture and Pedagogy." *Curriculum and Teaching* 16 (1986): 17–29.

Johnson, Barbara. "Teaching Deconstructively." Atkins and Johnson 144–48.

Kaufer, David and Gary Waller. "To Write Is to Read Is to Write, Right?" Atkins and Johnson 66–92.

Leitch, Vincent. "Deconstruction and Pedagogy." Atkins and Johnson 16–25.

McCormick, Kathleen. "Teaching Critical Thinking and Writing." *The Writing Instructor* 2 (1983): 137–44.

Miller, James and Stephen Tchudi. *Writing in Reality.* New York: Harper and Row, 1978.

Northam, Paul. "Heuristics and Beyond: Deconstruction/Inspiration and the Teaching of Writing Invention." Atkins and Johnson 115–28.

Petrosky, Anthony. "Critical Thinking: Qu'est-ce que C'est?" *The English Review* 37.3 (1986): 2–5.

Pogrebin, Letty Cottin. *Growing Up Free.* New York: McGraw-Hill, 1980.

Pollitt, Katha. "The Smurfette Principle." *New York Times Magazine* 7 April 1991: 22+.

Salvatori, Mariolina. "The Teaching of Writing as 'Problematization.'" *Teacher Education Quarterly* 10 (1983): 38–57.

Sheldon, Amy. "'Kings Are Royaler Than Queens': Language and Socialization." *Young Children* 45.2 (1990): 4–9.

Soltis, Jonas. "The Intersubjective World and Education." *American Journal of Education.* 93 (1985): 504–10.

Wilson, Marilyn. "Critical Thinking: Repackaging or Revolution." *Language Arts* 65 (1988): 543–51.

9

Collaborative Learning and Critical Thinking

Kate Sandberg

Imagine for a moment that you are a college student in a collaborative-learning situation. For you, life is not easy. Sure, you've worked in small groups before, but this collaborative-learning stuff is different. It's hard. The teacher asks you to listen carefully to what your group members say, wants you to have good reasons for your ideas, and then makes the group come to a consensus when no one agreed in the first place. Anyway, who needs it?

As the student's teacher, one way to answer this question is to look at the direct relationship of small-group learning to critical thinking. Critical-thinking skills such as listening analytically, attending to other points of view, negotiating, and evaluating one's own point of view are more likely to occur in small-group problem solving than if the student works alone. As Carnevale, Gainer, and Meltzer report, these skills, though they are difficult to learn, are deemed necessary for success in college and on the job. Of course, all of this doesn't happen automatically or easily. As teachers, we must plan with great care and detail before the class ever meets and must give the students responsibility for their own learning in the classroom. Students must learn to value their own and their peers' knowledge, use forgotten or new social skills, and negotiate. Yet the benefits, particularly critical-thinking empowerment, far outweigh these difficulties.

Both critical-thinking and small-group learning are young and burgeoning fields. According to Lauren Resnick in *Education and Learning to Think*, critical-thinking instruction for the elite has roots in ancient Greek culture, but the philosophy that all students can learn to think critically is new (7). Educators now realize the importance of teaching students from all economic and social classes to identify and solve complex problems. Within the last ten years, the critical-thinking field has grown at a rapid pace. Hundreds of books, videos, and prepackaged programs, and several annual international conferences devoted to the topic all demonstrate the current popularity of critical-thinking instruction.

Social psychologists have studied small groups in classrooms since the late 1930s. Within the last fifteen to twenty years, structured small-group learning has become increasingly popular in elementary, secondary, and college instruction. Although various advocates of this sort of learning use their own nomenclature (such as *cooperative learning, collaborative learning, learning in social contexts*, and *intentionally structured groups*), they have certain commonalities. Together, these proponents persuasively assert that small groups in classrooms create an environment conducive to both academic success and a disposition toward thinking critically.

This chapter summarizes the findings of these critical-thinking/small-group advocates, presents six elements of successful practice, and gives two examples of effective application of those elements.

Brief Review of Theory

Kenneth Bruffee, the chief advocate for collaborative learning in college composition classes, is familiar to most readers of this book. Among Bruffee's various reasons for supporting collaborative learning is the development of students' higher-order thinking skills. He draws from diverse philosophical sources to argue that conversation among peers is the appropriate vehicle for students to develop a thoughtful appreciation for any discipline. Bruffee states:

> To think well as individuals we must learn to think well collectively — that is, we must learn to converse well. The first steps to learning to think better, therefore, are learning to converse better and learning to establish and maintain the sorts of social context, the sorts of community life, that foster the sorts of conversation members of the community value. ("Conversation" 640)

According to Bruffee, this social conversation happens in the classroom only when small groups of students address problems and then reach a consensual solution. Bruffee frequently mentions M. L. J. Abercrombie's work with medical students who diagnosed faster and more accurately when they made hospital rounds in small groups than when they were alone. The groups discussed each case until the members agreed on the diagnosis. Bruffee asserts that the ability to make better judgments while in a group will transfer to situations when a person makes judgments alone, an assertion that has been substantiated by Lauren Resnick.

Cognitive psychologist Resnick is another advocate of small groups for encouraging critical thinking in the classroom. She writes, "There are striking points of similarity among those [thinking skills] programs that have shown some promising results. Many such programs rely on a social setting and social interaction for much of teaching and practice" (40). Although Resnick does not use the term *collaborative learning*, she echoes Bruffee's arguments. She reasons that the social setting is important to successful critical thinking because small groups of peers offer each other cognitive and affective support while solving complex problems. Support comes in the form of help in performing complex tasks, motivation to try new approaches to learning, and the creation of a disposition toward critical thinking. The habit of thinking critically is shaped when students see and hear peers posing questions, grappling with solutions, and dealing with uncertainty. If students observe the teacher and their peers valuing this process, the disposition toward higher-order thinking will be cultivated in students (42).

David and Roger Johnson have done extensive research with small groups in the classroom for more than twenty years and have established the concept of *cooperative learning*. Drawing from social and educational psychology research, the Johnsons emphasize the academic and social benefits of learning in small groups. Although most of their influence has been in the elementary and secondary schools, their research addresses the concerns of college students as well. They are particularly interested in constructive conflict in the classroom. According to the Johnsons' *Creative Conflict*, carefully controlled controversy in small groups brings higher levels of creativity, reasoning, interpersonal relations, and self-esteem than does either individualistic or competitive class instruction.

Several books on adult thought processes and critical thinking have made a significant impact on the critical-thinking field. Each of these books emphasizes the importance of small groups in the college classroom to encourage higher levels of thinking. Chet Meyers, in *Teaching Students to Think Critically*, addresses a multidisciplinary audience of college teachers interested in alternative teaching methods for fostering students' critical-thinking skills. He contends that the learner must be shaken from an egocentric perspective by interaction with peers (57). Meyers cautions us, however, that a teacher must understand group processes and have a well-planned discussion. He gives five keys to planning successful student interaction: begin each class with a problem or controversy, use silence to encourage reflection, arrange classroom space to encourage interaction, create a hospitable environment, and extend class time (61–68).

Stephen Brookfield, in *Developing Critical Thinkers* and *The Skillful Teacher*, asserts that peer support is crucial to thinking critically. Critical thinking depends on exposure to and working with points of view other than one's own. If students understand and feel the support of peers for the questioning and reflecting, then an atmosphere of safety is created. According to Brookfield, adult students are more likely to question and debate in small groups than in a large class.

Jack Mezirow argues in *Fostering Critical Reflection in Adulthood* that transforming one's thinking does not happen in an environment of isolation. Students' perspectives on issues change and mature in a social context of dialogue and exposure to other points of view (364). Other authors who contribute to this book agree. Examples of collaborative group work such as evaluating each other's efforts for revision, discussing life histories, or mapping out lifetime goals can be found throughout the book.

Although these advocates of small groups have varied backgrounds and priorities, each argues convincingly that learning to think well is essential for every student and that structured small groups are a primary vehicle for achieving this goal. They agree that a dynamic interaction between peers is necessary for the emotional support and motivation needed to question, to be questioned, to take risks, and to create new knowledge. Yet they disagree mightily as to models for teaching. The following section synthesizes some of these theories to create a basic model for teaching.

Six Elements of Successful Practice

Drawing from the theories and models of these disparate supporters — Bruffee, Johnson and Johnson, Resnick, Meyers, Brookfield, and Mezirow — we are able to create a single model for successful practice. Six elements for the model emerge as particularly important.

1. *A challenging, appropriate group goal.* Members of a group will see little reason for making an effort to work together if there is no common goal. This goal must be challenging enough that students see the advantages of working together rather than alone, but not so challenging as to be overwhelming. The teacher will need sound knowledge of the target population before designing the goal.

    Greg Myers argues that teachers who use some variation of collaborative learning must resolve the issue of consensus before they introduce the goal to the students (156). Students who are requested to reach a group consensus at the price of denying individual beliefs or values are not taught to think critically. If the teacher gives groups options for degrees of consensus or acceptable alternatives in the event of a lack of agreement, then individual students will not jeopardize their beliefs.

The issue, however, does not end there. One's beliefs are often misguided and should be scrutinized. If the students are taught how to question each other in a rational manner, individuals will realize that their beliefs are open to question. Understanding that one's beliefs and values may be ill-founded is an extremely painful process, and pseudo-consensus with the majority may be an easy way to avoid scrutiny. Again, this is not thinking critically. A teacher's watchfulness, knowledge of students, and ability to teach students to argue reasonably will help alleviate potential problems. But as John Trimbur shows us in "Consensus and Difference in Collaborative Learning," consensus is certainly one of the most controversial concerns of collaborative learning (602).

2. *Positive interdependence of group members.* When the teacher designs the goal, each student needs to have a specific role to play in order for the group to meet its goal. These roles are usually divided up by task, for example, director, writer, actor. Students soon realize that it is in the best interest of everyone if each member succeeds and learns.

3. *Briefing and debriefing with the entire class.* Briefing is the explanation of the goal and how to reach it; debriefing is the evaluation of the experience. Both are essential for learning; however, time constraints and other priorities often shortchange debriefing. When students learn in an active, emotionally charged atmosphere, debriefing helps to identify and summarize the learning outcomes and the interpersonal dynamics of group members. According to Margot Pearson and David Smith in "Debriefing in Experience-based Learning," this process centers on three questions: What happened? How do you feel about the experience? What does it mean? Answering these questions helps the learner understand more completely the recent learning experience and its affective and cognitive ramifications.

4. *Presentation and use of small-group skills.* Schools have psychologically and physically isolated the adult learner for so many years that highly developed social skills such as critical listening, negotiating, and trusting are rare among students. Teachers who use small-group learning cannot expect students to understand intuitively how to interact with each other. Small-group work should also incorporate instruction of these social skills.

5. *Individual accountability for mastery of learning the material.* Social loafing or the "Let everyone else do the work" mentality exists in small groups unless individuals are held accountable for their own

contributions. A student's total grade for collaborative work should include points or grades for participation, the group goal, *and* individual mastery of the subject matter. The individual mastery portion usually takes the form of papers, tests, quizzes, oral interviews, or random questioning. The essential factor is that all group members know that each one of them is accountable and will be graded accordingly.

6. *Group rewards.* Groups, like individuals, need recognition of effort and goal attainment. These rewards seem especially important to students who are not used to working effectively in small groups. Bonus points, verbal praise, and class presentations are forms of group rewards. Students need to know about the potential rewards before they start the collaborative experience.

By integrating these six elements into a collaborative problem-solving experience, we create a powerful environment for critical thinking. Within that environment, our students learn to think critically not only about the subject matter, but also about the process of reaching decisions and solutions. They learn the value of working together to solve problems and discover that results are more thoroughly thought out if everyone has a stake in the outcome.

Two Effective Applications

With a fair amount of planning, facilitators of workshops or teachers in classes can use these six elements to create successful small-group learning experiences. Essential to this planning process is accurate information about the current needs, interests, and skills of the potential audience. This knowledge then influences decisions about what concept(s) will be learned, how much time to allow for the experience, how groups will be selected, and how to incorporate all six elements into an instructional plan. Workshop facilitators do not ordinarily give grades, nor are their participants usually held accountable for their learning. Therefore, collaborative tasks for workshops are slightly different from those assigned in class.

In workshops, I have successfully used a short exercise that introduces participants to the six elements of collaborative learning. After a brief introduction to the workshop, participants select a partner whose eye color is different from their own. This type of criterion gets participants to look at each other, to talk, and to begin to feel at ease.

Then I spell out clearly the group goal by saying, "People in small groups have characteristics that help the group succeed. Your goal is to agree on four such characteristics. Each partner will alternately contribute two possible characteristics. Both partners will discuss each one until they reach a consensus. Each person is to keep a list." Four items is a realistic, nonthreatening goal in a workshop situation. The participants seem to understand the point of the exercise and are not overwhelmed.

After hearing an explanation of the goal, participants volunteer a few examples of such characteristics — for example, trust, dependability. I briefly discuss the social skills of how to disagree effectively — for example, how to show respect for others' thoughts and how to value the minority opinions. Then the pairs start to work. After approximately ten minutes, I stop the conversation and ask how many groups have agreed on four characteristics. I've made sure that all the groups finish, so each person usually raises his or her hand. This is the group reward. Then I use the debriefing questions mentioned in the last section: What happened? How did it feel? What does it mean? The ultimate goal is for the participants to realize what happened in the experience, how it felt, and what it meant in terms of elements of collaborative learning. Depending on my purposes, debriefing could also emphasize the kind of thinking used or the social skills necessary for this type of learning.

An example of successful application of collaboration in college classrooms comes from my critical/creative thinking course at the University of Alaska Anchorage. The entire three-week exercise is derived from Roger von Oech's book, *A Kick in the Seat of the Pants*, which is solidly based on current creative problem-solving theory. For two weeks, groups of four students design a product that could be sold in our university bookstore. This product cannot exist already, so my students must find a problem common to a fair number of peers and then create a solution. The third week is spent giving class presentations.

Von Oech's book focuses on four roles for identifying, creating, evaluating, and acting on solutions to problems: the Explorer, the Artist, the Judge, and the Warrior. One week before the class starts the group work, students receive a packet of materials that includes all the directions and assignments for the three weeks. After briefing by me at some length, the groups begin work. All the members of the group work together to create a product that solves a student problem, but the individual members have their own responsibilities as well. Each member selects one role — Explorer, Artist, Judge, or Warrior — to play for the two weeks (four class periods) and agrees to fulfill the requirements for that role. For instance, if a student chooses to be the Explorer, he knows he must accomplish three objectives: lead his group through the class period that focuses on the Explorer phase of the project, formally write answers to preassigned Explorer questions for an individual grade, and represent the Explorer phase during the group presentation to the class during a following third week. The other group members will have similar assignments for their respective roles as Artist, Judge, or Warrior.

In such long, complicated collaborative assignments, I give each student three grades for the project. I award one grade for social skills such as cooperation, participation, attendance, and listening. Students also receive one grade for an individual paper, which is a response to preassigned questions for their role. The third grade is a common grade for the group presentation. I give guidelines for the group presentations that leave plenty of room for creativity. I specify the minimum of information to be included in each member's portion of the presentation, but the group can deliver this information in any manner they see fit.

Students love this assignment. I arrange to have the groups begin work the second week of the semester so they have enough time to get adjusted to me and to each other but have not established their own friendships. After the project has ended, I sense a comradeship among the students that is stronger here than in my classes that don't have this type of collaborative experience. Many students tell me that this exercise is one of the highlights of the course. Some students take their project idea and try to patent it, to sell it, or to get financing. A large corporation even offered to buy one group's idea.

Conclusion

So — what *do* you say to the students who ask, "Who needs collaborative learning?" The chances are that these students are not interested in critical-thinking and collaborative-learning theory, six elements for successful practice, or even effective applications — all of which have been discussed in this chapter. These students will want to know what collaborative learning does for them now — in their personal, academic, and work environments.

You can start by saying that collaborative learning empowers them to know how to think critically in a manner that other ways of learning do not. Through collaboration, they will learn the interpersonal skills necessary for successfully solving problems in the workplace, and they will understand how knowledge is generated in social communities such as corporations and academic disciplines.

If that does not satisfy them, mention the fact that the peers in small groups offer emotional support. Hard assignments in your class and in their lives are less threatening, actually fun, when there's a support group working on the same task. You might also remind them that collaborative learning is only one part of the course, and that yes, you will lecture from time to time.

You, too, have a support group for collaborative learning. Kenneth Bruffee, Lauren Resnick, and the other researchers mentioned in this chapter firmly believe that you enable your students to think critically in today's world by teaching with collaborative learning.

Works Cited

Abercrombie, M. L. J. *The Anatomy of Judgement.* New York: Basic Books, 1960.

Brookfield, Stephen. *Developing Critical Thinkers: Challenging Adults to Explore Alternative Ways of Thinking and Acting.* San Francisco: Jossey-Bass, 1987.

———. *The Skillful Teacher: On Technique, Trust, and Responsiveness in the Classroom.* San Francisco: Jossey-Bass, 1990.

Bruffee, Kenneth A. "Collaborative Learning and the 'Conversation of Mankind.'" *College English* 46 (1984): 635–52.

———. "Collaborative Learning: Some Practical Models." *College English* 34 (1973): 634–43.

Carnevale, Anthony, Leila J. Gainer, and Ann S. Meltzer. *Work Place Basics: The Essential Skills Employers Want.* San Francisco: Jossey-Bass, 1990.

Johnson, David W., and Roger T. Johnson. *Creative Conflict.* Edina, NM: Interaction Book, 1987.

Meyers, Chet. *Teaching Students to Think Critically.* San Francisco: Jossey-Bass, 1986.

Mezirow, Jack, and Associates, eds. *Fostering Critical Reflection in Adulthood: A Guide to Transformative and Emancipatory Learning.* San Francisco: Jossey-Bass, 1990.

Myers, Greg. "Reality, Consensus, and Reform in the Rhetoric of Composition Teaching." *College English* 48 (1986): 154–72.

Pearson, Margot, and David Smith. "Debriefing in Experience-based Learning." *Reflection: Turning Experience into Learning.* Ed. David Boud, Rosemary Keogh and David Walker. New York: Nichols, 1985, 69–84.

Resnick, Lauren. *Education and Learning to Think.* Washington, DC: National Academy Press, 1987.

Trimbur, John. "Consensus and Difference in Collaborative Learning." *College English* 51 (1989): 602–16.

Von Oech, Roger. *A Kick in the Seat of the Pants.* New York: Harper & Row, 1986.

10

Critical Thinking and Computer-Mediated Writing Instruction

Joel Nydahl

As recently as 1986, a writing teacher related how her English department "dragged its first-year composition program into the computer age" (Simpson 11). Perhaps instigated by an early fear that computers might replace teachers, that reluctance is now an anomaly. Even those teaching in writing programs within traditional English departments have come to understand that the question now is not *whether* to use computers in the writing class, but *how* to use them wisely—not simply "as tutoring or editing machines, but as writing tools, at the center of an intelligent and imaginative curriculum" (Nash and Schwartz 45).

In general, this challenge means using computers in ways that will encourage critical thinking. In the words of Anthony Petrosky, if students are to become critical thinkers, they must engage in "interpretive encounters" with the material they are studying—encounters "different from rote learning," which simply "emphasizes . . . memorization or the use of algorithms which guarantee correct solutions if properly applied" (2). Instead, as a recent study points out, students need to participate in cognitive activities that stress "(1) integrating and synthesizing different bodies of information, (2) making critical judgments, and (3) developing and testing hypotheses"—in other words, the kinds of "activities generally identified in the literature on problem-solving" (Patterson and Smith 82).

In the writing class, that prescription would seem to translate, respectively, into activities that demand that students (1) deal both with feedback from others and with new judgments of their own; (2)

evaluate the worth of various possibilities for content, organization, and expression; and (3) try out those writing and revision strategies that seem most promising. Teaching critical thinking to novice writers, in other words, means helping them learn not simply the "know-what" but the "know-how" of writing (Foster 119); it means helping them move from being "knowledge tellers to knowledge transformers" (Kozma 33).

Ironically, for those of us in computerized classrooms who want to make knowledge transformers of our students, the most serious challenge is to surmount the computer's primary advantage: its ability to use, and its propensity to encourage, algorithmic thinking and rote learning. To enable inexperienced writers to become flexible, innovative, and self-reliant ones — writers capable of taking over their own writing instruction — we must use a tool closely associated with algorithmic tasks in such a way that we encourage a nonalgorithmic approach to learning and expose our students to more than drill-and-practice programs, which provide, in the words of Ann Duin, only "rigidly logical, sequential, lock-step control patterns" (78).

Ultimately, however, when we talk about a tool succeeding or failing to promote nonalgorithmic thinking, the computer itself isn't the tool we mean at all. A computer, after all, is a tool only to the extent that a brain is. Both are incomplete: one needs a mind, the other a program, in order to function. Using tools in the writing class to help students become independent thinkers and writers, then, means giving students the "right" writing software — software, I will claim, that doesn't detach responsibility from self or encourage dependence on external authority. In addition to giving students suitable writing software, however, we must also teach them how to use the new tools effectively. Finally, and somewhat paradoxically, we must make students tool-independent.

This last criterion is an important one. Teachers who are interested in developing self-reliant writers should not teach writing strategies that aren't translatable from computers to yellow pads and pencils. Those writing teachers skeptical about using computers as a teaching tool frequently argue that "there's nothing students can do with computers that they can't do without them." Exactly. That's precisely (if only partially) the point. Users of tools shouldn't be shackled to them. As I've pointed out elsewhere, as with a Nautilus machine, a computer "should extend students' powers" rather than make them dependent on it (Nydahl, "Teaching" 906).[1]

As we learn from other essays in this collection, critical thinking means a number of things — among them, being comfortable with ambiguity (Capossela) and with considering an issue from many sides (Zeiger). But if critical thinking predisposes an individual toward independence and autonomy — and that would seem self-evident — one said to be skilled in that area would have to be able to apply principles and exercise strategies, and to carry out operations learned under one set of circumstances when he or she encounters a different set.

In the writing class, then, critical thinking would imply the ability of a student to carry out composing and revising strategies learned in a computerized classroom to writing situations met in a computerless environment. Writing teachers need to be sensitive to that principle. Simply put, inexperienced writers need to develop "cognitive residue" — that is, they need to "internalize certain operations and strategies, explicitly encountered while interacting with a computer tool, such that [these strategies] can come to serve as [generalized] cognitive tools" (Salomon 2).

In this essay, I'll discuss how a number of college writing teachers use computers to develop students' critical thinking skills. Not surprisingly, their methods vary. Some call upon the untapped teaching potential of word processors; some write their own computer-assisted-instructional (CAI) writing software; some adapt CAI programs written by others; and some use local-area and distance networking to encourage collaborative learning.

The Philosophical Significance of Software

Writing teachers who want to develop critical thinking skills need to be concerned about possible deep-level effects — about what might happen in minds — when writers use computers, especially when they use ancillary writing tools.

In *Electric Language: A Philosophical Study of Word Processing*, Michael Heim asks whether "thought itself change[s] [when] the mind works with symbols under different conditions" (24). Since, as Plato knew (and Heim reminds us), "writing detaches memory from speech," is it possible that some CAI software — rigid drill-and-practice, textbook-on-a-screen software, for example, or programs that give a five-page single-spaced printout of advice to a perplexed student who's written a three-page, double-spaced paper — tends to detach responsibility from self? Is most CAI software likely to stultify or to enhance writers' imaginations? Will it discourage or encourage writers to take chances? Is it possible that inexperienced writers who use certain kinds of CAI software will become dependent on the programs? Might they ask, "Is the program the expert or am I?" or "Whose writing is it?" Even if questions like these never occur consciously, might they end up embedded in the psyches of inexperienced writers?

Heim's question about conditions changing the nature of thought is, of course, a rhetorical one. Certainly, the writing tools that students use will cause them to internalize processes, values, and ways of seeing. Certainly, these tools will affect not only the texts students produce but also the ways in which they understand the nature of text, of writing, and of thinking. As teachers of writing, we need to make certain that these internalizations encourage and reinforce strategies and techniques that make for self-reliant thinkers and writers. To produce self-reliant writers, we need to put our students in positions where they have to take responsibility for their own texts. To position students for achieving self-reliance, we need to free them, as much as possible, from dependence on writing aids; and, when writing aids are called for, we need to furnish nonprescriptive aids that prompt in an open-ended manner.

As we'll see, one way to accomplish these goals is to call upon the hidden potential of many off-the-shelf word processors to emulate CAI routines. Besides avoiding the expense of special writing software, utilizing such CAI potential has at least three other advantages: (1) Teachers can "build" customized writing aids right into their students' word processors; (2) teachers can create writing aids that don't interrupt writing processes by requiring students to exit the text-entry mode in order to enter a special editing mode; and (3) teachers can create writing aids that are passive, nonprescriptive, and open-ended — aids that encourage students to take questioning stances and test alternative possibilities for texts.

New Ways of Seeing Writing Software

Word processors represent a virtually untapped resource for teaching critical-thinking skills. Even though computers in general may encourage algorithmic thinking and rote learning, the very nature of word processing — including, but not limited to, the fluidity and evanescence of the text, the concomitant ease of imagining and executing revisions, and the degree of "play" generally encouraged — tends to undermine the kind of "rigidly logical, sequential, lock-step control patterns" of thinking that Duin warns about (78). To see and understand what is meant by the CAI potential of word processors, however, we need to re-place them (that is, "place them again") in the scheme of writing software.

Gail Hawisher argues that since the way we classify software indicates how we place "computers in the context of instruction," changing the paradigms we use to conceptualize software can change the ways we think about the roles that software plays. To illustrate how this insight helps us re-place word processors, let's consider one of the best known writing-software classification systems, Robert Taylor's. Taylor's categories are *tutors* (software that teaches something), *tools* (software that helps users accomplish something), and *tutees* (software that can be taught something) (Hawisher). Examples of each, in order, might be Writer's Helper, WordPerfect, and Hypercard.

But what a program *primarily* is should not obscure what it *potentially* is. We shouldn't allow ourselves to be trapped by limiting paradigms — such as the false dichotomy that sees word-processing programs and erasable ballpoint pens as "just tools for doing something" but sees "instructional computer materials [as] tools for teaching and learning something" (Southwell 223). The trouble here is that software classified as one kind can often be transformed into another. Word processors, for example, which we tend to think of only as powerful *tools*, can be transformed, first, into *tutees* and, then, into *tutors* by their being "taught" to carry out new and unexpected operations that in turn can be used to teach writers.

The potential of a word processor to become a tutee or a tutor resides mainly in its ability to execute *macros*. It's helpful to think of macros as a kind of programming language — one that's very powerful, yet easily accessible, even to computer novices. More specifically, a macro is "a way to record and quickly play back sequences of keystrokes" (Rinearson 463); these sequences can be of any length, can represent any combination of characters or commands, and can be of great complexity — even to the point of mimicking routines and performing operations on text that we usually associate only with special add-on CAI software.

Utilizing the Teaching Potential of Word Processors

Using macros to program and carry out CAI-like operations has at least two cognitive advantages, one for teachers and one for students. Both advantages involve the "higher order thinking skills of synthesis and evaluation": first, to modify and expand an analysis by Hawisher, in order to teach a word processor well the teacher "must first create a full understanding of what it is he or she wants [the word processor and the students] to learn"; second, because of the passive and non-prescriptive nature of macro routines, students must take responsibility for their own texts.

Here's a scenario from a first-year composition class at a college of business and management whose curriculum, since students need to write documents such as company policies and executive summaries, stresses a somewhat narrowly conceived mode of transactional writing. The teacher has introduced a sequence of thinking and writing strategies, which he encourages students to carry out in the process of coming up with topics on which to write, deriving theses, developing ideas, composing, revising globally and locally as they move through drafts, and editing for style and correctness. The teacher has also created a number of macros — applicable irrespective of writing content and in no pre-determined sequence — that will enable students to apply the strategies quickly and easily.

Bill has finished a draft of an essay on the presence of British troops in Northern Ireland. He's been taught to check for unity and organization of major ideas by evaluating a topic-sentence outline. To produce one, he activates a macro that carries out the following operations: (1) splits the screen; (2) copies the thesis sentence into the bottom window; (3) and copies all topic sentences, in order, after the thesis sentence.[2] On screen (or in hard copy), the result looks like this:

GREAT BRITAIN IS THE MAJOR CAUSE OF THE TURMOIL IN NORTHERN IRELAND AND IT SHOULD REMOVE ITS TROOPS OR ELSE THE IRA WILL CONTINUE TO WREAK HAVOC ON THE TROOPS.

Members of the IRA are an extremely nationalistic group that feel that they can achieve their goals only after there is complete removal of British troops from their homeland.

The goals the IRA wish to achieve are simple.

The IRA feel threatened and intimidated by the large number of British troops that are stationed in Ulster.

Great Britain should remove its troops from Northern Ireland because it has nothing political or economical to gain by remaining there.

Clearly, Great Britain should realize its presence in Northern Ireland is only encouraging more violence to occur.

After (presumably) attending to the lack of focus revealed in the essay, if Bill wants to work on less global concerns he can turn his attention to paragraph- or word-level matters. If, for example, he's had problems with paragraph cohesion, he can run a macro that randomly scrambles the order of sentences in any selected paragraph. Macros like these, which manipulate text in various ways, can help writers see their writing freshly, in new forms, and, in doing so, undermine preconceived relationships between form and function. For example, if a classmate has difficulty reconstructing the scrambled paragraph, Bill may discover that the sentences, although grouped to look like a paragraph, fail to act like a normative one because they don't meet minimal requirements of unity and cohesion.

Macros can also help Bill edit for grammar, punctuation, and usage by marking instances of *potential* surface-level problems. For example, if his teacher has noted a lack of action verbs in Bill's other writing, Bill might decide to run a macro that marks all instances of the verb *to be*, as in the following example:

The IRA feel threatened and intimidated by the large number of British troops that *are* stationed in Ulster. There *are* over 10,000 troops occupying Irish soil, while there *are* only 40 members of the IRA and 150 volunteers. The Catholics feel that they *are* being discriminated against and that the troops *are* there to support and protect only the Protestants. What *is* more, the Special Powers Act that *was* passed in 1933 gives British troops freedom to enforce curfews, search homes without warrants, and to arrest on suspicion. These rules *are* unfair because they discriminate against the Catholics, while they *are* rarely enforced against the Protestants.

If, as Paul LeBlanc claims, writing tools have "the power to drive the way our students think," clearly, macro routines can encourage critical thinking. They can relieve inexperienced writers of the sometimes overburdening task of "juggl[ing] ... the demands placed on short-and long-term memory" (Collier 150); and they can "assume part of the intellectual burden by handling lower-level [tasks], thus enabling learners to work at higher levels" (Kozma 34). In addition, combined with informed writing instruction, they can encourage writers to take control of their own writing. It's important to note, for example, that in the above scenario Bill initiated the routines; nothing prompted him to carry out any operations. Equally noteworthy, the macros were nonadvisory and nonjudgmental. Although Bill might have wanted some authority to speak omnisciently from the screen, none did. Because he received no prompts to go through a series of programmed steps, he had to identify problems, choose strategies for solving them, apply the strategies, and evaluate the results.

The expectation is that by being put in charge of teaching himself, Bill will develop what Gavriel Salomon calls "skill internalization." What Bill "accomplish[es] today with help and guidance," he ought to "be able to accomplish tomorrow, through the internalization of the help, on his ... own" (2). In other words, Bill has used a computerized writing tool that stresses, to use Robert Kozma's terms once again, being a knowledge transformer rather than a knowledge teller (33).

Using CAI Writing Software

Although the teaching potential of word processors can encourage the development of critical-thinking abilities, CAI software also has a role to play. Although most early CAI programs reflected an algorithmic approach to learning[3] — drill-and-practice software, of course, being the easiest to write — increasingly, programs began to appear that "engage[d] students in thinking, writing, organizing, and synthesizing material" (Hawisher). This approach grew out of a commitment to the idea that students should "experience the creation of ideas and knowledge" and, thus, develop "their metacognitive as well as cognitive abilities" (Montague 7).

Before committing ourselves to specific programs, however, we need to ask what identifies pedagogically sound CAI writing software. Literature in the field of critical thinking makes it clear that CAI software of any kind should encourage a "self-awareness of thinking and learning" (Patterson and Smith 81) and should focus on the "procedures in making choices . . . rather [than on] the making of a [particular] choice" (D'Angelo 19). In short, CAI software should be open-ended and nonprescriptive. And it should prompt, not preach.

Among the CAI software most likely to meet these criteria—and help students like Bill gain the insights and master the strategies they'll need to be competent revisors of their own writing—are what Stephen Marcus terms "second-generation programs" (writer aids) and "third-generation programs" (author systems). Second-generation programs focus "on one or the other stage of the basic composing-process model" (135); third-generation programs usually address all of the so-called stages by providing "direct instruction for prewriting, a word processor, and editing and rewriting aids" and by letting "writers move . . . freely among the various stages of the writing process" (136).[4]

Without recommending one third-generation program over others, we can get an overview of these programs by looking closely at one of the best known, Writer's Helper, by William Wresch. Writer's Helper assists students in finding topics, viewing topics from different perspectives, organizing ideas, adapting writing to specific audiences, and polishing. Properly used, and accompanied by informed writing instruction, Writer's Helper, like the best of other programs of this kind, encourages critical thinking by making students responsible for their own texts. When using Writer's Helper, students themselves must determine which tools are best at which times, which information the program should give them, and how to respond to the information they receive. Of primary importance, most of that information is descriptive rather than prescriptive; and most of the prompts are suggestive rather than imperative. In the words of its creator, there's no ideal "essay-in-a-box" for students to find; nor does the program claim to have answers for all questions that might arise in every writing situation. In dealing with word frequencies, diction level, and style, Writer's Helper reflects the same pedagogical commitment to self-reliance that undergirds the word-processing macros: it simply performs calculations and presents results that students can adopt, adapt, or ignore.

Finally, in judging the potential of CAI writing software to encourage critical thinking, we need to look beyond the programs themselves and ask how they're used. Since many second- and third-generation programs can be customized — for example, by "expand[ing] the list of phrases that the program searches for and [editing] its suggestions" (Thomas and Thomas 18) — teachers can skirt or minimize problems in writing pedagogy and make programs more class- or writer-specific. Some programs, in fact, such as Editor (Thiesmeyer and Thiesmeyer), encourage customizing.[5]

Using Local-Area and Distance Networking

Influenced by both postmodern pedagogy and theories of collaborative learning, many teachers have come to believe that knowledge "is something people make as they work and write and discuss together" and "the result of a community solving meaningful problems with language" (Petrosky 3). These teachers repudiate prosceniumlike classroom structures — where the teacher, standing in front, acts as a conduit for all knowledge — and "notions of education" that encourage "teachers talk[ing], students listen[ing]; teachers' contributions [being] privileged; [and] students respond[ing] in predictable, teacher-pleasing ways" (Hawisher and Selfe 55).

Recently, some writing teachers have moved toward using networked computers to validate "collaboration, intertextuality, and the polyphonous voices of many in negotiating meaning through writing" (Hawisher). This use of computers would seem to be a natural one since, as Marjorie Montague has pointed out, "technology-based education moves the educational process from a linear model to a multifaceted, dynamic, and interactive one" (9). As leaders within this movement, Thomas Barker and Fred Kemp have argued for a "postmodern pedagogy for the writing classroom" that emphasizes enfranchising the student by means of "communal . . . knowledge making" (2). Barker and Kemp claim that since, in traditional writing classes, students "often fail to 'internalize'" the information presented to them or to "transfer the information into productive behaviors" (7), writing teachers need to stress more than mere "knowledge transfusion" (10). Believing, as others have before them, that "we need to teach students not 'what' they need to know, but 'how' they will produce what they need to know when relevant occasions arise," Barker and Kemp propose a pedagogy that emphasizes "practice in recognizing situations in which new knowledge is required and . . . in producing knowledge by negotiating information within contexts" (9–10).

Based on network theory, Barker and Kemp's model utilizes a computerized classroom in which all computers are linked in a non-hierarchical fashion by a collaborative local-area-network (LAN) program. This program, called Interchange (Taylor et al.), allows an entire class to transact synchronous communication among all members, none of whom are privileged.[6] In fact, a teacher who wants to participate in the give-and-take of classroom discussion must get on-line and exchange messages with students. While students read a common text — comments by classmates — in the top window of a split screen, they are able to enter remarks in the bottom window and, when ready, share their ideas by posting their remarks to the class. The posted remarks then become part of the common, expanding text that participants can scroll through, save, or print. As Barker and Kemp put it, when using Interchange, "the writer reads the shared text of his classmates [and] becomes . . . aware of how his own ideas and his own presentation fit into the context of his particular discourse community" (18).

Some teachers have expanded beyond the restricted scope of local-area networks and enabled their students to critique the ideas and texts of students at other institutions by means of a distance network such as Bitnet. Believing that students often have little understanding of what it means to write to real audiences and that writing to strangers over a distance network would encourage students to "develop fully supported ideas" (Marx 26), Michael Marx (at Skidmore College [Saratoga Springs, NY]) and I (at Babson College [Wellesley, Mass.]) had our students exchange texts.

Prefatory to their handing in final versions of essays on the common subject of terrorism, students twice exchanged drafts and critique letters. Marx and I wanted to go beyond what we saw as two inherent limitations of synchronous networks: relatively short comments by writers; and an at-best-tenuous relationship between, on one hand, the extemporaneous writing usually fostered by synchronous communication and, on the other, the formal expository writing that students have to master in order to succeed in academia. Since our students would be writing to strangers to whom they owed neither intellectual nor emotional allegiance, we wanted an arrangement that would encourage an objectively critical stance and emphasize "the role of individual students as knowledge makers" (Barker and Kemp 17).

That computers can be effective tools for developing critical thinking, collaborative learning, and audience awareness is, of course, not a new idea. Marjorie Montague, for example, has written of using computers to "enhance the level of cognitive engagement of students by creating a rate of interaction more typical of small group learning" (18) and of helping writers "develop audience awareness by focusing on communication as the primary purpose of writing" (39). What is new, however, is the extent to which recent experiments with various kinds of networking stand as repudiations of the criticism that "using computers pedagogically in the classroom" removes students "from the effective instructional activity of the group [simply] to stare at video screens and to perform automated drill and practice" (Barker and Kemp 16).

What the Future Holds

The approaches to teaching critical-thinking skills that this essay investigates are practical possibilities for many of us, because they are electronic variations of classroom techniques we've used before. Only local-area and distance networking require an investment beyond computers and relatively simple and inexpensive software. Some teacher-researchers, however, are using computers in ways that are not practical for most of us today—but may be the day after tomorrow.

Diane Balestri, for example, has her students learn how to program in an artificial language. She believes that the intellectual effort needed to "make a program work right" can be harnessed to improve students' writing skills (36–37). By actually programming, for example, students learn that a program must be mechanically correct for it to work, that it "works to accomplish something," and that a problem must be understood before a program can be written to solve it (37–39).

If there is a "wave of the future" in developing students' critical thinking skills in writing classes, it is probably hypertext. For example, Michael Joyce's, Stuart Moulthrup's, and Nancy Kaplan's innovative work with interactive fiction will undoubtedly have direct classroom applications for writing teachers. Of more immediate interest—simply because it represents an attempt to break the "rigidly logical, sequential, lock-step control patterns" still evidenced in much software—are the speculations of Fred Kemp. In attempting to go beyond the work of Hugh Burns in delivering "open-ended instructional programming," Kemp believes it's "possible that a hypercard interactive questionnaire, with its extraordinary flexibility of screen action, [can] move considerably beyond sequential prompts" and make possible "a quasi-natural language interface." Such software might be able to demonstrate "interesting things about the way people generate knowledge about a topic, especially if the programs could have a feedback mechanism built in which would capture decision patterns on the part of the user" (Kemp).

This essay has only skimmed the surface of its subject. It has not, for example, speculated on what researchers in the field of artificial intelligence might develop tomorrow. It has, however, made clear that writing teachers down in the trenches here and now, working today within the confines of limited expertise and limited resources, can do a great deal with computers to ensure that their students are better writers because they are better thinkers, and better thinkers because they are better writers.

Endnotes

1. I owe the metaphor to Daniel C. Dennet.

2. Since this macro searches for character formatting, it's necessary for Bill to have formatted his thesis sentence in upper-case characters and his topic sentences in bold.

3. Although we've passed both into and through the "second generation" (writer-aids), "third generation" (author-systems), and "fourth generation" (idea-processors) (Marcus 134–36), much of the writing software available — including programs that accompany many student handbooks — still, in fact, stresses a "pigeon-training" pedagogy (Strohmer 6). Consider, for example, *Sentence Patterns*, a program based on the naive premise that the

> teaching of freshman composition has a logical progression: sentence to paragraph to theme. If the first entity — the sentence — is not mastered by beginning college writers, then paragraph and, consequently, theme writing is less than successful. (Cox 161)

Each program disk for *Sentence Patterns* inevitably follows a set format which provides a "definition of the [sentence] pattern, [an] example of the pattern, word banks for writing sentences, checks for each sentence, and a quiz over each pattern" (Cox 162).

4. Most effective, I believe, would be CAI programs embedded within the word processors — for example, Microsoft Word and WordPerfect — which students actually use. The word processors in many third-generation programs are unsophisticated and limited in their power. (See my review of *HBJ Writer*.)

5. For insightful suggestions on modifying and using style-checking software, see Crew.

6. The term *synchronous communication* indicates that a message is received as soon as it is transmitted, with no lapse of time — as in the case of a telephone conversation; *asynchronous communication* indicates that a certain amount of time — anywhere from a few seconds to a few minutes or longer — elapses between the time a message is sent and the time it is received.

Works Cited

Balestri, Diane P. "Algorithms and Arguments: A Programming Metaphor for Composition." Gerrard. 36–44.

Barker, Thomas T., and Fred O. Kemp. "Network Theory: A Postmodern Pedagogy for the Writing Classroom." *Computers and Community: Teaching Composition in the Twenty-first Century*. Ed. Carolyn Handa. Portsmouth, NH: Boynton/Cook, 1990.

Collier, Richard M. "The Word Processor and Revision Strategies." *College Composition and Communication* 34 (1983): 149–155.

Cox, Diana. "Developing Software for Freshman Composition Students." *Collegiate Microcomputer* 6 (1989): 161–64.

Crew, Louie. "Style-Checker as Tonic, Not Tranquilizer." *Journal of Advanced Composition* 8 (1988): 66—70.

D'Angelo, Edward. *The Teaching of Critical Thinking*. Philosophical Currents 1. Amsterdam: B. R. Grüner, 1971.

Dennet, Daniel C. Lecture. "The Computer as a Trojan Horse." Babson College, Wellesley, MA, 17 November 1987.

Duin, Anne. "Computer Exercises to Encourage Rethinking and Revision." *Computers and Composition* 4.2 (1987): 66—105.

Foster, David. *A Primer for Writing Teachers: Theories, Theorists, Issues, Problems*. Portsmouth NH: Boynton/Cook, 1983.

Gerrard, Lisa, ed. *Writing at Century's End: Essays on Computer-Assisted Composition*. New York: Random House, 1987.

Hawisher, Gail E. "Blinding Insights: Classification Schemes and Software for Literacy Instruction." *Computers and Literacy*. Eds. Cynthia Selfe and Susan Hilligoss. New York: Modern Language Association, forthcoming, 1993.

Hawisher, Gail E., and Cynthia L. Selfe. "The Rhetoric of Technology and the Electronic Writing Class." *College Composition and Communication* 42 (1991): 55—65.

Heim, Michael. *Electric Language: A Philosophical Study of Word Processing*. New Haven: Yale University Press, 1987.

Kemp, Fred. Megabyte University. Computer network. August 2, 1991.

Kozma, Robert B. "Computer-Based Writing Tools and the Cognitive Needs of Novice Writers." *Computers and Composition* 8.2 (1991): 31—45.

LeBlanc, Paul. "Roundtable: Computers and Composing: New Paradigms for Instructional Design." Conference on College Composition and Communication. Chicago, 22 March 1990.

Marcus, Stephen. "Computers in Thinking, Writing, and Literature." Gerrard. 131—40.

Marx, Michael Steven. "Distant Writers, Distant Critics, and Close Readings: Linking Composition Classes Through a Peer-Critiquing Network." *Computers and Composition* 8.1 (1990): 23—39.

Montague, Marjorie. *Computers, Cognition, and Writing Instruction*. Albany, NY: State University of New York, 1990.

Nash, James, and Lawrence Schwartz. "Computers and the Writing Process." *Collegiate Microcomputer* 5 (1987): 45—48.

Nydahl, Joel. "Teaching Word Processors to Be CAI Programs." *College English* 52 (1990): 904—15.

———. "Writing Instruction Software with HBJ Writer." Research in Word Processing Newsletter (1986): 12—16.

Patterson, Janice. H., and Marshall S. Smith. "The Role of Computers in Higher-Order Thinking." *Microcomputers and Higher Education*, Part I. Ed. Jack A. Culbertson and Luvern L. Cunningham. National Society for the Study of Education. Chicago: University of Chicago Press, 1986. 81—108.

Petrosky, Anthony. "Critical Thinking: Qu' est-ce que c'est?" *The English Record*. 37.3 (1986): 2−5.

Rinearson, Peter. *Word Processing Power with Microsoft Word*. 3rd Ed. Redmond, WA: Microsoft Press, 1989.

Salomon, Gavriel. "Discontinuity Between Controlled Study and Implementation of Computers in Classrooms: A Letter to a Young Friend." *Technology and Learning* 3.3 (1989): 1−5.

Simpson, Jeanne. "Word Processing in Freshman Composition." *Computer-Assisted Composition Journal* 3.1 (1988): 11−16.

Southwell, Michael G. "Appropriate Uses for Instructional Software." *Collegiate Microcomputer* 4 (1986): 223−27.

Strohmer, Joanne C. "Are We Using Technology to Train Pigeons or Thinkers?" *Principal* 67.2 (1987): 6−7.

Taylor, Paul, et al. *Interchange* Software program. Austin, TX: The Daedelus Group, Inc., 1990.

Taylor, Robert. *The Computer in the School: Tutor, Tool, and Tutee*. New York: Teachers College Press, 1980.

Thiesmeyer, Elaine, and John E. Thiesmeyer *Editor*. Software program. New York: Modern Language Association, 1990.

Thomas, Gordon P., and Dene Kay Thomas. "Judging and Adapting Style-Analysis Software." *Computers and Composition* 8.2 (1991): 17−30.

Wresch, William. *Writer's Helper*. Software program. Iowa City: CONDUIT/ The University of Iowa. 1991.

11

Making Meaning Through Journal Writing: A Look at Two Teachers and Their Classrooms

Sandra M. Lawrence

My interest in journal writing stems from my evolution as a teacher of first-year college students, from study in cognitive psychology and composition theory, and from my experiences using various forms of writing to enhance student thinking and promote student learning. Like many of my colleagues at the college level, I was often dismayed by first-year students who, though intelligent, seemed unengaged with learning and seldom understood subject matter in deep or meaningful ways. For the most part, students focused primarily on memorizing facts and principles in order to pass exams, and they paid scant attention to how concepts operated or how they might apply such information to other situations. My dismay, coupled with uncertainty about how to help students better understand the content of their courses, prompted me to study teaching and learning processes more carefully.

Through my own thinking about the work of Dewey, Freire, Piaget, and Vygotsky, I began to see the importance of interactive teaching methods. At the same time, scholars in the field of composition such as Ann Berthoff, James Britton, Janet Emig, Toby Fulwiler, James Moffett, and Donald Murray convinced me that writing could be used to make classrooms interactive and could encourage students to think critically about the material under study.

As the connections between writing, thinking, and learning became more apparent, I began to explore different pedagogical strategies to assist students with their thinking and learning. I considered various forms of writing — essays, letters, journals, and reaction papers — to engage students. Yet the literature that inspired these explorations provided little practical information on how to use them, because readings on the topic tended to be theoretical or uncritically laudatory. It made sense to me that writing about subject matter in particular ways enabled students to interpret knowledge and make it their own, but I needed more. I wanted to know what I could do in my classroom with my students to help writing function in those ways.

At that point, I realized that if I wanted definitive answers to my questions, I would have to find them myself. Since I agreed with the view that different kinds of writing seem to necessitate different ways of thinking and hence lead to different types of learning (Langer and Applebee 101), I decided that a study of the processes of using one form of writing might yield useful results. And since many teachers at all levels of instruction and in a wide variety of courses use journal writing with the belief that it functions as a thinking, learning tool (Berthoff, Fulwiler, Gere, Herrington, Tchudi), I decided to examine how teachers use journal writing to achieve the claimed effects on thinking and learning.

Journal assignments are often discussed in terms of their end products or intended benefits (Goodkin, North, Selfe et al., Tierney, Wotring) with less attention given to *how* journal writing promotes those benefits (i.e., student thinking and learning). To understand how journal writing works the way it does, I decided to look into actual college classrooms in which teachers assigned journal writing to help students think critically about the course content. I selected two teachers — one from psychology and one from computer programming — to be teacher-participants, and I selected several students from each course to be representative case studies. The data from this investigation came from semesterlong classroom observations, interviews, and questionnaires with teachers and students, and samples of student writing. My inquiry into these classrooms focused on the journal-writing tasks assigned; the teachers' expectations, goals, and pedagogical practices for these tasks; and students' views on the influence of journal writing on their thinking and learning (for a full description of methods and findings, see Lawrence).

Carol's Use of Journal Writing in Her Psychology Course

Carol, a member of the Psychology Department at an urban college, taught Psychology and Management of Stress (PSY105), a three-credit elective course. Carol had been teaching for fourteen years and had assigned some type of journal writing for many of those years. For this course, she assigned two types of journals — the in-class and the at-home journal — and had very different expectations for each. She viewed in-class journal assignments as a way for students to assess what they knew or didn't know about a topic and to make sense of that information by relating it to their own lives. For Carol, students indicated that they had learned by showing that they had thought about, processed, and applied the information to some new situation.

Carol incorporated seven- to twelve-minute journal-writing sessions as part of her class and ended the sessions by asking students to share their entries. She believed (and related this belief to students) that the oral sharing helped students to learn from one another. In addition, such sharing enabled her to build on what students wrote as a way to initiate class discussion or present new information.

Carol viewed the at-home journal as a place where students could react to what they had read, heard in class, or experienced in their lives concerning the course content. Such reactions were intended to help students think more deeply about, make connections with, and hence better understand subject matter. Carol assigned various types of writing for the at-home journal: reactions to material presented in class and in the text, reviews of chapters in the text, and deeper questions about specific concepts or topics.

Alex's Use of Journal Writing in His Computer Programming Course

Alex taught Programming in Pascal II (CP104), a four-credit course offered by the Computer Sciences Department at a suburban college. He had been teaching in the department for six years and had been using journal writing for two years. Like Carol, he assigned two types of journals for his course. In class, he used journals to focus student thinking on a topic to "help them get their thoughts out." During class, he gave specific questions for students to think and write about. Sometimes he asked questions before and in the middle of a topic discussion, but most often he asked students to write in journals after he had finished reviewing a topic. At the conclusion of the five-minute writing period, he asked for volunteers to read or talk about what they had written; on most occasions, he read his entry as well.

Alex also assigned out-of-class journal writing, which was to be completed in conjunction with writing computer programs in the lab. He felt that lab assignments were an essential part of any programming course and that much of the learning of the course came from students interacting with the computer. His intention in assigning journal writing was for students to think and focus more on what they were doing in problem-solving situations. He hoped that the journal would give students the opportunity to stop and reflect, and that this reflection would provide some new insights into the solution. He instructed students to write in the journal five times for each of the problems he assigned. The first entry was to include initial thoughts or feelings on the problem; for the middle three entries, students were to write about their difficulties in solving the problem and how the program was progressing; the last entry was to be a reflection on what they did to solve the problem.

Successes and Failures with Journal Writing

Both Carol and Alex assigned journal writing because they expected it to foster student thinking and enhance student learning. Additionally, they intended the journal to be a vehicle for expressing thoughts, feelings, and speculations about the content, and for integrating past knowledge with new knowledge. They believed that the reflective, critical thinking students did in conjunction with journal writing would then help them to learn course content in various ways.

Both teachers, however, experienced varying degrees of success with the types of journal writing they assigned. Generally, in-class assignments appeared to be more successful than those written out of class. Carol's in-class assignments seemed somewhat more successful than Alex's, while out-of-class assignments were equally unsuccessful for both teachers.

The Success with In-Class Journal Writing

Examination of the in-class journal entries from both classes reveals evidence of critical thinking and meaning making: there are expressions of ideas, feelings, and opinions about the topic under discussion; some entries also demonstrate integration of prior knowledge with newly presented information and the construction of new knowledge. For example, when Carol asked her students to write briefly about something new that they had learned from an assigned chapter—something that they had not known before—one student wrote the following:

> The effects of stress on the cardiovascular system are much greater than I had imagined. On the other hand, functions of the skin, muscles, and autonomic nervous system are parts which are not new to me as I had an introduction to these parts of the body and what stress does to them in Intro. to Psychology. (Polly's Journal, PSY105)

In this excerpt Polly is trying to make sense of what she has read by relating the new information to what she has previously learned. She also gives her opinion about the content and expresses amazement at the extent of the physiological effects of stress. Through her writing,

Polly has personalized the content, interacted with it, and categorized it to make learning easier. Instead of memorizing textbook material, she is taking a reflective, critical stance toward understanding.

On another occasion, Carol asked students a general question dealing with the topic of the course: "What does stress mean to you?" In response, one student wrote the following:

> When I think of stress I think of feeling nervous and uptight. Somewhat unsure of what I'm doing. When under stress you just don't feel right. Some physical symptoms may be headaches, stomach aches, rapid heart beats, and just whole feeling of uneasiness. (Ruth's Journal, PSY105)

Ruth personalizes the content by recalling past experiences with stressful situations and using her own language to express her ideas. Because there is no single correct answer to Carol's question, Ruth takes this opportunity to interpret the content in a way that is meaningful to her.

Other student entries from in-class journals illuminate areas of understanding and misunderstanding of content and/or illustrate speculation about certain aspects of the topic. For instance, before they began to work through some examples on a problem sheet, Alex asked students to take out their journals and "jot down some approaches" to a particular problem. One student wrote the following:

> The problem at hand is to write 2 arrays and we are to find as many matches between the two as possible. Because A RAY is unique — no same #s and B RAY is not unique, we have to count how many same #s, we find in B RAY and match it to a single # in A RAY. Actually we'll look at the 1st # in A RAY, go to B RAY and look for that number, count how many times it occurs, and that is the # of matches for that specific #. Then we took the 2nd # in A RAY, went to B RAY and counted how many times that occurred, etc. (Peggy's Journal, CP104)

In this entry Peggy restates the problem in her own words and speculates about what is needed to solve the problem. Then she hypothesizes what a possible approach might be — she must first set up a two-dimensional array — and outlines several steps involved in the approach. This journal assignment gives Peggy the opportunity to come up with her own approach to a problem before she hears the approaches used by others in the class, including the teacher. She can then examine and compare her solution with those of others, thinking about what works and what doesn't, as the class works through the various steps to the solution. This writing, thinking, and comparing enables students to see that there are many approaches to solving problems.

During another class, when Alex attempted to work out a solution to a problem on the board, he asked for a volunteer to offer a beginning step. When there was no response, he said, "I want you to take out your journals and write about this problem." One student entry began as follows:

> We are going over a problem to find an odd number and print this out. It sounds easy, but accutly [*sic*] it isn't. I know you'll need a couple of loops like "for" and you need a "hold" to hold this number as you go until there is a smaller prime number. (Susan's Journal, CP104)

In this entry, Susan describes what she believes is the task of the problem; then she gives her opinion about the difficulty of the problem. Although she isn't quite sure of an approach, she does speculate about what she thinks is needed: she believes that in order to accomplish the task some loop commands will be needed, as will a holding command. Like the previous journal-writing assignment, this one gives students the opportunity to recall what they know from past experience and apply it to new situations. Susan has learned about loops in previous courses and speculates that loop commands can be applied in this new situation. Through this assignment, Alex encourages Susan and other students to think critically about problem situations and to construct their own meaning as they proceed through problem-solving steps.

Both teachers felt that the type of in-class journal writing that resulted in speculating, hypothesizing, and personalizing the content was successful. When the factors surrounding the use of in-class journals are examined, it appears that the structure and format of assignments, together with the degree of integration of journals with other class activities, contributes to the success of journal assignments.

Students were given a considerable amount of structure and assistance in understanding and completing assignments to be written in class. Each teacher specified a limited amount of time for writing and gave students topics on which to focus their thinking. In fact, "reflective" guiding questions were the central component of Carol's and Alex's in-class journal assignments. Both teachers used similar types of questions to guide student thinking about a topic, such as, "Free write on this topic. What do you know about . . . ? What do you understand? What did you learn?" During the five-to-ten minute writing period, students were expected to focus on the topic and to write. And they did. It seems that the open-ended nature of the in-class questions, combined with the specified structure and allotted writing times outlined by the teachers, were conducive to getting students to write in their journals. After journal-writing sessions, students read entries aloud in both classes as teachers either asked for volunteers or called on students.

Even though both groups of students shared written entries, and the two teachers expected that hearing other points of view would be valuable to students, the reading of entries seems to have had a more pronounced purpose and effect in PSY105. For Carol, the writing, reading, and summarizing of entries formed the basis of her mini-lecture/discussion format. During the second class session, for example, after assigning a chapter that surveyed leading psychologists, physicians, and theorists in the field, she had students write about two people in the chapter who had impressed them, and why they had been impressed. Carol then began the discussion by asking for a volunteer to read or summarize her entry. One student responded as follows:

> Okay, here is what I wrote: Two people I was impressed about after reading chapter one. I am impressed with the author of the book, Jerold Greenberg, who cared enough about other people to share his wisdom and knowledge on the subject of stress. Also, how he shared his life situations with the intent to help us identify and cope with stress and all that it brings. I am impressed with Carl Simonton who believes that personality is related to cancer. He came up with a different approach to treating cancer by using visualization in addition to the usual therapy. He had the patient visualize that the treatment he was receiving had good effects on beating the cancer battle.

After the reading, Carol complimented the student, then wrote "Simonton" on the board. Then she described his research and explained the applications of his work. After this minilecture, she called on another student, who shared the following entry:

> I'll read just one: Walter Cannon impressed me because it was he who first recognized the physiological changes in the body caused by stress. This opened up a door for several methods of relaxation and releviation [sic] of these symptoms. I feel the fight or flight response is a very accurate measure of the typical reaction to a stressor.

After the reading, Carol wrote "Cannon" on the board and proceeded to give a minilecture about his work. The remainder of the class proceeded in a similar manner, with students bringing up names and Carol adding information to their written entries. Thus, the journal writing and reading were integral parts of class sessions. Students remarked during interviews that they liked sharing information, that they learned from one another, and that hearing other perspectives helped them remember more about a particular topic.

During the times when Alex used in-class writing as a way for students to approach a programming problem, the writing and subsequent reading of entries, as in Carol's class, was the basis of class discussions. Students commented that sharing entries about possible solutions to programming situations was helpful because it enabled them to see that there were many ways to "tackle a problem." Usually, however, the journal in Alex's class was *not* used to lead students to brainstorm approaches to problems; instead, it was used to get students to summarize material that had just been covered. During the brief oral sharing sessions after the writing, Alex rarely expanded on what students wrote. Typically he began a new topic or ended class sessions at those points. As a result, many of the journal-writing assignments were not well integrated into the class sessions. Even though a few students noted that such reading aloud was interesting, for most it was not particularly useful.

It seems, then, that the degree of integration of writing assignments with other class activities influenced the journal's effectiveness as a learning tool. When the teacher used journals as a structure for learning about course concepts and topics, and illustrated how learning from others during sharing sessions could be useful, students found journals helpful.

The specific times during class sessions when journal writing was assigned also had relevance. The integration of journal entries with class activities, as well as the usefulness of those entries, was more effective in both classes when the journal assignment occurred *before* discussion of a topic or *during* a problem-solving session, rather than at the conclusion of those activities. For PSY105, most in-class assignments fell into the former category; Carol asked students what they knew before she began a topic. She then built upon their responses to present new information; consequently, many students participated in the presentations/discussions and found the sessions helpful. Similarly, during the few times when Alex used in-class writing to brainstorm solutions so that journal entries formed the basis of the "trial and error" problem-solving sessions, the different approaches that students shared gave them new insights into problem solutions. It would appear that journal writing that required that students brainstorm, speculate, or scan prior knowledge before class discussion provided valuable occasions for discussion and information sharing — activities that, in turn, reinforced the importance of the journal's purposes and enhanced its usefulness.

Failures with Out-of-Class Journal Writing

When I examined a few students' out-of-class journals, I found that they contained many kinds of entries: expressions of feelings, opinions, and ideas; speculation and reflection on past activities; examination of areas of misunderstanding or difficulty; the integration of past knowledge with new information; the use of personal language. For example, John's entry illustrates his thinking about the first lab assignment:

Lab 1 (#2). This sort of thing can keep a person up at night. I've taken to carrying paper around with me in case I get a hot idea. I did today for the management of the calendar section.

Using 2 nested loops and a case statement to control the 3rd variable I can print the calendar! I will use a WRITE _____: VARIABLE and keep increasing the variable to follow the days. I will also use an array 1 ... 12 of JAN..DEC. to store the names of the months. I can use this in all sections (make it global) whenever I want to substitute the name for the #. Good—I can sleep tonight!

(John's Journal, for Lab #1, CP104)

In this entry, John alludes to the difficulty he is having solving problems and states one method he is using to "catch" ideas as they arise. He then goes on to outline what he did to solve one part of the lab problem, the one dealing with setting up a calendar. He used his previous knowledge of nested loops and combined it with newly learned information about case statements to set up the one-dimensional array to solve and print the calendar segment. John now has a record of this procedure and can refer to it for other sections of the problem whenever necessary. His thinking about the problem, rather than the teacher's thinking or a textbook, gives him a meaningful solution that he can repeat or alter as necessary.

When *all* entries from out-of-class assignments are examined and compared to all in-class entries, however, a major difference becomes obvious: most students did not complete out-of-class entries as instructed. The noncompletion of assignments was manifested in a variety of ways. In Carol's class, for example, students waited until the last minute to write journal entries; some wrote only particular parts, and others did not write them at all. The reflective thinking that Carol hoped students would do in the journal was often lost in the last-minute scramble to complete required assignments.

The lab entry/out-of-class component of the journal in CP104 was difficult for most students as well. Most did not write in the journal during problem solving, as Alex had instructed. Instead, they wrote entries *after* the programs had been finished or not at all, thereby eliminating the use of the journal as a way to think through problems. Thus, in both classes, except for a few students who completed journal entries as instructed, the use of the out-of-class journal as a critical thinking, reflective, and learning tool was of questionable value.

Several factors seemed to affect the noncompletion of assignments. One factor was the inadequate explanations that teachers gave students about the purposes of journal writing. Both teachers expected that students would write in journals on their own outside of class, and that such writing would further enhance learning of course content. For the out-of-class journal, Alex directed students to use their writing to reflect on their process of solving problems and to write about "stuck points" as they arose. He expected that reflecting on previous computer programs and principles would assist them in thinking through current programming problems. Carol, in contrast, directed students to do a variety of assignments in the at-home journal: writing about chapters in the text, pondering certain questions, writing critiques, and so on. Her intent was that students would draw upon their personal experience to make sense of the content while writing in these various modes; she hoped such writing would provide them with numerous opportunities to think about the content and how it related to their lives.

Yet neither teacher explicitly articulated these expectations for journal writing to the students. Carol, for example, didn't clearly vocalize the *ways* in which the journal would be useful. Alex mentioned generally that the journal would help students write programs and solve problems, but as in Carol's case, did not explain *how* the writing would serve that function. As a result, it seems that many students had difficulty discerning the teachers' intended purposes of the out-of-class journals, so they used their own notions of journal writing to complete assignments. For example, some students came to their classes with established definitions of journal writing. For them, the journal was like a diary — a place for writing feelings and expressing opinions. They believed that such writing had some value in one's personal life, but could not see how writing about feelings was related to learning. For example, when students in CP104 were asked at the end of the semester whether journal writing influenced or affected their learning of the material of the course, one student replied:

> No. What I was going to learn, I learned. I don't feel that putting my feelings on paper helped me with Pascal material at all. I didn't write in it all during my labs and I never referred to it. (Questionnaire #2, Maureen, CP104)

Another student responded similarly:

> Myself, I don't think it influenced or affected my learning of this material. This type of course is of a logical type and doesn't really need an opinion to help you understand it. (Questionnaire #2, Frank, CP104)

For both Maureen and Frank (and for other members of the class as well) journal writing was of little help in learning content; for them, journals were about feelings and opinions, which they felt had little to do with thinking or learning. Because of these perceptions of the journal as a repository for feelings and opinions, students relegated the completion of journal assignments to a low priority.

Other students' perceptions of the journal evolved during the semester. For example, perceptions of journal writing in CP104 were influenced by what the teacher said and did with journals. When Alex introduced the journal, he mentioned that journal writing, in general, was a tool that would help them focus on their learning. He also said it was a way that he could get feedback, and he told students, "You can let me know how you're feeling about things." Thereafter, he emphasized the "feedback" features of journal writing more than its learning capabilities. As a result of hearing journal writing referred to in this manner, many students believed that Alex assigned the journal in order to determine how they were progressing in the course and as a way for him to obtain feedback on his teaching. The student remarks below, given during end-of-semester interviews, capture this belief about the journal's purpose:

> I think the teacher cares for the student, and this [the journal] helps him to see the student's character. Because you express your character there. And it makes him understand the person that you are; he sees your reactions to this course. So, sometimes if he has made a mistake or something or this assignment was too hard, too abstract, or something, it makes him think, "Next time, I won't do it this way." or he may revise it. This helps a teacher to revise his work ... by seeing the students reaction. Helps the teacher to see how he can treat his students or he can relate to them." (Interview with Nick, CP104)

For Nick, the journal's main purpose is to help the teacher, not him. Believing that Alex was the primary beneficiary of the journal writing, most students like Nick, when they had time, used the journal to write personal communications to him and to give him feedback on the course. Yet they paid little attention to writing about their thinking and learning processes. Although many of the students felt that this type of writing was helpful for the teacher and for getting changes made in the course, the majority of these students did not view journal writing as necessarily helpful to *their* learning.

It seems that students' perceptions of the journal and the teachers' unexplained expectations for journal writing were instrumental in affecting the noncompletion of out-of-class assignments. Without a clear understanding of what journals were or what benefits they were to gain from them, students' own definitions of journal writing guided their responses to assignments. In most cases, however, those definitions detracted from the use of the journal as a thinking/learning tool.

Yet even for those few students who understood the teachers' purposes in assigning journals and wrote in them as instructed, finishing assignments appeared to be problematic. Both teachers reviewed journals only twice during the semester, and students generally found it a constant struggle to write on their own, without the benefit of frequent monitoring. It was easier for them to overlook the assignments, or procrastinate, than it was to begin. Although a journal gives students the freedom to write at their own pace, it also gives them the freedom to procrastinate, or not write at all. Journal entries that are put off or done at the last minute seldom allow for the level of thinking and reflection that journal writing can command.

Can Journal Writing Work?

The attributes accorded to journal writing give it great appeal as a learning tool; many teachers, myself included, want to help students with learning and thinking, and journal writing can be a way to do that. Yet from this study I learned that the successful incorporation of journals into the curriculum is not easy; further, journal writing can be difficult even for the most motivated students. I believe that journals *can* work as thinking, learning tools; journal assignments can help students make sense of what they read and hear, and can engage students with knowledge. But teachers who assign journals must first create the climate and conditions that enable reflective thinking and learning to occur. As this study of two teachers and their classrooms demonstrates, journal writing, to be effective, requires clear instructions, well-articulated expectations for learning, and careful integration with other course activities.

Works Cited

Berthoff, Ann E. "Dialectical Notebooks and the Audit of Meaning." *The Journal Book*. Ed. Toby Fulwiler. Portsmouth, NH: Boynton/Cook, 1987, 11–18.

Britton, James et al. *The Development of Writing Abilities (11–18)*. London: Macmillan Education, 1975.

Dewey, John. *Experience and Education*. New York: Macmillan, 1959.

Emig, Janet. "Writing as a Mode of Learning." *College Composition and Communication* 28 (1977): 122–28.

Freire, Paulo. *Pedagogy of the Oppressed*. New York: Continuum, 1970.

Fulwiler, Toby, ed. *The Journal Book*. Portsmouth, NH: Boynton/Cook, 1987.

Gere, Anne R., ed. *Roots in the Sawdust: Writing To Learn Across the Disciplines*. Urbana, IL: NCTE, 1985.

Goodkin, Vera. *The Intellectual Consequences of Writing:Writing as a Tool for Learning*. Diss. Rutgers, 1982. Ann Arbor: U of MI 1982, 8313441.

Herrington, Anne J. "Writing to Learn: Writing Across the Disciplines." *College English* 43 (1981): 379–87.

Langer, Judith A., and Arthur N. Applebee. *How Writing Shapes Thinking: A Study of Teaching and Learning*. Urbana, IL: NCTE, 1987.

Lawrence, Sandra M. "Journal Writing as a Tool for Learning in College Classrooms." Diss. Harvard Univ. 1988.

Moffett, James. *Active Voices IV*. Upper Montclair, NJ: Boynton/Cook, 1986.

Murray, Donald M. "First Silence, Then Paper." *fforum: Essays on Theory and Practice in the Teaching of Writing*. Ed. Patricia L. Stock. Portsmouth, NH: Boynton/Cook, 1983, 227–33.

North, Stephen M. "The Philosophical Journal: Three Case Studies." *The Journal Book*. Ed. Toby Fulwiler. Portsmouth, NH: Heinemann, 1987, 278–88.

Piaget, Jean. *The Language and Thought of the Child*. New York, New American Library, 1955.

Selfe, Cynthia et al. "Journal Writing in Mathematics." *Writing Across the Disciplines: Research into Practice*. Ed. Art Young and Toby Fulwiler. Portsmouth, NH: Boynton/Cook, 1986. 184–207.

Tchudi, Stephen. "The Hidden Agendas in Writing Across the Curriculum." *English Journal* 75 (1986): 22–25.

Tierney, Robert. "Using Expressive Writing to Teach Biology." *Two Studies of Writing in High School Science: Classroom Research Study No. 5*. Berkeley: Bay Area Writing Project, 1981.

Wotring, Ann. "Writing to Think About High School Chemistry." *Two Studies of Writing in High School Science: Classroom Research Study No. 5*. Berkeley: Bay Area Writing Project, 1981.

Vygotsky, Lev S. *Thought and Language*. Trans. Eugenia Hanfmann and Gertrude Vakar. Cambridge, MA: MIT Press, 1962.

12

Saturation Research: An Alternative Approach to the Research Paper

Carol Booth Olson

Picture this ... It's nearing the end of the semester and those research papers you felt honor-bound to assign are about to come due. Weeks ago, you sent your students off to the library, 3″ × 5″ cards in hand, and they have been busily collecting and organizing data on topics which they feel befit the seriousness of something as lofty and formal as the *research paper*. Ahead of you, you have twenty-two or thirty-six or forty-eight of these products to respond to.

Now, be honest. How do you *really* feel as you face the thought of an entire weekend — and then some — consumed by such questions as *Should we legislate gun control?* and *What is the impact of television on American society?*

Why is it that we have come to dread reading and responding to our students' research papers almost as much as they have come to dread writing them? Perhaps the answer to this question is rooted in the answer to another: *Is what we are asking the students to do in the name of "research" really research?* I think not. My sense is that what we have been asking students to do as they compose what Carol Jago, a UCLA Writing Project teacher/consultant, calls the Termpapasaurus Rex is to conduct research of research. That is, instead of being actively engaged in a genuine problem-solving and discovery process, many students merely analyze and restate the results of someone else's intellectual inquiry, an inquiry in which they may have no personal investment.

This picture of students passively summarizing someone else's in-depth investigation or experimentation gives rise to another question: *What are we teaching when we teach research of research?* If our goal is to foster critical thinking in our students and to encourage them to take what Anthony Petrosky calls a "speculative or questioning stance toward knowledge and experiences," then we may be doing them a disservice by teaching research of research (3). The nature and scope of most research topics that students elect to pursue, their lack of ownership in those topics, and the strict time constraints under which they must operate, relegate many students to "strip mining" for "veri-fiable information and facts," to use Petrosky's metaphor. There is little opportunity or incentive for reflection and interpretation. In fact, students are often not expected or encouraged to make their own meaning. The students' presumption, and sometimes the teacher's as well, is that the answers to their questions reside in something that is external to them, in the "findings" of someone else.

If the traditional research paper, as it is commonly taught, does not promote a spirit of reflection or foster our students' ability "to respond interpretively, to make sense of people, events, books and ideas" (Petrosky 3), then we must ask ourselves, *How can we frame assignments that enable and encourage students to select topics for research and inquiry in which they have a genuine personal stake and from which they can make their own meaning?*

What Is the Saturation Research Paper?

> It was 1849, the year I got my freedom. Mind you, it wasn't given to me. The only thing Master Ed and Miss Susan ever give me was a sore whippin' an' I's got scars an' callouses all over my stocky black body to show for it (Petry, 45). It weren't many a poor Negro slave that got freedom given to him, Lord no. He had to go on out and run to catch his freedom. Run faster and farther than he'd ever pray he'd run agin. And that's just what I did, that night in 1849 (Humphreville, 129).

So begins the transformation of Alyse Rome, a twenty-three-year-old, white teaching credential candidate at the University of California at Irvine into Harriet Tubman, an elderly black woman in Auburn, New York, looking back upon her escape from slavery in 1849 and her journey on the Underground Railroad *"Through Freedom's Gate"* — the title of Alyse's saturation research paper.

The saturation research paper gives students like Alyse a personal stake in research. It enables students to immerse themselves in a historical figure through library research, to select one significant incident in that person's life, and to bring that incident to life as if it were happening now — either by becoming that person and speaking through his or her voice or by becoming a witness to the event. I am indebted to my colleague Catherine D'Aoust, co-director of the UCI Writing Project, for sharing this concept at our Summer Institute on the Teaching of Composition. It was Catherine's description of the project, the uniqueness and the potential of her idea, the exemplary student models from El Toro High School in Saddleback Valley Unified School District from which she read excerpts, and her discussion of the powerful impact of the assignment on her students that convinced me to adapt and implement the saturation research paper.

In calling upon students to use library research to make their own meaning of a historical incident, the saturation research paper addresses a concern about research raised by Ken Macrorie. Macrorie has pointed out that the dictionary definition of research as a "patient study and investigation in some field of knowledge, undertaken to establish facts and principles" leaves out "the basic motivation for the whole effort" (162). I agree. It seems to me that the point of having students conduct research is not just to learn how to systematically collect, organize, and report data to establish facts and principles, but to experience some of the excitement of hunting for and grappling with that information to make their own connections and discover new insights. What we're after in the saturation research paper, then, is not just transmission but transaction. We want students to interact with the information they are compiling — not just to search but to re-search, to see anew.

But how does one help students to see anew? In "Reforming Your Teaching for Thinking," Dan Kirby remarks, "If you're going to develop your students as thinkers, you must begin to look at knowledge and knowing in new ways". He goes on to say, "This new view of knowledge doesn't mean you have nothing to teach students or that textbooks are no longer important or that old knowledge is no longer valuable. What it does mean is that we have to plan for and structure our classrooms in such a way that students construct their own versions of old knowledge in new and more personal ways." The saturation research paper offers students just such an opportunity to construct their own personalized versions of history by inviting them not only to step outside themselves to examine a moment in time through someone else's point of view, but to speculate about and articulate what that person might have thought, felt, and said. The word *might* is an important one here because although the student engages in a research process in order to write this paper, the product of that research is historical fiction. The writer's goal, simply put, is to bring history to life by turning it into literature.

Preparing Students to Write the Saturation Research Paper

In order to ensure that students put the most into and get the most out of their saturation research papers, I take them through a sequence of activities that will enable them to select a topic, conduct their research, organize their ideas, and write and revise their paper. Selected activities from that sequence are provided below.

Introducing the Saturation Research Paper

Because I believe that "think time" is crucial to letting a topic of genuine interest emerge for students, I let them know several weeks in advance that they will have an opportunity to saturate themselves in a historical figure who is of interest to them, choose a significant event in that person's life, and bring that event to life, as if it were happening now, either by becoming that person and speaking through his or her voice or by becoming a witness to the event. I stress that although their paper must be based upon and weave in factual information derived from their research, they will be writing historical fiction. They are to *approximate* what might have happened based upon the resources available and upon their own best speculative and reflective thinking. For example, much less is known about Harriet Tubman's escape from slavery than about the assassination of John F. Kennedy. However, in either case, the writer cannot know, with any certainty, what Harriet Tubman was thinking as her song rang out among the slave quarters to signal the hour of her escape; or what ran through Jacqueline Kennedy's mind as an assassin's bullet caught her husband in the temple and sent him reeling into her lap, his blood splattering her pink suit. What the writer can do is to create an interior monologue for the character that is plausible, given the circumstances and based upon what *is* known factually.

At this point, I pass out a list of key features of a saturation research paper, which I have adapted from Catherine D'Aoust. This list becomes the foundation for a scoring guide, based on a nine-point scale that I use as an evaluative tool.

A saturation research paper involves ...

- choosing a historical figure that you can saturate yourself in through library research (and firsthand sources, if available);
- selecting one significant event in that person's life to dramatize as if it were happening now, either by becoming that person and speaking through his or her voice or by becoming a witness to the event; and

- weaving factual information together with fictional techniques such as dialogue, interior monologue, and showing-not-telling description that reflect your best speculative and reflective thinking in order to bring that event to life and to create a *you are there* feeling in the reader.

The most effective saturation research papers will ...

- demonstrate that the writer has genuinely "saturated" himself or herself in the historical figure;
- highlight an event in that person's life that is clearly significant;
- adopt a discernible point of view that is consistent throughout the narrative;
- capture the event in present tense, as if it were happening now, using past tense if and where appropriate;
- display insight into and critical thinking about that person and convey judgments and opinions about that person through showing rather than telling;
- weave accurate, factual information derived from library research together with sensory/descriptive details about setting, character-ization, and plot in order to create a *you are there* feeling in the reader;
- reveal the person's thoughts and feelings through dialogue, interior monologue, use of showing-not-telling description, use of symbol-ism, and other fictional/cinematic techniques, such as flashback;
- document sources with parenthetical references and a list of works cited;
- vary sentence structure and length; and
- use the conventions of written English effectively (spelling, punctu-ation, grammar, sentence structure, dialogue form, etc.)

Finding a Topic

One good way to help students identify a historical figure who is of genuine interest to them is to ask them to cluster the names of people they can recall from their history classes, from independent reading, from current events, or from conversations with friends, and then to free write about the names they come up with. These activities often help students not only to recall names of historical figures but to get in touch with their own values and preoccupations. For example, through her cluster, reproduced on the next page, Alyse Rome found out early on that she was attracted to individuals of culturally diverse background who have fought against oppression and to strong women who can serve as positive role models. She combined these interests in her choice of Harriet Tubman.

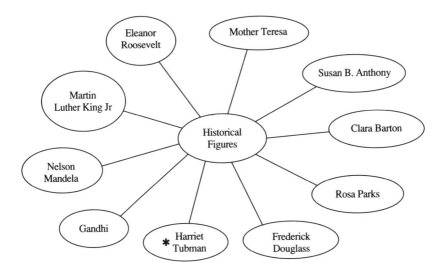

The idea of exposing students to cultures and races other than that of the white Anglo Saxon Protestant majority of Middle America really appeals to me. Especially because of the current emphasis on multicultural education in the classroom, it's important to know how all the cultures represented here in America contributed to our history. So, I guess I'm getting clear that it's someone who figures in U.S. history that I want to focus on.

Equally important to me is the concern I share with many others about the lack of historical data on great women leaders and shapers of history. I feel it is necessary to offer more positive role models (not simply more of the proverbial victim) for girls and women of the world to emulate.

I think maybe Harriet Tubman, from what little I know about her, is the kind of strong woman whose story all the kids in the classes I'll be teaching could learn from.

After students have let the possibilities for this report percolate for a week or two, I provide them with several student models to read and discuss in class. It is important for students to see how a range of papers are structured and to explore the literary strategies the writers use to portray their historical figure and bring the event to life. From one perspective, the saturation research paper is an exercise in problem solving. Exposing students to multiple approaches to solving a problem — in this case, of how to dramatize history — as they are devising their own, broadens their options. In Alyse's paper, for example, students notice how she uses the point of view of the elderly Harriet Tubman as a framing device to flash back to a pivotal event in her life — her escape from slavery. They comment upon the effectiveness of her use of black dialect and the immediacy and the poignancy of the dialogue. And they are able to trace the pictures they formed in their own minds as they heard the narrative back to her rich use of sensory/descriptive language, and the way she shows rather than tells about the feelings of her character by using figurative language. (The complete text of Alyse's paper is appended to this essay.)

Becoming the Object of Your Research

After students have selected a historical figure to saturate themselves in and have a good feel for what the saturation research paper entails, they need several weeks not just to conduct their research but to walk around in their character's shoes, so to speak, in order to take on their persona. In *Forms of Intellectual and Ethical Development in the College Years*, William Perry notes that one sign of cognitive growth is the ability to move from the stage of *basic duality*, in which the world is perceived in absolutes; through the stage of *multiplicity*, in which one recognizes that there is more than one approach to an idea, problem, or issue; and finally to the advanced stages of *relativism* and *commitment*, which include the ability to negotiate with uncertainty, consider alternatives, and commit to one's choices (57–176). The saturation research paper can assist students as they move along this developmental continuum from concrete and somewhat simplistic to more abstract and complex thinking, because it requires that they make what is simultaneously a cognitive and an affective leap: they must decenter to assume someone else's point of view and to *become* subjectively the object of their research. This requires a high degree of empathy on the part of the student and a great deal of knowledge — both about the subject and about the craft of writing.

Since most students choose historical figures who are long since deceased, they have to rely on library books and their own imaginations as resources. I encourage them, however, to research and take advantage of whatever other sources of information are available. For example, Alyse checked out an audiotape of the book *To Be A Slave*, featuring readings of slave narratives by famous African American actors. She also watched a videotape about Harriet Tubman from the television news series, "You Are There." These auditory and visual aids helped her not only to develop Harriet's character but also to capture the black dialect that she felt would lend authenticity to her piece. In the metacognitive learning log entry that Alyse wrote after completing her paper, she described the process she went through to bring Harriet Tubman to life:

> I had to think about how a black slave woman in the mid-nineteenth century would have sounded, appeared, thought, felt, lived, and acted. I not only thought about what it would be like to be the person, Harriet

Tubman, but about the history and the setting. I tried to imagine the time and place, the plantation grounds in Maryland, the feel of the air, the lighting, the sounds, the smells, the danger . . .

In order to include the relationship between Harriet and her brothers, I had to learn as much as I could about the slaves' family lives in general, as I found little specific reference to Harriet's family in my research. From there, I created the relationship between Harriet and her brothers for the purpose of writing my flashback. Since I could find nothing written about the circumstances of the escape but I did find evidence that Harriet came back to help her brothers escape, I had to invent my scene, making it as lifelike as possible.

Only after I totally "saturated" myself in all these details did I feel capable of writing my paper. If I hadn't thought and felt my way through all of this, I would have felt I was cheating both myself and my audience and my paper would have, subsequently, suffered.

Notice that Alyse had to empathize with Harriet Tubman's plight, assume her point of view, "negotiate" with her own uncertainty about the circumstances of the escape, and consider a variety of approaches to creating her scene before she could write her paper. Her process was both cognitive and affective. As she says, "I . . . thought and felt my way through all of this."

Prewriting for the Saturation Research Paper

While students are conducting their research, I take them through a series of brief, guided exercises that enable them to practice some of the thinking and writing tasks called for in the assignment. For example, in order to help students make a connection between their own lives and the life of their chosen character, I ask them to think about a significant moment in their personal history — something that was a watermark of some kind and left a lasting impression — and to cluster and free write about it. Then, to provide practice in decentering and in point of view, I ask them to put their free writes away and to tell their significant event to a partner. (*Note: Students need to be told in advance that they will be sharing these pieces with a partner.*) The partner, after listening carefully, must re-create in writing the event he or she has just listened to. To do this it is necessary to become the person who has just told the story and to assume his or her voice. Building upon James Moffett's discourse schema, which progresses from "immediate subjects of small time-space scope to remote subjects far flung in time and space" (12), this practice in adopting the persona of a known subject helps students make the transition to becoming someone they can come to know only secondhand.

In order to prepare students to show the incident in their historical figure's life and not just to tell about it, I expose them to a variety of showing-not-telling activities, including a trust walk. During this walk, each student is blindfolded and experiences deprivation of sight and also guides a blindfolded student. After the walk, the students cluster the sensations and feelings they have associated with the word *blind*, and then write a sensory/descriptive paragraph to show the telling sentence, *"Being blind was _____,"* after adding their descriptor of choice, such as *"scary," "disorienting," "enlightening."* After students have internalized the concept of showing, not telling, I ask them to write a telling sentence that will capture some central message they would like to convey about their historical figure and to show that telling sentence in a paragraph. For Alyse, it was Harriet Tubman's determination to secure her freedom that stood out.

> **Telling sentence: Harriet Tubman was determined to gain her freedom**
>
> I slipped out of the cabin into the shelter of darkness, my teeth clamped so tightly in my jaws, they set my ears to ringing. The whisper-like sound of the wind sweeping through the branches of the cypresses stirred my nerves, but my mind refused to hear the echoes of fear which rattled nerves shook loose in my body.
>
> The wind seemed to blow harder, pushing me back toward my cramped cell-of-a-cabin. With a violent shiver, I pulled my tattered coat closer to my body, lowered my head and pushed forward into the wind — each step driving me into the next. I could feel my desire for freedom stronger than ever now, for I knew that each step forward meant one step closer to that great Promised Land in the North. Couldn't stop now . . . I could almost feel my hand pushing open Freedom's Gate . . .

These show-not-tell descriptions often provide students with the focus and the point of departure they need to begin writing their papers.

Writing and Sharing the Saturation Research Paper

Because I have found that students benefit more from receiving feedback during the writing process than after they have completed a final product, and because getting off to a good start is so critical to the success of a paper, I ask them to write an opening page or scene of their paper which is read around silently in class and commented upon in a two-minute "quick write" by at least eight other students. This reading around allows students to see the strategies that eight other writers used to set the stage for their historical incident; to receive eight quick writes on what in their own opening page or scene engaged their readers' attention and what questions, concerns, advice or encouragement those readers have regarding the remainder of the piece; and to meet in small groups to discuss and list key features of an effective opening of a saturation research paper. This preliminary feedback

validates some students and sends others back to the drawing board —
but at a stage where they are usually still willing to consider making
adjustments.

About a week after this first set of responses, student drafts are
scored by three of their peers, using the response sheet reproduced in
Figure 1.

This "in-progress" score that my students receive from their peers
has a dramatic effect on the final products I receive one week later. It
gives students a chance to find out where they stand on a 1–9 point
scale *before* their final draft is due for evaluation, to think about why
their paper received the score it did, to seek advice from writing group
partners and from me, and to hone and refine their work.

Reading Saturation Research Papers

Picture this ... It's nearing the end of the semester and those
saturation research papers that you decided to assign as an experiment
are about to come due. Weeks ago, you sent your students off to the
library, 3″ × 5″ cards in hand, and they have been busily collecting,
reflecting upon, interpreting, and constructing their versions of the
data as they figure out how to assume the persona and consciousness
of another human being during a pivotal time in that person's life.
Ahead of you, you have twenty-two or thirty-six or forty-eight of
these products to respond to.

As you face the thought of an entire weekend — and then some —
consumed in reliving significant moments in the lives and minds of
Charles Darwin, Amelia Earhart, Dorothea Lange, Mark Twain,
Marie Curie, Abraham Lincoln, Sacajawea, the cave painters of
Lascaux, Ethel Rosenberg, Jackie Robinson, Joan of Arc, and more,
you find yourself genuinely looking forward to receiving these papers
and taking them home to read and evaluate.

Why is it that the saturation research paper is so engaging to
students and teachers alike? Although I am already aware of how
powerful this assignment is, I never cease to be surprised and impressed
by the richness, depth, and quality of my students' writing. It strikes
me that what prompts students to stretch intellectually and inspires
them to produce some of their finest work is as much affective as
cognitive in nature. Anthony Petrosky points out that "reflective thinking
has its source in our interpretive encounters with experiences" (2). The
saturation research paper is not just a research paper; it is an interpretive
encounter. Students must take what they learn from secondary sources
and then look within to see history anew. They must make their own
meaning. And, in the process, they make personal connections with
the subjects of their research that often leave lasting impressions upon
them. These impressions, in turn, can inspire them to take the kind of

Figure 1

Saturation Research Paper

To the author of _____. We gave the first draft of your Saturation Research paper a score of _____.

	Excellent	Pretty Good	Needs Improvement
You clearly saturated yourself in your historical person.			
You highlighted an event in your person's life that was clearly significant and displayed insight into the person and the event.			
As readers, we felt like we were there.			
You wore your facts into your narrative well.			
Your paper is well crafted and uses different fictional/ cinematic techniques.			
You use showing writing to dramatize your character's moments and to convey your judgments and opinions.			
You use ample citations from research sources.			
You have few, if any, errors in the conventions of written English.			
What we liked best about your paper was ...			
You might want to consider the following suggestions when you revise ...			

"speculative or questioning stance toward knowledge and experiences" that Petrosky calls for, a stance that can ultimately lead them to the "commitment" that Perry identifies as a sign of cognitive maturity. Perhaps Alyse Rome's final reflection about her interaction with Harriet Tubman demonstrates this best:

> In researching the life of Harriet Tubman, I found that the more I discovered about her emotional life, her feelings, motivations and thoughts, the more she was transformed from simply a character in what seemed like a fascinating fiction into a living, breathing human being. I learned to respect Harriet for her incredible strength, courage and her determination and through studying accounts of the daily abuse and injustice suffered by her and the other slaves, I gained an appreciation of how dire circumstances can lead someone to such daring acts of bravery.
>
> I could not help but feel a deep empathy as I immersed myself further and further into accounts of her life. Ultimately, it was as if I had shared in her hardship and her joy. I found myself rejoicing at the glorious triumph of an oppressed spirit rising up and prevailing against overwhelming odds.
>
> Above all, Harriet Tubman has taught me what a true sense of social responsibility and commitment to a cause can bring. Her actions teach that we must continue to fight for the causes in which we believe. How secure are my personal freedoms when those of my sisters and brothers have been denied?

Appendix

Through Freedom's Gate: A Saturation Research Paper
by Alyse Rome

It was 1849, the year I got my freedom. Mind you, it wasn't given to me. The only thing Master Ed and Miss Susan ever give me was a sore whippin', an' I's got scars an' callouses all over my stocky black body to show for it (Petry, 5). It weren't many a poor Negro slave that got freedom given to him. Lord no. He had to go on out and run to catch his freedom. Run faster and farther than he ever did from Master's whip. Faster and farther than he'd ever pray he'd run agin. And that's just what I did, that night in 1849 (Humphreville, 129).

I had reasoned this out in my mind, after hearin' those forbidden stories whispered agin and agin, quietly around the fire—stories of the slave revolt brought on by Nat Turner (Jackson, 121; Stoddard, 422) and of the runaways ridin' to freedom on the Underground Railroad. I figured they was one of two things I had a right to: liberty or death. If I could not have one, I would have the other. No man should take Harriet Tubman alive. I should fight for my liberty as long as my strength lasted; and when the time came for me to go, the Lord would let them take me (Sterling, 60).

It was my visions and my faith in the Lord that got me through that first time, and the times after (Heidish, 305). The gash on my forehead, from the two-pound weight that nasty overseer done throw at me when I was fifteen, may have counted for somethin' after all (Jackson, 12). My sleepin' spells, when I'd black out and see my visions were a 'cause of that gash. Mebbe it was the Lord's way of speakin' to me.

1849 .... I'd been brewin' in my head how I's to get out. Brewin' an' thinkin' till I thought I'd bust. My brothers, Benjamin and William knew what I was schemin' (Sterling, 59). It was only at the very last minute that they changed their plannin' to come with me. The very last minute ....

> "I's bound for de Promised Land.
> Friends, I's gwine to leave you.
> I'm sorry, friends, to leave you.
> Farewell Oh, farewell" (Sterling, 63).

My hoarse-soundin' voice floated through the still night air (Humphreville, inside book jacket) softly signalin' to the cabins in the slave quarter that this was the time, the time I'd told em' all about. The time Harriet Tubman was finally gwine to leave them and catch the Freedom train.

"Shh, William. Listen! ... That'd be Hatt. You ready?" Benjamin stuffed the last bit of ashcake and salt herring in his makeshift satchel while he waited for brother Will to answer (Heldish, p. 96). William stood for a piece, as if he was waitin' for a sign from God. Finally, he grunted.

"Uh ya. I's ready."

They pulled their satchels over their shoulders and slipped silently out of their cramped cabin into the shadowless black of the moonless night. The sparklin' stars above were the only light they had to lead their way to Freedom's door.

They reached the meetin' place in the boneyard, between the meadow and the swamplands (Heidish, 4, 132). I slipped out of the thick shelter of nearby trees and demanded,

"Le's move it! They's no time to waste!" (Heidish, 12). We held tightly to our satchels, which held the necessities of life we would need to see us through the long journey, Lord willin'. Lord knows when the next chance for a real meal and a warm bed might come.

Silently, we ran through the cool, damp grass of the pasture till we reached the thickened stand of trees which signaled the beginning of the forest land.

William was the first to break the silence, as his thoughts turned from freedom to danger.

"Ssst! Hold on," he whispered hoarsely. "I thinks I hears somethin'."

Benjamin and I stopped, an' turned to face William. We listened, 'spectin' to hear the hoofbeats of the patroller's horses comin' at us from behind. We heard nothin' but the cool breeze rattlin' the leaves around us.

"Will!" I gritted through my teeth. "We cain't be stoppin' every minute to be listenin' to your fool 'magin's! Now le's move!"

'Ventually, my brothers did come North with me, as did Ol' Rit an' Ben, my mama n' papa, even though by then, they was well into their eighties (Smith, Jeffers, 41).

I worked for the Northern army durin' the War, as both a spy an' a nurse, on account of I knew the Southern territory better than most of the commandin' generals. I's been told I was the first Negro to be allowed to join the army, and I was the only woman to fight on the battlefield. I guess I did all right. The only thing that bothered ol' Hatt was my long skirts gettin' in the way, as we marched Southward into battle (Petry, 227). Lord, sometimes I thinks I was meant to be a man 'riginally.

This here house I lives in now, I built from money I got workin' as a cleanin' woman (Harding, 153) and I brought Ol' Rit n' Ben here to Auburn, New York, to live out their last years (Smith, Jeffers, 41). It shore was a blessin' from God, them livin' their final days here in peace, knowin' they was free at last. An' Lord willin', I 'spect that is 'xactly what I'm a goin' to do here, too.

List of Works Cited

Harding, Vincent. *There is a River*. New York: Harcourt Brace Jovanovich, 1981.

Heidish, Marcy. *A Woman Called Moses*. Boston: Houghton Mifflin, 1976.

Humphreville, Frances T. *Harriet Tubman, Flame of Freedom*. Boston: Houghton Mifflin, 1967.

Jackson, George F. *Black Women Makers of History: A Portrait*. Oakland: Jackson, 1985.

Petry, Ann. *Harriet Tubman, Conductor on the Underground Railroad*. New York: Crowell, 1955.

Smith, Senator Margret Chase, and H. Paul Jeffers. *Gallant Women*. New York: McGraw-Hill, 1968.

Sterling, Dorothy. *Freedom Train*. New York: Doubleday, 1954.

Stoddard, Hope. *Famous American Women*. New York: Crowell, 1970.

Works Cited

Kirby, Dan. "Reforming Your Teaching for Thinking: The Studio Approach." *Practical Ideas for Teaching Writing as a Process*, Ed. Carol Booth Olsen. Sacramento, CA: California State Department of Education, 1992. Revised edition in press.

Macrorie, Ken. *Searching Writing*. Portsmouth, NH: Boynton/Cook, 1984.

Moffett, James. *Active Voice*. Portsmouth NH: Boynton/Cook, 1981.

Perry, William. *Forms of Intellectual and Ethical Development in the College Years*. New York: Holt, Rinehart and Winston, 1970.

Petrosky, Anthony. "Critical Thinking: *Qu'est-ce que c'est?*" *The English Record*. 37.3 (1986): 2–5.

Annotated Bibliography

An ERIC search for works discussing critical thinking and writing yielded 459 items between 1982 and September, 1991; obviously it would be redundant — and not very helpful — to repeat them all. What follows is a selective list of sources that consider the connection between writing and holistic critical thinking. Textbooks are not included, nor are discussions of pedagogy that do not emphasize college teaching. Many issues which impinge closely on critical thinking (e.g., literacy, developmental theory) are also omitted, as are basic works on critical thinking that do not connect it to writing. For sources in these areas, consult the Works Cited pages of the relevant chapters. A useful source for relevant empirical studies is the annotated annual bibliography of *Research in the Teaching of English*, which includes in its classification system the category "Writing and Learning."

Activities to Promote Critical Thinking. Classroom Practices in Teaching English. Evanston, IL: NCTE, 1986.
   A collection of teaching ideas to encourage "significant thinking" in students of all ages. Subjects include metaphor, sentences, thesis statements, protocol analysis, conference techniques, collaboration, logic, and writing within particular disciplines.

Applebee, Arthur N. "Writing and Reasoning." *Review of Educational Research.* 54 (1984): 577–96.
   Critiques the degree to which research to date has assumed, rather than examined or empirically documented, the connection between writing and reasoning, on both a cultural and an individual level.

Bean, John. "Summary Writing, Rogerian Listening, and Dialectical Thinking." *College Composition and Communication* 37 (1986): 343–46.
   Explains how a summary-writing sequence can reduce egocentrism and promote dialectical thinking.

Bizzell, Patricia. "Cognition, Convention, and Certainty: What We Need to Know about Writing." *Pre/Text* 3 (1982): 213–43.
   Critiques as incomplete the "inner-directed" approach to thinking and writing described by cognitive and information-processing models, and advocates supplementing this approach with the "outer-directed" models of sociolinguistics and discourse analysis.

Britton, James. *Prospect and Retrospect: Selected Essays of James Britton.* Ed. Gordon M. Pradl. Montclair, NJ: Boynton/Cook, 1982.

Britton's influential theory of expressive writing as the matrix that nourishes both transactional and poetic writing supports the connection between writing and many kinds of thinking, including ordering, reflection, and meaning making.

Brookfield, Stephen D. *Developing Critical Thinkers: Challenging Adults To Explore Alternative Ways of Thinking and Acting.* San Francisco: Jossey-Bass, 1987.
Organized into three topics: what critical thinking is, (a useful and thorough summary of definitions from many sources), how people can be helped to become critical thinkers, and how to develop critical thinking in specific contexts. Describes techniques for teaching critical thinking to adult learners in ways that relate to life experiences.

Bruner, Jerome. *Toward a Theory of Instruction.* Cambridge, MA: Harvard University Press, 1966.
Discusses the relationship between thinking, language, and writing, particularly as it relates to teaching.

Carter, Michael. "Problem Solving Reconsidered: A Pluralistic Theory of Problems." *College English* 50 (1988): 551–65.
Traces disagreements between the information-processing and the epistemic models of the thinking-writing connection to two conflicting problem theories, and describes a "pluralistic theory of problems" as the grounds for consensus.

Coe, Richard M. "If Not to Narrow, Then How to Focus: Two Techniques for Focusing." *College Composition and Communication* 32 (1981): 272–77.
Discusses the oversimplification that may result from confusing narrowing with focusing; proposes instead a dialectic method (find two conflicting statements and figure out how to accommodate them), which also promotes Dewey's "attitude of suspended solution."

Collins, James L. "Speaking, Writing, and Teaching for Meaning." *Exploring Speaking-Writing Relationships.* Ed. Barry Kroll and Roberta Vann. Evanston, IL: NCTE, 1981. 198–214.
Sees the need for writing teachers to emphasize "the meaning latent in language" because of the semantic and developmental distinctions between speaking and writing.

Comley, Nancy. "Review: Critical Thinking/Critical Teaching." *College English* 51 (1989): 623–27.
A review of five texts about critical thinking, which also summarizes current thought about the role of writing in critical thinking.

Dewey, John. *How We Think.* Boston: D.C. Heath, 1933.
The original source of the term *critical thinking*, and a thorough discussion of some of its synonyms and its pedagogical implications.

Dilworth, Collett B. *Critical Thinking and the Experience of Literature.* ERIC, 1985, ED 266 477.
Identifies *contrasting* as the most fundamental component of critical thinking, then shows how students can use reader's journals to contrast their understanding of a text with the text's assumed coherence.

Dinkelman, Todd. "Critical Thinking and Educational Reform in the 1980's." *Illinois Schools Journal* 69 (1990): 5–14.

Looks in detail at three educational reform proposals (*A Nation at Risk, High School,* and *An Imperiled Generation Saving Urban Schools*) and concludes that they contain "little substantive emphasis on the development of critical thinking."

Dowst, Kenneth. "The Epistemic Approach: Writing, Knowing and Learning." *Eight Approaches to Teaching Composition.* Ed. Timothy Donovan and Ben McClelland. Urbana, IL: NCTE, 1980, 65–85.

Explains the connection between writing and thinking that underlies epistemic rhetoric, and draws examples from student writing.

Emig, Janet. "Writing as a Mode of Learning." 1977. *The Web of Meaning.* Ed. Dixie Goswami and Maureen Butler. Montclair, NJ: Boynton/Cook. 123–31.

Explores the ways in which writing, which Emig describes as "not merely valuable, not merely special, but unique" as a form of learning, exhibits the characteristics common to all powerful learning strategies.

Farris, Christine. *Using Literature to Encourage Academic Thinking in a Basic Writing Course.* ERIC, 1985, ED 266 486.

Describes a course that uses Purves four steps in responding to literature "to broaden, deepen, and sharpen students' critical thinking" and to "draw them into wider and wider public and academic world views."

Flower, Linda, and John Hayes. "Images, Plans, and Prose: The Representation of Meaning in Writing." *Written Communication* 1 (1984): 120–60.

The best-known proponents of the information-processing model of writing examine from three perspectives (philosophical, cognitive, process-oriented) the question, "How can we describe the form of thinking called writing?" The "multiple-representation thesis" is proposed as a frame for investigating the movements from thought to formal prose.

Goodkin, V. *The Intellectual Consequences of Writing as a Tool for Learning.* Diss. Rutgers U, 1982.

Reports the results of an ethnographic case study of a writing classroom, using journals, logbooks, notes, reaction papers, and in-class writings; concludes that writing is particularly important in abstracting and making connections.

Gregg, Lee W., and Erwin R. Steinberg, eds. *Cognitive Processes in Writing.* Hillsdale, NJ: Erlbaum, 1980.

A collection that originated in the 1978 Carnegie-Mellon symposium of psychologists, English teachers, and linguists; heavily weighted towards the information-processing model of writing.

Hahn, Stephen. "Counter-Statement: Using Written Dialogue to Develop Critical Thinking and Writing." *College Composition and Communication* 38 (1987): 97–100.

Asserts that students' critical thinking skills improve when they practice written dialogue, a form that combines exposition, analysis, and argumentation, and that addresses their tendency to "under-conceptualize the context in which controversy occurs."

Hays, Janice N. "Socio-Cognitive Development and Argumentative Writing: Issues and Implications from One Research Project." *Journal of Basic Writing* 7.2 (1988): 42–67.
Studies the connection between cognitive maturity and effective argumentative writing, and concludes that accommodation to a hostile audience is closely related to more advanced levels of cognitive development.

———. "Intellectual Parenting and a Developmental Feminist Pedagogy of Writing." *Feminine Principles and Women's Experience in American Composition and Rhetoric.* Ed. Janet Emig and Louise W. Phelps. Pittsburgh: Pittsburgh University Press. In press.
Applies general principles of developmental instruction to the teaching of writing, incorporating a feminist pedagogy.

Hays, Janice N. et al., eds. *The Writer's Mind: Writing as a Mode of Thinking.* Urbana, IL: NCTE, 1983.
A collection originating in and named after the 1980 conference at Skidmore sponsored by the New York College English Association Information processing, epistemic, and social constructionist approaches are represented.

Herrington, Ann, and Deborah Cadman. "Peer Review and Revising in an Anthropology Course: Lessons in Learning." *College Composition and Communication* 42 (1991): 184–99.
Shows how peer reviewing promotes decision-making and other critical thinking skills more effectively than can be accomplished by teacher response to student writing.

Hollis, Karyn. "Building a Context for Critical Literacy: Student Writers as Critical Theorists." *The Writing Instructor* 7 (1988): 122–30.
Gives a thorough summary of the controversy about literacy and its connection to higher-order thinking skills; describes Hollis's own efforts to build critical thinking and writing skills through a course based on Raymond Geuss's Idea of a Critical Theory, which gives students "the epistemological tools they need to discover and analyze the ideological basis of institutionalized inequalities."

Hubbuch, Susan. "The Writer's Stance: An Exploration of Context in Invention and Critical Thinking." *Journal of Advanced Composition* 10 (1990): 73–86.
Uses Hubbuch's experience as a writing center tutor to examine the phenomenon of "intellectual vertigo," a difficulty students often encounter when attempting to assume "the writer's stance" with its necessity to encompass a specific vantage point.

Kiniry, Malcolm, and Ellen Strenski. "Sequencing Expository Writing: A Recursive Approach." *College Composition and Communication* 36 (1985): 191–202.
Describes a UCLA course designed to prepare freshmen for college writing; presents a sequence of writing assignments as "problem-solving exercises of gradually increasing difficulty," which "stretch what is at first a relatively mechanical skill to make it a versatile instrument."

Kirby, Dan, and Carol Kuykendall. *Mind Matters: Teaching for Thinking.* Portsmouth, NH: Boynton/Cook, 1991.
This interactive, participatory book, which is based on the belief that "real learning theorists live in classrooms." offers illustrations, models, and suggestions for a critical thinking pedagogy, but encourages readers to develop their own materials and course material.

Kurfiss, Joanne G. *Critical Thinking: Theory, Research, Practice, and Possibilities.* ASHE-ERIC Higher Education Report No. 2. Washington, D.C.: Association for the Study of Higher Education, 1988.
Describes the three basic approaches to critical thinking (logical, cognitive, and epistemic), examines the strengths and weaknesses of each, then discusses pedagogical implications and recent efforts to implement critical thinking on an institutional level.

Lagana, J.R. *The Development, Implementation, and Evaluation of a Model for Teaching Composition Which Utilizes Individual Learning and Peer Grouping.* Diss. U Pittsburgh, 1973.
Concludes that writing students who work in groups develop stronger critical thinking skills than students who work alone.

Lamb, Catherine E. "Beyond Argument in Feminist Composition." *College Composition and Communication* 42 (1991): 11–25.
Recommends mediation techniques as a basis for teaching argumentation; such mediation encourages the multiple perspectives required of critical thinking.

Larson, Richard. "Problem-Solving, Composing, and Liberal Education." *College English* 33 (1972): 628–35.
Argues that if composition teachers are to promote the aims of liberal education, they should use problem-solving as heuristics, organizing principles, and analytic tools.

Lauer, Janice. "Writing as Inquiry and Some Questions for Teachers." *College Composition and Communication* 33 (1982): 89–93.
Reviews several recent studies of the inquiry process (Lonergan, Piaget, Festinger, Rothenburg, Wallas) and poses questions that composition teachers should ask themselves about their goals and methods.

Maimon, Elaine, Barbara Nodine, and Finbarr O'Connor. eds. *Thinking, Reasoning, and Writing.* New York: Longman, 1989.
An anthology examining the thinking-writing connection from the vantage points of logic, psychology, and composition theory. Composition theorists include Bruffee, Flower, Kinneavy, and Maimon. Information-processing, epistemic, semiotic, and social constructionist approaches are represented by some of their most eloquent proponents.

Marble, Meredith. "A Critical Thinking Heuristic for the Argumentative Essay." *Rhetoric Society Quarterly* 16.2 (1986): 67–78.
Shows how similarities between critical thinking and current composition theory suggest heuristics for argumentation.

Matthews, Dorothy, ed. *On Teaching Critical Thinking. Cognitive Strategies*

for Teaching: Poetry, Short Story, Composition, the Research Paper, Critical Reading. Urbana, IL: Illinois Assn. of Teachers of English, 1986.
A special issue of the Illinois English Bulletin, with an admirably self-explanatory title.

McPeck, John. *Critical Thinking and Education.* New York: St. Martin's, 1981.
A philosopher's explanation of why critical thinking is not a generalizable skill, let alone a set of subskills, and why it must be taught in connection with a discipline or context.

Meyers, Chet. *Teaching Students To Think Critically.* San Francisco, Jossey-Bass, 1986.
Employs a holistic approach, and concludes that critical thinking must be taught within a discipline; thoughtful recommendations for teaching.

Newkirk, Thomas. *Critical Thinking and Writing: Reclaiming the Essay.* ERIC/RCS and NCTE, 1989.
Examines the limitations of the "school essay," a simplified version of the classical argumentative form defending a position, as opposed to the personal essay, which leaves room for "the art of wondering" and encourages reflection. Recommends that open-ended assignments (e.g., reading narrative, reflective essay, parallel narrative) be added to the composition classroom.

Nystrand, Martin, ed. *Language as a Way of Knowing.* Symposium Series No. 8. Ontario: Ontario Language Institute for Studies in Education, 1977.
Contributors (including Bruner, Ornstein, Polanyi, Kuhn, and Britton) share a psycholinguistic approach, through which they explore the assumption that language is "a unique and powerful strategy for knowing."

Odell, Lee. "Piaget, Problem-Solving, and Freshman Composition." *College Composition and Communication* 24 (1973): 36−42.
Describes a writing/problem-solving class at the University of Michigan, and argues that problem-solving belongs in the writing classroom because problem-solving skills are required of successful readers and writers.

———. "The Process of Writing and the Process of Learning." *College Composition and Communication* 31 (1980): 42−50.
As a response to colleagues in other disciplines interested in using writing to help their students learn, Odell scrutinizes particular writing tasks to see what conceptual activities they require.

Petrosky, Anthony. "Critical Thinking: Qu'est-ce Que C'est?" *The English Record* 37.3 (1986): 2−5.
Argues for holistic critical thinking as an approach to both ill-structured and well-structured problems; describes the pedagogical implications of holistic critical thinking.

Pollard, Rita, ed. *The English Record* 23.3 (1986).
A special issue consisting of articles that examine reading/writing/thinking/learning connections.

Quinn, Mary. *Critical Thinking and Writing: An Approach to the Teaching of Composition.* Diss. U of Michigan, 1983.
    Uses developmental instruction principles to generate "conscious and learnable methods by which students can learn to deal with the inevitability of change that thinking creates"; proposes four rhetorical heuristics (form, purpose, audience, and arrangement) to guide thinking in writing courses.

Resnick, Lauren. *Education and Learning to Think.* Washington, D.C.: National Academy Press, 1987.
    Reports on research conducted by the Committee on Mathematics, Science, and Technology Education, the Commission on Behavioral and Social Sciences and Education, and the Educational Research Council; concludes that higher-order thinking skills are best taught in conjunction with a discipline, rather than in a separate course.

Rosen, Joan. "Problem-Solving and Reflective Thinking: John Dewey, Linda Flower, Richard Young." *Journal of Teaching Writing* 6.1 (1987): 69–78.
    Looks at three formulations of the process of inquiry (Dewey's reflective thinking, Young's tagmemics, and Flower and Haye's problem solving), all of which define it as a way of dealing with incongruity.

Salvatori, Mariolina. "The Teaching of Writing as 'Problematization.'" *Teacher Education Quarterly* 10 (1983): 38–57.
    Investigates important theoretical and pedagogical connections between critical thinking and recent poststructuralist ideas about knowledge, meaning, and text.

Scribner, Sylvia, and Michael Coles. "Literacy Without Schooling." *Harvard Educational Review* 48 (1978): 448–61.
    Distinguishes between literacy and schooling in terms of their effects on higher-order reasoning skills. Concludes from a study of members of the Vai tribe that literate subjects demonstrated no significant differences in any of the study's cognitive measures, nor did the illiterate subjects demonstrate a significant decrease in metalinguistic skills.

Shor, Ira, ed. *Freire for the Classroom: A Sourcebook for Liberatory Teaching.* Portsmouth, NH: Boynton/Cook, 1987.
    A collection of essays in which teachers describe their applications of Paulo Freire's liberatory, problem-posing philosophy of education and explore its political implications; particularly useful are discussions of the relevance of "the pedagogy of the oppressed" to privileged mainstream students.

Siegel, Marjorie, and Robert F. Carey. *Critical Thinking: A Semiotic Perspective.* ERIC, 1989. ED 303 802.
    Uses Peirce's semiotic theory to argue for holistic rather than subskills approach to critical thinking, which is seen as "a special case of semiotics in which thought itself becomes the object under consideration."

Smagorinsky, Peter. "The Writer's Knowledge and the Writing Process." *Research in the Teaching of English* 25 (1991): 339–64.
    Presents a protocol analysis study asserting that task-specific procedures

for promoting knowledge lead to more critical thinking and writing than a models or a general procedures approach.

Tierney, Robert, et al. "The Effects of Reading and Writing upon Thinking Critically." *Reading Research Quarterly* 126 (1989): 234–73.
Attempts the kind of empirical research that Applebee calls for; concludes that a combination of reading and writing activities results in dialectical thought: writing allows ideas to come to fruition and helps resolve disputes, while reading provides students with opposing ideas and additional support.

Young, Richard. "Problems and the Composing Process." *Writing: The Nature, Development, and Teaching of Written Communication.* Ed. Carl Frederickssen and Joseph Dominic. Hillsdale, NJ: Erlbaum, 1981. 59–66.
Explores the ways in which the shift from product to process gives prominence to writing as problem solving. Suggests a set of questions that can help students articulate problems (see chapter 6 of this volume).

Young, Robert E., ed. *Fostering Critical Thinking.* San Francisco: Jossey Bass, 1980.
A collection of essays by philosophers, psychologists, and educators, each asking whether critical thinking can be taught.

Conferences

The following conferences feature numerous presentations on the connections between writing and critical thinking.

Bard, The Institute for Writing and Thinking, Annandale-on-Hudson, New York, 12504. 914–758–7484. Annual conference in the spring; weekend, weeklong, and special-interest workshops throughout the year.

Center for Critical Thinking and Moral Critique, Sonoma State University, Rohnert Park, CA 94928. 707–664–2940. Conference on Critical Thinking and Educational Reform in the summer.

Conference on College Composition and Communication, c/o National Conference of Teachers of English, 1111 Kenyon Rd., Evanston, IL 61801. 217–328–3870. Annual conference in March; location changes.

University of Chicago, Institute on Cognitive Frameworks and Higher Order Reasoning, 5801 S. Ellis Ave., Chicago, IL 60637. Fall and spring workshop/conferences.

Notes on Contributors

Marcia Birken is currently associate professor and assistant department head of the Mathematics Department at Rochester Institute of Technology. She has published articles on writing and mathematics, problem solving, and teaching students how to study mathematics. Her most recent publication, is "Using Writing to Assist Learning in College Mathematics Classes" in *The Role of Writing in Learning Mathematics and Science.*

Toni-Lee Capossela teaches writing at Stonehill College, where she is also coordinator of the Writing Center. She has published in *College Composition and Communication* and *The English Record*, and her research interests, in addition to critical thinking, include collaborative learning and assignment sequencing.

Anne C. Coon is currently associate professor and director of writing in the College of Liberal Arts at Rochester Institute of Technology. She has published articles on problem solving, collaboration, and student research. Her most recent publication is "Using Ethical Questions to Develop Autonomy in Student Researchers" in *College Composition and Communication*. She is currently editing a collection of speeches by Amelia Bloomer.

Richard Jenseth received his Ph.D. from the University of Iowa, where he was also a member of the Writers' Workshop in Poetry. His current projects include a booklength study of epistemic pedagogies and an article on the politics of theory in composition studies. He is currently director of University Writing Programs at St. Lawrence University in Canton, NY.

Libby Falk Jones is director of the Center for Effective Communication and associate professor of English at Berea College. She has published widely in the areas of the rhetoric of utopia, feminist pedagogy, learning communities, and faculty development. She is co-editor, with Sarah Webster Goodwin, of *Feminism, Utopia, and Narrative* (University of Tennessee, 1990).

Sandra Lawrence holds an Ed.D. from Harvard Graduate School of Education, and is assistant professor of psychology and education at Mt. Holyoke College. Her research interests include interdisciplinary writing and learning, collaborative learning, peer response groups, and community-based adult literacy instruction. She has published articles about writing to learn, classroom contexts for teaching and learning, and teacher education.

Joel Nydahl is Writing Program administrator and director of the Peer-Consultant-in-Writing Program at Babson College. He has published in *College*

English and *Computers and Composition*. His research interests, in addition to computer-assisted instruction, include the theory and practice of peer tutoring and collaborative learning.

Carol Booth Olson is director of the Writing Project at the University of California, Irvine, and coordinator of UCI's outreach unit, Project Radius. She has published in many journals, and recently edited *Thinking/Writing: Fostering Critical Thinking Skills Through Writing* for Scott Foresman.

Betty P. Pytlik, university composition coordinator and director of composition at Ohio University, has published articles about writing assessment, collaboration between high schools and colleges, teacher preparation, sequenced writing assignments, and teaching critical thinking skills.

Lois Rubin is assistant professor of English at Penn State University, New Kensington Campus, where she teaches writing, leads workshops in assignment design across the curriculum, and develops composition courses with a multicultural emphasis. Her articles on teaching writing and investigating students' reflections on their writing have appeared in *College Composition and Communication*, *The Writing Instructor*, *The English Record*, *College Teaching*, and *Teaching English in the Two-Year College*.

Kate Sandberg, associate professor of English, teaches courses in learning and critical/creative thinking skills at the University of Alaska Anchorage, where she has served as co-director of both the Reading-Writing Center and the Teaching Excellence Program. She had led workshops on collaborative learning at national and international conferences.

William Zeiger, assistant professor of English at Slippery Rock University, has given workshops on dialectic methods of teaching and on the role of narrative and oral story telling in the teaching of writing and literature. He has published in *College English, Rhetoric Review*, and *Freshman English News*, as well as contributing a chapter, "The Personal Essay and Egalitarian Rhetoric," to *Literary Nonfiction* (Southern Illinois University Press).